Student Study Guide

Kelli Jade Hammer

Broward Community College

Intermediate Algebra

for College Students

Sixth Edition

Allen R. ANGEL

PEARSON
Prentice
Hall

PEARSON EDUCATION, INC.
Upper Saddle River, NJ 07458

Editor-in-Chief: Chris Hoag
Senior Acquisitions Editor: Paul Murphy
Supplement Editor: Kerri-Ann O'Donnell
Assistant Managing Editor: John Matthews
Production Editor: Allyson Kloss
Supplement Cover Manager: Paul Gourhan
Supplement Cover Designer: Joanne Alexandris
Manufacturing Buyer: Ilene Kahn

© 2004 Pearson Education, Inc.
Pearson Prentice Hall
Pearson Education, Inc.
Upper Saddle River, NJ 07458

Printed in the United States of America

10 9 8 7 6 5 4 3 2 1

ISBN 0-13-141758-4

Pearson Education Ltd., *London*
Pearson Education Australia Pty. Ltd., *Sydney*
Pearson Education Singapore, Pte. Ltd.
Pearson Education North Asia Ltd., *Hong Kong*
Pearson Education Canada, Inc., *Toronto*
Pearson Educación de Mexico, S.A. de C.V.
Pearson Education—Japan, *Tokyo*
Pearson Education Malaysia, Pte. Ltd.
Pearson Education, *Upper Saddle River, New Jersey*

Table of Contents

Chapter 1

1.1 Study Skills for Success in Mathematics, and Using a Calculator

Mathematics is relevant to your everyday life. Throughout this course we will use data from real-life examples to demonstrate this to you. A thorough understanding of algebra will make it easier for you to succeed in later mathematics courses and in life. For many students, this section may be the most important section in the book. *Read it carefully and follow the advice given.* Your chances for success will be greatly enhanced.

Have a Positive Attitude

Due to your past experiences in mathematics you may at times think to yourself, "I hate math" or "What do I need this class for?" You may have 'math anxiety'. Many students fall into this same category. However, you are more mature now than when you took previous math courses. This maturity combined with your desire to learn will make a tremendous difference. Give yourself and this math course a fair chance. Go into it with an open mind. Most of all, believe in yourself! You can be successful in this course. Just believe it!

Prepare for and Attend Class

Preview the Material

Preview any new material in the textbook before class. Get a feeling for the definitions and concepts that will be discussed. Even if you do not fully understand what you have read, doing this will help you understand what your instructor is explaining during class.

Read the Text

A mathematics text should be read carefully and slowly. Do not skim over the material. You may wish to underline or highlight a new concept or definition. When you come across an example, read and follow it line by line. Then work the *Now Try Exercises* that appear in the text next to the example.

Pay close attention to the special features in the book. The *Avoid Common Errors* boxes point out the most common errors made by students. Make sure you understand what is explained. By avoiding these common errors you will increase your chance of success. The *Helpful Hints* offer techniques for working certain problems. They may show an alternative way to work a problem. Ask your instructor about anything you do not understand.

Do the Homework

Make sure you do all your homework assignments. Do them as soon as possible, when the material presented is fresh in your mind. This will improve your retention and performance. Even if you understand what is presented in class, it is crucial to the learning process that you do all the homework assigned. Only then will you truly learn the material.

When doing your homework, make sure that you write it neatly and carefully. Work each problem step by step. Show all of your work. When you are done, check your answers. You can find the answers to the odd-numbered problems in the back of the textbook. In addition, you can also find the answers to the cumulative reviews, chapter reviews, chapter tests, and cumulative review tests. Make sure you ask questions at the next class meeting about any homework problems that you didn't understand.

Attend and Participate in Class

Plan to attend every class. If you miss a class, you miss important information. The more absences you have, the lower your grade will be. While in class, pay close attention. If you do not understand something, ask questions of your instructor. If you do not ask questions, your instructor will not know you have difficulties.

Take careful notes. Only copy the major points and the examples that do not appear in the text. Don't frantically take notes and lose track of what your instructor is saying.

Study

Study in the proper atmosphere, where you will have no distractions. Make sure that you have sufficient desk space to spread out all materials that you need.

In order to understand the process of working out a problem, it is important to follow the specific steps that lead to the correct answer. Doing this will enable you to know how to solve similar problems.

Time Management

It is recommended that you study and do homework for at least two hours for each hour of class time. Finding the necessary time to study is not always easy. Following are some suggestions that you may find helpful.

- Plan ahead for times when you can study and do your homework. Space these time periods out evenly over the week, and do not schedule other activities during these times.
- Be organized. Have books, pen, calculator, and notes ready to go so you do not spend your homework time looking for your supplies.
- Save time by using a calculator for tedious calculations.
- When your study session is over, clearly mark the page at which you stopped. This will allow you to quickly continue from where you left off when you begin your next study session.
- Try not to take on added responsibilities. Make your education a top priority and give it the time it needs.
- Do not take on more courses than you can handle. If you do not have sufficient time to study, your grades in all your courses may suffer.

Prepare for and Take Examinations

To Study for an Exam

Do some studying each day, so you will not need to cram the night before an exam. Waiting for the last minute to prepare for a test will not give you enough time to seek the help you may need.

- Read your class notes.
- Review your homework assignments.
- Study formulas, definitions, and procedures you will need for the exam.
- Read the *Avoiding Common Errors* boxes and *Helpful Hints* boxes carefully.
- Read the summary at the end of each chapter.
- Work the review exercises at the end of each chapter. If you have difficulties, restudy those sections. If you still have trouble, seek help.
- Work the chapter practice test.
- Rework quizzes previously given if that material will be included on the test.
- If your exam is a cumulative exam, work the Cumulative Review Test.

To Take an Exam

- Make sure you get sufficient sleep the night before.
- Arrive early so you have a few minutes to relax.
- Carefully write down any formulas or ideas you want to remember.
- Look over the entire exam quickly to get an idea of its length. Make sure no pages are missing.
- Read all directions.
- Read each question carefully and answer each question completely. Make sure you answer the specific question asked.
- Work the questions you understand first, then go back and work the ones you are not sure of. Do not spend too much time on any one problem or you may not finish the exam.
- Work carefully step by step. Be sure to copy all signs and exponents correctly.
- Write clearly. If your writing is not clear, it is easy to make a mistake when working from one step to another. In addition, you may lose credit if your instructor cannot read your work.
- If you have time, check your work and answers.
- Stay calm. Do not be concerned if others finish before you. Use the extra time to check your work.

Find Help

Use the Supplements

Your textbook comes with supplements. Find out from your instructor which supplements would be beneficial to you. Supplements should not replace the text, but should enhance your understanding of the material.

Seek Help

You must thoroughly understand the material. In mathematics courses, the material you learn is cumulative: New material is built on material previously presented. Do not fall behind. If you have any difficulties, seek help immediately. Utilize the following services as soon as you need them.

- Your instructor: Know your instructor's office hours and seek help from your instructor when you need it. Be prepared and ask specific questions.
- Form a study group with other students in your class. Discussing the concepts and homework with your classmates will reinforce your own understanding of the material.
- Many colleges have a math learning center where tutoring is available. Find out where and when you can be tutored.

Learn to Use a Calculator

Find out which calculator, if any, your instructor expects you to use. Some instructors require a scientific calculator while others require a graphing calculator. Keep in mind the calculator requirements for any future math classes that you may take. Consider purchasing a calculator that you can use for other courses as well. Always read and save the user's manual for whatever calculator you purchase.

1.2 Sets and Other Basic Concepts

Summary

Terminology of Sets

1. A **set** is a collection of objects.

2. Objects in the set are called **elements** of the set.

3. When the elements of a set are listed within braces, the set is said to be in **roster form**.

4. The symbol ∈ represents "is a member of" or "belongs to."

5. If the elements of a set can be counted, the set is a **finite set**.

6. If it is impossible to list all elements of a set, the set is called **infinite.**

Example 1
The set of **natural numbers**, $N = \{1, 2, 3, 4, 5 \ldots\}$, is an infinite set since it is impossible to list the elements of the set.

Example 2
The set $\{1, 5, 9, 17\}$ is a finite set having four elements.

Subsets, Null set

1. The **null set** or **empty set** is the set which contains **no** elements. It is symbolized as { } or ∅.

2. Set A is a **subset** of set B, symbolized by $A \subseteq B$, if every element of A is also an element of B.

Example 3
The set $\{a, c, d\}$ is a subset of $\{a, b, c, d, e, f\}$ since every element of the first set is an element of the second set.

Example 4
The set $\{1, 2, 5, 9\}$ is not a subset of $\{1, 2, 4, 6, 9, 10\}$ since the element 5 from the first set is not an element of the second set.

Example 5
Find the set of **whole number** solutions of $x + 2 = 0$.

Solution
Since $x = -2$ is the only solution of $x + 2 = 0$, and $x = -2$ is **not** a whole number (it is an integer), the solution set of $x + 2 = 0$ in the set of whole numbers is $\{\ \}$ (null set).

Summary

Greater than, Less than

1. The symbol ">" is read "is greater than."

2. The symbol "$\geq$" is read "is greater than or equal to."

3. The symbol "<" is read "is less than."

4. The symbol "$\leq$" is read "is less than or equal to."

5. If $a > b$, then a lies to the right of b on the real number line.

6. If a is not equal to b, then either $a > b$ or $a < b$.

Example 6
Insert > or < symbol between the numbers to make a true statement.

    a. 10 7   **b.** −17 −23   **c.** −5 0

Solution:

    a. $10 > 7$ since 10 lies to the right of 7 on the real number line.

    b. $-17 > -23$ since −17 lies to the right of −23 on the number line.

    c. $-5 < 0$ since −5 lies to the left of 0 on the number line.

Summary

Union and Intersection of Sets

1. The **union** of set A and set B, written $A \cup B$, is the set of elements that belong to either set A or set B.

2. The **intersection** of set A and set B, written $A \cap B$, is the set of elements that are common to both set A and set B.

Example 7
Find $A \cup B$ and $A \cap B$ if $A = \{3, 4, 5, 7, 9\}$ and $B = \{5, 7, 11, 13\}$.

Solution
$A \cup B = \{3, 4, 5, 7, 9, 11, 13\}$; $A \cap B = \{5, 7\}$

Summary

Important Sets of Numbers

1. **Natural or Counting numbers** are represented by $N = \{1, 2, 3, 4, 5, \ldots\}$.

2. **Whole numbers** are represented by $W = \{0, 1, 2, 3, 4, 5, \ldots\}$.

3. **Integers** are denoted by $I = \{\ldots -3, -2, -1, 0, 1, 2, 3, \ldots\}$.

4. **Rational numbers**
    A number is rational if it can be written in the form $\dfrac{p}{q}$ where p and q are integers and q is not equal to zero.

5. **Irrational numbers** are those real numbers which are not rational.

6. **Real numbers** are denoted by $\{x | x$ is a point on the real number line$\}$. Real numbers consist of the union of the set of rational numbers with the set of irrational numbers.

7. Every rational number, when written as a decimal number, will either be a repeating or terminating decimal.

Example 7

Consider set $S = \{-3, 0, 0.6, 3.4, \sqrt{5}, 19, -43, \pi\}$.

List the elements of the set that are:

    a. Natural numbers   **b.** Whole numbers   **c.** Integers

    d. Rational numbers   **e.** Irrational numbers   **f.** Real numbers

Solution

    a. 19   **b.** 0, 19   **c.** –3, 0, 19, –43

    d. –3, 0, 0.6, 3.4, 19, –43   **e.** $\sqrt{5}, \pi$ **f.** entire set S

Example 8

Illustrate the set $\{x | -2 \le x < 3 \text{ and } x \in I\}$ on a number line.

Solution

Example 9

Illustrate the set $\{x | -2 \le x < 3\}$ on a number line.

Solution

Exercise Set 1.2

    1. Is $\dfrac{2}{5}$ a rational number?

    2. Is $\sqrt{7}$ an integer?

    3. Is –13.2 a real number?

    4. Consider the set $\left\{-7, 0, 1.6, \dfrac{3}{4}, \sqrt{11}, \pi, 23\right\}$. List the elements that are:

        a. Natural numbers   **b.** Whole numbers   **c.** Integers

        d. Rational numbers   **e.** Irrational numbers   **f.** Real numbers

    5. List the set $\{x | x \text{ is a whole number greater than } 9\}$ in roster form.

    6. List the set $\{x | x \text{ is an integer between } -4 \text{ and } 7.9\}$ in roster form.

    7. Is the set of whole numbers a subset of the set of integers?

8. Is the set of rational numbers a subset of the set of natural numbers?

9. Is the set of rational numbers a subset of the set of irrational numbers?

10. Is the set of real numbers the union of the set of rational numbers and the set of irrational numbers?

Find $A \cup B$ and $A \cap B$ for sets A and B.

11. $A = \{-2, 3, 5\}$; $B = \{-3, -2, 4, 5, 6\}$

12. $A = \{\ \ \}$; $B = \{-3, -2, -1, 0, 1\}$

Insert $<$ or $>$ between the two numbers to make a true statement.

13. $-7 \quad -7.5$

14. $-\dfrac{11}{7} \quad -3$

15. $-\pi \quad \pi$

16. $\dfrac{17}{4} \quad \dfrac{9}{2}$

17. Describe the set $\{5, 6, 7, 8, \ldots\}$.

18. Illustrate the set $\{x|x > 5 \text{ and } x \in N\}$ on a number line.

19. Illustrate the set $\{x|x > 5\}$ on a number line.

20. Express in set builder notation.

Answers to Exercise Set 1.2

1. Yes	2. No	3. Yes
4. **a.** 23	**b.** 0, 23	**c.** $-7, 0, 23$

    d. $-7, 0, 1.6, \dfrac{3}{4}, 23$ **e.** $\sqrt{11}, \pi$ **f.** entire set

5. $\{10, 11, 12, 13, 14, \ldots\}$

6. $\{-3, -2, -1, 0, 1, 2, 3, 4, 5, 6, 7\}$

7. Yes	8. No	9. No

10. Yes

11. $A \cup B = \{-3, -2, 3, 4, 5, 6\}$; $A \cap B = \{-2, 5\}$

12. $A \cup B = \{-3, -2, -1, 0, 1\}$; $A \cap B = \{ \quad \}$ or $\varnothing$

13. $>$ **14.** $>$ **15.** $<$

16. $<$

17. The set of natural numbers greater than 4.

18.

19.

20. $\{x | -3 \leq x \leq 1 \text{ and } x \in I\}$

1.3 Properties of and Operations with Real Numbers

Summary

Definitions and Properties

1. **Additive inverse**
   For any real number a, its additive inverse is $-a$.

2. **Double negative property**
   For any real number a, $-(-a) = a$.

3. The **absolute value** of any real number is its distance from the number zero on the real number line.

4. The **absolute value** of any nonzero number will always be **positive**, while the absolute value of zero is **zero**.

5. $|a| = \begin{cases} a \text{ if } a \geq 0 \\ -a \text{ if } a < 0 \end{cases}$

Example 1
Evaluate each of the following:

    a. $|-7.65|$ **b.** $-|-8|$ **c.** $-|7|$

Solution

    a. $|-7.65| = -(-7.65) = 7.65$ since $-7.65 < 0$.

    b. $-|-8|$; first, $|-8| = -(-8) = 8$ since $-8 < 0$. Thus, $-|-8| = -(8) = -8$.

c.　$-|7|$; first, $|7| = 7$ since $7 > 0$. Thus, $-|7| = -(7) = -7$.

Summary

Addition of Real Numbers

1. **To add two numbers with the same sign**, add their absolute values and place the common sign before the sum.

2. **To add two numbers with different signs**, take the difference of the absolute values. The answer will have the same sign as the number which has the larger absolute value.

Example 2
Find the sums.

　　a.　$-8 + (-9)$　　　　**b.**　$4 + (-11)$　　　　**c.**　$-34 + 67$

　　d.　$-6.5 + (-9.8)$　　**e.**　$\dfrac{5}{6} + \left(-\dfrac{4}{5}\right)$

Solution

a. Since both numbers being added are negative, the sum will be negative. Add their absolute values and place a negative sign (or common sign) before the sum:
$|-8| = 8$, $|-9| = 9$, $8 + 9 = 17$ (sum of absolute values). Final answer is -17.

b. Since the numbers have different signs, subtract their absolute values: $|-11| = 11$, $|4| = 4$, $11 - 4 = 7$. The sign of the answer will be the same as the sign of the number with the larger absolute value. Thus, the answer will be -7.

c. Since the numbers have different signs, subtract their absolute values: $67 - 34 = 33$. The answer will have the same sign as the sign of the number with the larger absolute value. Thus, the final answer is 33.

d. Same rules apply for decimal numbers. The numbers have the same sign so add their absolute values: $6.5 + 9.8 = 16.3$. Place the common sign before the sum. Thus, the final answer is -16.3.

e. Find the LCD of 6 and 5, which is 30. Rename each fraction using a denominator of 30: $\dfrac{5}{6} = \dfrac{25}{30}$, $-\dfrac{4}{5} = -\dfrac{24}{30}$. To add $\dfrac{25}{30} + \dfrac{-24}{30}$, add the numerators $25 + (-24) = 1$ and place result over 30. Final answer is $\dfrac{1}{30}$.

Summary

Subtraction of Real Numbers

1. To subtract real numbers, change the subtraction symbol to an addition symbol, find the opposite or the second number, and add the two numbers.

2. In symbols, $a - b = a + (-b)$.

Example 3
Subtract as indicated.

   a. $8 - 12$ **b.** $-9 - (-17)$ **c.** $3 - (7 - 9) - 10$

Solution

   a. $8 - 12 = 8 + (-12) = -4$, or, better yet, $8 - 12 = -4$.

   b. $-9 - (-17) = -9 + 17 = 8$

   c. $3 - (7 - 9) - 10 = 3 - (-2) - 10$

$$= 3 + 2 - 10$$

$$= 5 - 10$$

$$= -5$$

Summary

Multiplication and Division of Real Numbers

1. The **product** or **quotient** of two real numbers with like signs is a **positive** number.

2. The **product** or **quotient** of two real numbers with **unlike** signs is a **negative** number.

3. For any number a, $a \cdot 0 = 0 \cdot a = 0$.

Example 4
Find the product or quotient as indicated.

   a. $4(-12)$ **b.** $-16\left(\dfrac{-3}{4}\right)$ **c.** $\left(\dfrac{-2}{3}\right)\left|\dfrac{-6}{10}\right|$

   d. $(-36) \div 9$ **e.** $(-5.1) \div (-1.7)$ **f.** $\dfrac{-2}{7} \div \left|\dfrac{-8}{7}\right|$

Solution

a. $4(-12) = -48$; the product is negative since the numbers have different signs.

b. $-16\left(\dfrac{-3}{4}\right) = \dfrac{-16}{1}\left(\dfrac{-3}{4}\right) = \dfrac{(-16)(-3)}{4} = \dfrac{48}{4} = 12$; the product of -16 and -3 is positive, since the numbers have like signs.

c. Since $\left|\dfrac{-6}{10}\right| = \dfrac{6}{10}$, the problem becomes $\left(\dfrac{-2}{3}\right)\left(\dfrac{6}{10}\right) = \dfrac{-2 \cdot 6}{3 \cdot 10} = \dfrac{-12}{30} = \dfrac{-2}{5}$ or $-\dfrac{2}{5}$.

d. $(-36) \div 9 = -4$ since the quotient of two numbers with unlike signs is negative.

e. $-5.1 \div (-1.7) = 3$ since the quotient of two numbers with like signs is positive.

f. $\dfrac{-2}{7} \div \left|\dfrac{-8}{7}\right| = -\dfrac{2}{7} \div \dfrac{8}{7} = -\dfrac{2}{7} \cdot \dfrac{7}{8} = \dfrac{-2 \cdot 7}{7 \cdot 8} = \dfrac{-14}{56} = -\dfrac{1}{4}$

Summary

Properties of Real Numbers

1. **Commutative Properties**
   $a + b = b + a$; $ab = ba$
   Changing the order in which you add or multiply two numbers does not change the result.

2. **Associative Properties**
   $a + (b + c) = (a + b) + c$; $(ab) \cdot c = a(b \cdot c)$
   Changing the grouping when adding or multiplying three numbers does not affect the result.

3. **Identity Properties**
   $a + 0 = 0 + a = a$; $a \cdot 1 = 1 \cdot a = a$
   0 is called the **additive identity**. The number 1 is called the **multiplicative identity**.

4. **Distributive Property**
   $a \cdot (b + c) = a \cdot b + a \cdot c$

5. **Inverse Properties**
   $a + (-a) = (-a) + a = 0$; $a \cdot \dfrac{1}{a} = \dfrac{1}{a} \cdot a = 1$ for $a \neq 0$

Example 5
Name each property illustrated.

a. $(x + y) \cdot 9 = 9 \cdot (x + y)$ **b.** $(3 + (-2)) + 2 = 3 + (-2 + 2)$

c. $(ab) \cdot 1 = ab$ **d.** $-2(x + 3y) = -2x + (-2)3y$

e. $-17 + 0 = -17$ **f.** $x + (-x) = 0$

Solution

a. Commutative property of multiplication since the order of multiplication was changed

b. Associative property of addition since a change in grouping symbols was involved.

c. Identity property of multiplication (1 is called the multiplication identity.)

d. Distributive property

e. Identity property of addition (Zero is the additive identity.)

f. Inverse property of addition

Exercise Set 1.3

Evaluate the absolute value expression.

1. $-|-8|$ **2.** $\left| \dfrac{-4}{9} \right|$ **3.** $|-5.89|$ **4.** $|0|$

Insert > or < symbol between the numbers to make a true statement.

5. $|-8|$ 3   **6.** $-|-4|$ $|-7|$ **7.** $-|-25|$ -31

List values from smallest to largest.

8. $5, -8, -4, |-3|, -|5|, |0|$

9. $-3.1, -3, -3.4, |-3.8|, -|3.9|$

Evaluate.

10. $5 + (-7)$ **11.** $18 - (-19)$ **12.** $\dfrac{6}{7} - \dfrac{9}{10}$

13. $-4 + (-12)$ **14.** $-6.23 - 4.5$ **15.** $-|-4| - |7|$

16. $\dfrac{4}{5} - \left(\dfrac{3}{5} - \dfrac{2}{3} \right)$ **17.** $\left| -\dfrac{3}{4} \right| \cdot \left| \dfrac{8}{27} \right|$ **18.** $-20 \div (-4)$

19. $\left(25 - |36|\right) \cdot (-7 - 8)$ **20.** $-\dfrac{5}{9} \div \left(-\dfrac{18}{25}\right)$

Name the property of real numbers.

21. $8 + 5 = 5 + 8$ **22.** $(a + b) + [-(a + b)] = 0$

23. $-4(x + y) = -4x + (-4)y$ **24.** $a + b = 1 \cdot (a + b)$

25. $x + (15 + y) = (x + 15) + y$

Answers to Exercise Set 1.3

1. -8 **2.** $-\dfrac{4}{9}$ **3.** 5.89

4. 0 **5.** $>$ **6.** $<$

7. $>$ **8.** $-8, -|5|, -4, |0|, |-3|, 5$ **9.** $-|3.9|, -3.4, -3.1, -3, |-3.8|$

10. -2 **11.** 37 **12.** $-\dfrac{3}{70}$

13. -16 **14.** -10.73 **15.** -11

16. $\dfrac{13}{15}$ **17.** $\dfrac{2}{9}$ **18.** 5

19. 165 **20.** $\dfrac{125}{162}$

21. Commutative property of addition

22. Inverse property of addition

23. Distributive property

24. Identity property of multiplication

25. Associative property of addition

1.4 Order of Operations

Summary

+---+

Base and Exponent

1. Exponential expression
$b^n = b \cdot b \cdot b \cdot \cdots \cdot b$, ($n$ factors of b)

2. b is called the **base** and n is called the **exponent**. The exponent tells the number of times the base is multiplied by itself.

+---+

Example 1
Evaluate each of the following:

a. 4^3 **b.** $(-2)^4$ **c.** 1^{50}

d. $\left(\dfrac{-2}{3}\right)^4$ **e.** $(0.4)^3$

Solution

a. $4^3 = (4)(4)(4) = 64$

b. $(-2)^4 = (-2)(-2)(-2)(-2) = 16$

c. $1^{50} = (1)(1)(1)\cdots(1) = 1$ (1 is multiplied by itself 50 times.)

d. $\left(\dfrac{-2}{3}\right)^4 = \dfrac{(-2)\cdot(-2)\cdot(-2)\cdot(-2)}{3\cdot3\cdot3\cdot3} = \dfrac{16}{81}$

e. $(0.4)^3 = (0.4)(0.4)(0.4) = 0.064$

Example 2
Evaluate $-4^2 + (-3)^3 - 2^2 + (-3)^2$

Solution
$$-4^2 + (-3)^3 - 2^2 + (-3)^2 = -(4)(4) + (-3)(-3)(-3) - (2)(2) + (-3)(-3)$$
$$= -16 + (-27) - 4 + 9$$
$$= -38$$
(Common error: Remember not to evaluate -4^2 as $(-4)^2 = 16$. In -4^2, the base is 4, not -4.)

Summary

Radicals

1. The **principal** or **positive square root** of a number a is written as $\sqrt{a}$ and represents that positive number when multiplied by itself gives n.

2. The symbol $\sqrt{}$ is called a **radical sign**. The expression underneath the radical sign is called the **radicand**. The number used to indicate the root is called the **index**.

Example 3
Evaluate the following:

a. $\sqrt[3]{-64}$

b. $\sqrt[5]{32}$

c. $\sqrt[5]{-32}$

d. $\sqrt[4]{81}$

e. $\sqrt[3]{\dfrac{-1}{64}}$

f. $-\sqrt[4]{1}$

g. $-\sqrt[3]{\dfrac{27}{64}}$

Solution

a. $\sqrt[3]{-64} = -4$

b. $\sqrt[5]{32} = 2$

c. $\sqrt[5]{-32} = -2$

d. $\sqrt[4]{81} = 3$

e. $\sqrt[3]{\dfrac{-1}{64}} = \dfrac{-1}{4}$ or $-\dfrac{1}{4}$

f. $-\sqrt[4]{1} = -1$

g. $-\sqrt[3]{\dfrac{27}{64}} = -\dfrac{3}{4}$

Summary

Order of Operations

To evaluate mathematical expressions the following order is used:

1. First, evaluate the expressions within grouping symbols. If the expression contains nested grouping symbols, evaluate the expression within the innermost set of grouping symbols first.

2. Next, evaluate all expressions containing exponents or roots.

3. Next, evaluate all multiplications or divisions in the order in which they occur, working from left to right.

4. Finally, evaluate all additions and subtractions in the order in which they occur, working from left to right.

5. A fraction bar acts as a grouping symbol.

Example 4

Evaluate $7 + 4 \cdot 2^3 - 5$.

Solution

$$
\begin{aligned}
7 + 4 \cdot 2^3 - 5 &= 7 + 4 \cdot 8 - 5 \text{ (exponents first)} \\
&= 7 + 32 - 5 \quad \text{(multiplication next)} \\
&= 39 - 5 \qquad \text{(addition and subtraction from left to right)} \\
&= 34
\end{aligned}
$$

Example 5

Evaluate $25 + 3\left[(7-4) \div \dfrac{1}{3}\right]$.

Solution

$$
\begin{aligned}
25 + 3\left[(7-4) \div \frac{1}{3}\right] &= 25 + 3\left(3 \div \frac{1}{3}\right) \\
&= 25 + 3(3 \cdot 3) \\
&= 25 + 3(9) \\
&= 25 + 27 \\
&= 52
\end{aligned}
$$

Example 6

Evaluate $\dfrac{8 \div 4 + 7|2 - 5|}{3 + (-6) \div 2}$.

Solution

$$\dfrac{8 \div 4 + 7|2 - 5|}{3 + (-6) \div 2} = \dfrac{2 + 7|-3|}{3 + -3}$$

$$= \dfrac{2 + 7(3)}{0}$$

$$= \dfrac{23}{0}$$

Since division by zero is not allowed, this expression is undefined.

Example 7

Evaluate $18 \div 2 \cdot 3 - \dfrac{5^2 \div 5 + |-10|}{|-20 - 25|}$.

Solution

$$18 \div 2 \cdot 3 - \dfrac{5^2 \div 5 + |-10|}{|-20 - 25|} = 18 \div 2 \cdot 3 - \dfrac{25 \div 5 + 10}{|-45|}$$

$$= 18 \div 2 \cdot 3 - \dfrac{5 + 10}{45}$$

$$= 18 \div 2 \cdot 3 - \dfrac{15}{45}$$

$$= 9 \cdot 3 - \dfrac{1}{3}$$

$$= 27 - \dfrac{1}{3}$$

$$= 26\dfrac{2}{3}$$

Example 8

Evaluate the expression $-x^3 - 2xy - y^4$ at $x = -3$ and $y = 2$.

Solution

Substitute $x = -3$ and $y = 2$ into the expression $-x^3 - 2xy - y^4$ and use the correct order of operations.

$$-(-3)^3 - 2(-3)(2) - (2)^4 = -(-27) - 2(-3)(2) - 16$$

$$= 27 + 12 - 16$$

$$= 23$$

Exercise Set 1.4

Evaluate the following.

1. 5^2

2. -5^2

3. $(0.2)^4$

4. $-\sqrt{64}$

5. $\sqrt[3]{-125}$

6. $(-1)^2 + (-1)^3 + (-1)^{50} + 1^{10}$

Evaluate the following.

7. $-3^2 - 2^2 - 4^3 + (5-5)^2$

8. $\left(\dfrac{3}{4}\right)^2 - \dfrac{1}{16}$

9. $2(4-1)^2 + 8$

10. $\dfrac{9-2^2}{7-11}$

11. $\dfrac{\sqrt{25} - 3 \cdot 2 + 8}{4^2 - 2(7) - 1}$

12. $\dfrac{4 - |-12| \div 3}{2(4 - |5|) + 9}$

13. $\dfrac{3}{4} \div \dfrac{1}{6} + \dfrac{1}{2} \cdot \dfrac{7}{4}$

14. $\dfrac{4 - \frac{3}{5}}{1 - \frac{1}{5}}$

15. $\dfrac{-1}{4}\left[8 - |-5| \div 5 - 3\right]^2$

Evaluate the expression at the indicated value(s) of the variable(s).

16. $-3x^2 + 5;\ x = -4$

17. $-2x^2 + 5x + 9;\ x = 3$

18. $2(2a + b)^2 - 4(a + b);\ a = -2,\ b = 5$

19. $4x^2 - 3xy - 2y^2;\ x = -2,\ y = 1$

20. $\dfrac{-b + \sqrt{b^2 - 4ac}}{2a};\ a = 3,\ b = -1,\ c = -10$

Answers to Exercise Set 1.4

1. 25

2. −25

3. 0.0016

4. −8

5. −5

6. 2

7. −77

8. $\dfrac{1}{2}$

9. 26

10. $-\dfrac{5}{4}$

11. 7

12. 0

13. $\dfrac{43}{8}$

14. $\dfrac{17}{4}$

15. −4

16. -43 **17.** 6 **18.** -10

19. 20 **20.** 2

1.5 Exponents

Summary

Rules for Exponents

1. The expression $x^m = x \cdot x \cdot x \cdot x \cdot \cdots \cdot x$ where x is multiplied by itself m times is called an exponential expression. x is called the base and m is called the exponent.

2. **Product Rule for Exponents**
   If m, n are natural numbers and a is any real number, then $a^m \cdot a^n = a^{m+n}$.

3. **Quotient Rule for Exponents**
   If a is any nonzero real number, and m and n are nonzero integers, then $\dfrac{a^m}{a^n} = a^{m-n}$.

4. **Negative Exponent Rule**
   For any nonzero real number a and any whole number m, $a^{-m} = \dfrac{1}{a^m}$.

5. **Zero Exponent Rule**
   If a is any nonzero real number, then $a^0 = 1$.

Example 1
Simplify each expression using the rules of exponents. Write the answer without negative exponents.

a. $y^9 \cdot y^4$ **b.** $\dfrac{x^{13}}{x^4}$ **c.** s^{-5}

d. $-3^2 xy^{-2}$ **e.** $(-3)^2 a^{-3} b c^{-2}$ **f.** $\dfrac{x^{-4} \cdot 2 \cdot x^2}{x^{-5}}$

Solution

  a. Use the product rule of exponents. Keep the base, y, and add the exponents: $y^9 \cdot y^4 = y^{9+4} = y^{13}$

  b. Use the quotient rule of exponents. Maintain the base, x, and subtract exponents: $\dfrac{x^{13}}{x^4} = x^{13-4} = x^9$

c. Use the negative exponent rule: $s^{-5} = \dfrac{1}{s^5}$

d. $-3^2 xy^{-1} = -\left(\dfrac{1}{3^2}\right) \cdot x \cdot \dfrac{1}{y} = -\dfrac{x}{9y}$

Remember, the exponent 2 refers to the number or variable **immediately preceding it**.

e. $(-3)^2 a^{-3} bc^{-2} = 9 \cdot \dfrac{1}{a^3} \cdot b \cdot \dfrac{1}{c^2} = \dfrac{9b}{a^3 c^2}$

f. We can move **factors** from numerator to denominator or from denominator to numerator by changing the sign of the exponent. The key word here is **factors**. If a number or variable is part of a sum or difference of terms, it is **incorrect** to move this number or variable from numerator to denominator or vice versa.

$$\frac{x^{-4} 2x^2}{x^{-5}} = \frac{x^5 \cdot 2x^2}{x^4} = \frac{2x^7}{x^4} = 2x^3$$

The following problem is **incorrect**: $\dfrac{y^3 + y^{-4}}{x^{-2} + y^2} = \dfrac{y^3 + x^2}{y^4 + y^2}$

This problem is incorrect because the variable terms are not factors but are part of a sum.

Example 2
Simplify.

    a. $3^{-1} - 2 \cdot 3^{-2}$ **b.** $-5^{-1} - 3 \cdot 2^{-1} - (4^3 \cdot 5)^0$

    c. $-13x^0 + y^0$ **d.** $(6x)^0 - 5y^0$

Solution

    a. $\begin{aligned}[t] 3^{-1} - 2 \cdot 3^{-2} &= \frac{1}{3} - 2 \cdot \frac{1}{3^2} \\ &= \frac{1}{3} - 2 \cdot \frac{1}{9} \\ &= \frac{1}{3} - \frac{2}{9} \\ &= \frac{3}{9} - \frac{2}{9} \\ &= \frac{1}{9} \end{aligned}$

b. $-5^{-1} - 3 \cdot 2^{-1} - (4^3 \cdot 5)^0 = -\dfrac{1}{5} - 3 \cdot \dfrac{1}{2} - (1)$

$$= -\dfrac{1}{5} - \dfrac{3}{2} - 1$$

$$= -\dfrac{2}{10} - \dfrac{15}{10} - \dfrac{10}{10}$$

$$= -\dfrac{27}{10}$$

c. $-13x^0 + y^0 = -13(1) + 1 = -12$

d. $(6x)^0 - 5y^0 = 1 - 5(1) = -4$

Example 3
Simplify the following and write the final result without negative exponents.

a. $\dfrac{4x^{-2}yz^3}{16x^5y^{-4}z}$

b. $\left(\dfrac{2x^{-2}y^{-4}}{z^3}\right)\left(\dfrac{x^3y^5}{z^{-3}}\right)$

Solution

a. $\dfrac{4x^{-2}yz^3}{16x^5y^{-4}z} = \dfrac{y \cdot y^4 \cdot z^3}{4x^5 \cdot x^2 \cdot z}$ (move factors across fraction bar and change signs of the exponents)

$$= \dfrac{y^5 z^2}{4x^7} \qquad \text{(product and quotient rules)}$$

b. $\left(\dfrac{2x^{-2}y^{-4}}{z^3}\right)\left(\dfrac{x^3y^5}{z^{-3}}\right) = \left(\dfrac{2}{x^2y^4z^3}\right)\left(\dfrac{x^3y^5z^3}{1}\right)$ (move factors across fraction bar and change

$$\text{signs of exponents)}$$

$$= \dfrac{2x^3y^5z^3}{x^2y^4z^3}$$

$$= 2xy \text{ (quotient rule)}$$

Summary

┌───┐

More Rules for Exponents

1. **Raising a Power to a Power**
   If a is a real number and m and n are integers,
   then $(a^m)^n = a^{m \cdot n}$.

2. **Raising a Product to a Power**
   If a and b are real numbers and m is an integer,
   then $(ab)^m = a^m b^m$.

3. **Raising a Quotient to a Power**
   If a and b are real numbers and m is an integer,

   then $\left(\dfrac{a}{b}\right)^m = \dfrac{a^m}{b^m}$, $b \neq 0$.

└───┘

Example 4
Simplify.

    a. $(4x^{-2}y^5)^{-3}$ **b.** $\left(\dfrac{6x^2 y^{-3}}{z^{-4}}\right)^{-2}$

Solution

a. $(4x^{-2}y^5)^{-3} = 4^{-3}(x^{-2})^{-3}(y^{-5})^{-3}$ Use raising a product to a power rule first.

$\qquad\qquad\qquad = 4^{-3}(x^6)(y^{15})$ Then use raising a power to a power rule.

$\qquad\qquad\qquad = \dfrac{x^6 y^{15}}{64}$ Finally use the negative exponent rule.

b. $\left(\dfrac{6x^2 y^{-3}}{z^{-4}}\right)^{-2} = \dfrac{6^{-2}(x^2)^{-2}(y^{-3})^{-2}}{(z^{-4})^{-2}}$ Use raising a product to a power and a quotient to a power rules first.

$\qquad\qquad\qquad = \dfrac{6^{-2}x^{-4}y^6}{z^8}$ Then use raising a power to a power rule.

$\qquad\qquad\qquad = \dfrac{y^6}{36x^4 z^8}$ Finally use the negative exponent rule.

Example 5
Simplify.

    a. $\left(\dfrac{6x^5 y^{-4}}{2xy^5}\right)^2$ **b.** $\dfrac{(3x^{-3}y^5)^{-2}}{(x^{-4}y^5)^{-5}}$

Solution

a. First simplify the expression within the parentheses and the raise to the second power.

$$\left(\frac{6x^5y^{-4}}{2xy^5}\right)^2 = \left(\frac{3x^4}{y^9}\right)^2$$

$$= \frac{9x^8}{y^{18}}$$

b. First, use raising a power to a power rule, then simplify.

$$\frac{(3x^{-3}y^5)^{-2}}{(x^{-4}y^5)^{-5}} = \frac{3^{-2}x^6y^{-10}}{x^{20}y^{-25}}$$

$$= \frac{x^6y^{25}}{3^2x^{20}y^{10}}$$

$$= \frac{y^{15}}{9x^{14}}$$

Exercise Set 1.5

Simplify and write the answer without any negative exponents. Assume all bases represented by variables are nonzero.

1. $\dfrac{4}{6x^{-2}}$

2. $\dfrac{3^{-1} \cdot x^{-1}}{y^3}$

3. $\dfrac{4x^{-2} \cdot y}{10x^5 \cdot y^{-4}}$

4. $-3(x^0 + 5y^0)$

5. $-3x^0 + (5y)^0$

Evaluate.

6. 3^{-4}

7. -4^{-3}

8. $-(-3^{-3})$

9. $2^{-4} - 3 \cdot 5^{-2} - (4^2 - 3)^0$

10. $3^{-2} - 2^{-3} - 4 \cdot 2^{-1}$

Simplify and write the answer without any negative exponents. Assume all bases represented by variables are nonzero.

11. $\left(\dfrac{3x^{-2} \cdot y^{-1}}{z^4}\right) \cdot \left(\dfrac{x^3y^5}{6 \cdot z^{-4}}\right)$

12. $\dfrac{(6x^4y^{-2}z) \cdot (5 \cdot x^{-3}y^4z^{-3})}{(9x^3y^{-4}z)}$

13. $w^{3x-2} \cdot w^{2x+3}$

14. $\dfrac{s^{2x-3}}{s^{3x+4}}$

Simplify and write answers without negative exponents.

15. $(2x^{-3}y)^{-4}$

16. $\left(\dfrac{3xy}{y^4}\right)^{-3}$

17. $(3x^2y)(2x^4y^2)^3$

18. $3(x^3y^{-4})^{-2}$

19. $\left(\dfrac{2x^2y^4}{3z^{-1}}\right)\left(\dfrac{3z^3}{2xy^4}\right)^4$

20. $\dfrac{(2x^4y)^3(4x^4y^2)^2}{(2x^{-3}y^{-2})^{-2}}$

21. $\left(\dfrac{6x^4y^{-6}z^4}{2xy^{-6}z^{-2}}\right)^{-2}$

22. $\dfrac{(4x^{-1}y^{-2})^{-3}}{(3x^{-1}y^3)^2}$

Answers to Exercise Set 1.5

1. $\dfrac{2x^2}{3}$

2. $\dfrac{1}{3xy^3}$

3. $\dfrac{2y^5}{5x^7}$

4. -18

5. -2

6. $\dfrac{1}{81}$

7. $-\dfrac{1}{64}$

8. $\dfrac{1}{27}$

9. $-\dfrac{423}{400}$

10. $-\dfrac{145}{72}$

11. $\dfrac{xy^4}{2}$

12. $\dfrac{10y^6}{3x^2z^3}$

13. w^{5x+1}

14. $\dfrac{1}{s^{x+7}}$

15. $\dfrac{x^{12}}{16y^4}$

16. $\dfrac{y^9}{27x^3}$

17. $24x^{14}y^7$

18. $\dfrac{3y^8}{x^6}$

19. $\dfrac{27z^{13}}{8x^2y^{12}}$

20. $512x^{14}y^3$

21. $\dfrac{1}{9x^6z^{12}}$

22. $\dfrac{x^5}{576}$

1.6 Scientific Notation

Summary

To write a number in scientific notation

1. Move the decimal point in the number to the right of the first nonzero digit. This will give you a number greater than or equal to 1 and less than 10.

2. Count the number of places you moved the decimal point in step 1. If the original number was 10 or greater, the count is to be considered positive. If the original number was less than 1, the count is to be considered negative.

3. Multiply the number obtained in step 1 by 10 raised to the count (power) found in step 2.

Example 4
Write the following numbers in scientific notation.

   a. 53,800   **b.** 0.000123

   c. 573,000   **d.** 0.0085

Solution

   a. 53,800 becomes 5.3800 when the decimal point is moved to the right of 5 (the first nonzero digit). Since the original number is greater than 10, the count is positive. The answer is 5.38×10^4.

   b. 0.000123 becomes 1.23 when the decimal point is moved to the right of 1. Since the original number is less than 1, our count is –4. The final answer is 1.23×10^{-4}.

   c. 573,000 becomes 5.73×10^5. The count is 5 since the original number is greater than 10.

   d. 0.0085 becomes 8.5×10^{-3}. The count is –3 since the original number is less than 1.

Summary

To convert a number in scientific notation to decimal form

1. Observe the exponent of the base 10.

2. **a.** If the exponent is positive, move the decimal point in the number to the right the same number of places as the exponent. It may be necessary to add zeros to the number. This will result in a number greater than or equal to 10.

   b. If the exponent is zero, the decimal in the number does not move from its present position. This will result in a number greater than or equal to 1 but less than 10.

   c. If the exponent is negative, move the decimal point in the number to the left the same number of places as the exponent. It may be necessary to add zeros. This will result in a number less than 1.

Example 5
Write each number without exponents.

    a. 3.8×10^4 **b.** 8.98×10^{-5} **c.** 5.6×10^0

Solution

    a. Since the exponent is positive, the decimal point in 3.8 is moved 4 places to the right and the decimal form of the number is 38,000.

    b. Since the exponent is negative, the decimal point in 8.98 is moved 5 places to the left. It will necessary to add 4 leading zeros to the number 8.98. The decimal form of the number is 0.0000898.

    c. Since the exponent is zero, do not move the decimal point in the number. The decimal form of this number is simply 5.6.

Example 6
Simplify the expression using scientific notation.
$$\frac{51{,}000{,}000}{0.0003}$$

Solution
Divide by first converting the numbers to scientific notation.
$$51{,}000{,}000 = 5.1 \times 10^7; \quad 0.0003 = 3.0 \times 10^{-4}$$

$$\frac{51{,}000{,}000}{0.0003} = \frac{5.1 \times 10^7}{3.0 \times 10^{-4}} = \frac{5.1}{3.0} \times 10^{11} = 1.7 \times 10^{11}$$

Exercise Set 1.6

Express each number in scientific notation.

1. 84,000   **2.** 0.000194

Express each number in decimal form without exponents.

3. 3.8×10^5 **4.** 4.9×10^{-3}

Find the value using scientific notation.

5. $\dfrac{64,000,000}{0.00004}$

Use scientific notation to solve the following problem.

6. A piece of paper is 0.0003 inches thick. How many sheets of this paper would be in a stack which is one mile high? There are 1,760 yards in a mile.

Answers to Exercise Set 1.6

1. 8.4×10^4 **2.** 1.94×10^{-4} **3.** 380,000

4. 0.0049   **5.** 1.6×10^{12} **6.** 2.112×10^8

Chapter 1 Practice Test

1. Find $A \cup B$ and $A \cap B$ for the sets $A = \{-5, -3, 0, 1, 2, 4\}$ and $B = \{-4, -3, 2, 5, 6\}$

2. a. Illustrate the set $\{x | -1 \le x < 4\}$ on a number line.

   b. Illustrate the set $\{x | -1 \le x < 4 \text{ and } x \in I\}$ on a number line.

3. Consider the set $\left\{-6, 0, 1.8, \dfrac{1}{5}, \sqrt{13}, \pi, 79\right\}$. List the elements that are

   a. Natural numbers   **b.** Whole numbers   **c.** Integers

   d. Rational numbers   **e.** Irrational numbers   **f.** Real numbers

4. Insert $<$ or $>$ between the two numbers to make a true statement.

   a. -8 -8.6 **b.** $-\dfrac{13}{2}$ -6 **c.** $\dfrac{7}{2}$ $\dfrac{11}{4}$

   d. $-|-16|$ $|15|$ **e.** $|-5|$ 3

5. Name the property of real numbers.

    a. $6 + 2 = 2 + 6$ **b.** $2x + (-2x) = 0$

    c. $7 = 1 \cdot 7$ **d.** $x + (17 + y) = (x + 17) + y$

6. Evaluate.

    a. $\dfrac{6}{5} - \dfrac{3}{10}$ **b.** $+|-7| - |8|$ **c.** $(30 - |31|)(-3 - 11)$

    d. $-\dfrac{5}{6} \div \left(-\dfrac{35}{24}\right)$ **e.** $\left(\dfrac{3}{5}\right)^2 - \dfrac{1}{25}$ **f.** $\sqrt{25} - 4 \cdot 2 + 23$

    g. $3(3 - 1)^4 + 1$ **h.** $\dfrac{3 - |-11| + 6}{2(4 + |-5|) \div 9}$ **i.** $\left[6 - \sqrt{100} \div 5 + 1\right]^3$

7. Evaluate each expression at the indicated values of the variables.

    a. $2(a - b)^2 + 3(a + b)$ for $a = 4$, $b = 6$

    b. $3x^2 - 2xy - 5y^2$ for $x = -1$, $y = 3$

8. Simplify and write the answer without any negative exponents.

    a. $\dfrac{8x^{-3}y}{16x^7 y^{-11}}$ **b.** $7x^0 + (10y)^0$ **c.** $\left(\dfrac{7x^{-5}y^{-3}}{z^4}\right)\left(\dfrac{x^6 y^7}{14z^{-2}}\right)$

    d. $\left(\dfrac{4xy}{y^5}\right)^{-2}$ **e.** $\dfrac{(3x^3 y)^2 (2x^5 y^3)^3}{(x^{-5} y^{-1})^{-2}}$ **f.** $\dfrac{(3x^{-1} y^{-4})^{-3}}{(9x^{-2} y^3)^2}$

9. Express each number in scientific notation.

    a. $692{,}000$ **b.** 0.047

10. Express each number in decimal form without exponents.

    a. 8.97×10^7 **b.** 5.3×10^{-4}

Answers to Chapter 1 Practice Test

1. $A \cup B = \{-5, -4, -3, 0, 1, 2, 4, 5, 6\}$, $A \cap B = \{-3, 2\}$

2. a.

    -2 -1   0   1   2   3   4   5   6

  b.

    -2 -1   0   1   2   3   4   5   6

3. a.   79   **b.**   0, 79   **c.**   −6, 0, 79

      d. $-6, 0, 1.8, \dfrac{1}{5}, 79$ **e.** $\sqrt{13}, \pi$ **f.** $-6, 0, 1.8, \dfrac{1}{5}, \sqrt{13}, \pi, 79$

4. a.   >   **b.**   <   **c.**   >

      d.   <   **e.**   >

5. a.   commutative property for addition

      b.   additive inverse property

      c.   identity property for multiplication

      d.   associative property for addition

6. a. $\dfrac{9}{10}$ **b.**   −15   **c.**   14

      d. $\dfrac{4}{7}$ **e.** $\dfrac{8}{25}$ **f.**   20

      g.   49   **h.**   −1   **i.**   125

7. a.   38   **b.**   −36

8. a. $\dfrac{y^{12}}{2x^{10}}$ **b.**   8   **c.** $\dfrac{xy^{4}}{2z^{2}}$

      d. $\dfrac{y^{8}}{16x^{2}}$ **e.** $72x^{11}y^{9}$ **f.** $\dfrac{x^{7}y^{2}}{2187}$

9. a. 6.92×10^{5} **b.** 4.7×10^{-2}

10. a.   89,700,000   **b.**   0.00053

CHAPTER 1 SUMMARY

IMPORTANT FACTS

Sets of Numbers

- Real numbers: $\{x \mid x$ is a point on a number line$\}$

- Natural or counting numbers: $\{1, 2, 3, 4, 5, \ldots\}$

- Whole numbers: $\{0, 1, 2, 3, 4 \ldots\}$

- Integers: $\{\ldots, -3, -2, -1, 0\ 1, 2, 3, \ldots\}$

- Rational numbers: $\left\{\dfrac{p}{q}\,\middle|\, p$ and q are integers, $q \neq 0\right\}$

- Irrational numbers: $\{x \mid x$ is a real number that is not rational$\}$

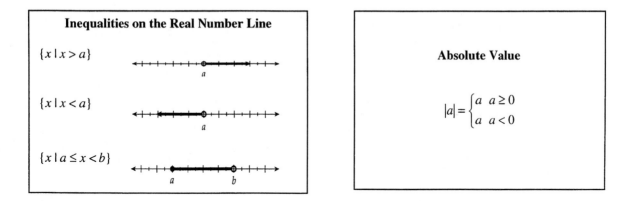

Inequalities on the Real Number Line
$\{x \mid x > a\}$
$\{x \mid x < a\}$
$\{x \mid a \leq x < b\}$

Absolute Value

$$|a| = \begin{cases} a & a \geq 0 \\ a & a < 0 \end{cases}$$

Operations with Real Numbers

- *To add two numbers with the same sign:* Add their absolute values and use the common sign.

- *To add two numbers with different signs:* Subtract the smaller absolute from the larger absolute value, and use the sign of the number with the larger absolute value.

- *Subtraction of real numbers:* Add the opposite of b to a, as in $a - b = a + (-b)$

- *When multiplying and dividing two numbers with the same signs:* The answer is positive.

- *When multiplying and dividing two numbers with different signs:* The answer is negative.

Properties of the Real Number System

- Commutative Properties: $a + b = b + a,\ ab = ba$

- Associative Properties: $(a + b) + c = a + (b + c),\ (ab)c = a\,(bc)$

- Identity Properties: $a + 0 = 0 + a = a,\ a \cdot 1 = 1 \cdot a = a$

- Inverse Properties: $a + (-a) = (-a) + a = 0,\ a \cdot \dfrac{1}{a} = \dfrac{1}{a} \cdot a = 1\ \ (a \neq 0)$

- Distributive Property: $a(b + c) = ab + ac$

- Multiplicative Property of 0: $a \cdot 0 = 0 \cdot a = 0$

- Double Negative Property: $-(-a) = a$

Order of Operations

1. Parentheses or other grouping symbols, such as brackets, braces, or a fraction bar

2. Exponents and roots

3. Multiplication or division from left to right

4. Addition or subtraction from left to right

Exponents and Roots

$$b^n = b \cdot b \cdot b \cdot \cdots \cdot b\ \ (n \text{ factors of } b)$$

$$\sqrt[n]{a} = b \text{ if } b \cdot b \cdot b \cdot \cdots \cdot b\ (n \text{ factors of } b) = a$$

Rules for Exponents -- For all real numbers a and b and all integers m and n:

- Product rule: $a^m \cdot a^n = a^{m+n}$

- Quotient rule: $\dfrac{a^m}{a^n} = a^{m-n},\ \ a \neq 0$

- Negative exponent rule: $a^{-m} = \dfrac{1}{a^m},\ \ a \neq 0$

- Zero exponent rule: $a^0 = 1,\ \ a \neq 0$

- Raising a power to a power: $(a^m)^n = a^{m \cdot n}$

- Raising a product to a power: $(ab)^m = a^m b^m$

- Raising a quotient to a power: $\left(\dfrac{a}{b}\right)^m = \dfrac{a^m}{b^m}, \quad b \neq 0$

HELPFUL HINTS

- Be very careful when writing or copying exponents. Since exponents are small, it is very easy to write or copy an exponent and then later not recognize what you have written.

- Always review your calculator screen to make sure that no keys were pressed incorrectly, and no keys were omitted. It is not necessary to enter the 0 before the decimal point in terms such as 0.56.

- In general, for any nonzero real number a and any whole number m, $\dfrac{1}{a^{-m}} = a^m$. When a base in the numerator or the denominator is raised to any power, that base can be moved to the other side of the fraction bar provided the sign of the exponent is changed. For example, $\dfrac{x^{-2}y^4}{z^{-6}} = \dfrac{y^4 z^6}{x^2}$.

- Don't confuse the *product rule*, $a^m \cdot a^n = a^{m+n}$, with the *power rule*, $\left(a^m\right)^n = a^{m \cdot n}$. For example, $\left(x^2\right)^4 = x^8$, not x^6.

Chapter 2

2.1 Solving Linear Equations

Summary

Properties of Equality

For all real numbers a, b, and c:

1. $a = a$
   Reflexive Property

2. If $a = b$ then $b = a$
   Symmetric Property

3. If $a = b$ and $b = c$, then $a = c$
   Transitive Property

Example 1
Identify the property of equality.

    a. If $5 = b$ and $b = c$, then $5 = c$.

    b. $x = x$

    c. If $x = 2$, then $2 = x$.

Solution

    a. Transitive property

    b. Reflexive property

    c. Symmetric property

Summary

Combining Terms

The **degree of a term** is the sum of the exponents on the variables in the term.

Like terms are terms that have the same variables with the same exponents.

To **simplify an expression** means to combine all like terms in the expression.

Example 2
Give the degree of the term.

   a. $2x^2$　　　　　　　　　　　　　**b.** $3a^3b$

Solution

   a. 2　　　　　　　　　　　　　　　**b.** 4

Example 3
Simplify each expression. If an expression cannot be simplified, so state.

   a. $2x - 7 + 6x + 3$

   b. $6a^2 + b^2 + ab$

   c. $4(x^2 + 3x - 1) + 2(x^2 - 7x + 6)$

Solution

   a. $2x - 7 + 6x + 3 = 8x - 4$

   b. Cannot be simplified

   c. $4(x^2 + 3x - 1) + 2(x^2 - 7x + 6) = 4x^2 + 12x - 4 + 2x^2 - 14x + 12$
$$= 6x^2 - 2x + 8$$

Summary

Properties of Equalities (continued)

For any real number a, b, and c:

  1. If $a = b$, then $a + c = b + c$
     Addition property of equality

  2. If $a = b$, then $a \cdot c = b \cdot c$
     Multiplication property of equality

Since subtraction is defined in terms of addition, the addition property of equality also allows us to subtract the same number from both sides of an equation.

Since division is defined in terms of multiplication, the multiplication property of equality also allows us to divide both sides of an equation by the same nonzero number.

Summary

To Solve Linear Equations

1. **Clear fractions.** If the equation contains fractions, eliminate the fractions by multiplying both sides of the equation by the least common denominator.

2. **Simplify each side separately.** Simplify each side of the equation as much as possible. Use the distributive property to clear parentheses and combine like terms as needed.

3. **Isolate the variable term on one side.** Use the addition property to get all terms with the variable on one side of the equation and all constant terms on the other side. It may be necessary to use the addition property a number of times to accomplish this.

4. **Solve for a variable.** Use the multiplication property to get an equation having just the variable (with a coefficient of 1) on one side.

5. **Check.** Check by substituting the value obtained in step 4 back into the original equation.

Example 4
Solve ech equation.

   a. $4x + 6 = 18$

   b. $3(3x - 4) = 33$

   c. $\dfrac{x+1}{2} - \dfrac{3}{4} = \dfrac{2x+3}{6}$

   d. $\dfrac{1}{5}(2x - 3) = \dfrac{3}{10}(x + 2)$

Solution

a. $4x + 6 = 18$

$4x + 6 - 6 = 18 - 6 \text{ (step 3)}$

$4x = 12$

$\dfrac{4x}{4} = \dfrac{12}{4} \quad \text{(step 4)}$

$x = 3$

Check:

$4x + 6 = 18$

$4(3) + 6 = 18$

$12 + 6 = 18$

$18 = 18 \text{ True}$

b. $3(3x - 4) = 33$

$9x - 12 = 33 \quad\quad \text{(step 2)}$

$9x - 12 + 12 = 33 + 12 \text{ (step 3)}$

$\dfrac{9x}{9} = \dfrac{45}{9} \quad\quad \text{(step 4)}$

$x = 5$

c. $\dfrac{x+1}{2} - \dfrac{3}{4} = \dfrac{2x+3}{6}$

$12\left(\dfrac{x+1}{2} - \dfrac{3}{4}\right) = 12\left(\dfrac{2x+3}{6}\right) \text{(step 1)}$

$6(x+1) - 3(3) = 2(2x+3)$

$6x - 6 - 9 = 4x + 6 \quad\quad \text{(step 2)}$

$6x - 15 = 4x + 6 \quad\quad \text{(step 2)}$

$2x - 15 = 6 \quad\quad\quad\quad \text{(step 3)}$

$2x = 21 \quad\quad\quad\quad\quad \text{(step 3)}$

$x = \dfrac{21}{2} \quad\quad\quad\quad\quad \text{(step 4)}$

d. $\dfrac{1}{5}(2x - 3) = \dfrac{3}{10}(x + 2)$

$10\left[\dfrac{1}{5}(2x-3)\right] = 10\left[\dfrac{3}{10}(x+2)\right] \text{(step 1)}$

$2(2x - 3) = 3(x + 2)$

$4x - 6 = 3x + 6 \quad\quad \text{(step 2)}$

$x - 6 = 6 \quad\quad\quad\quad \text{(step 3)}$

$x = 12 \quad\quad\quad\quad\quad \text{(step 3)}$

Summary

Types of Linear Equation Solutions:

1. A **conditional equation** has exactly one real solution.

2. An **identity** is true for every real number.

3. A **contradiction** has no solution.

Example 6
State whether each equation is a contradiction or an identity.

    a. $2x - 5 = 2(x + 2)$

    b. $4x + 3 = x + 3(x + 1)$

    c. $\dfrac{x+2}{5} = \dfrac{3x+6}{15}$

Solution

    a. Contradiction

    b. Identity

    c. Identity

Exercise Set 2.1

Name the property indicated.

    1. $y = y$

    2. If $a = b$ and $b = 3$, then $a = 3$.

    3. If $x + 2 = 5$, then $5 = x + 2$.

    4. If $2x = 3$, then $\dfrac{2x}{2} = \dfrac{3}{2}$.

    5. If $a = 2$, then $a + b = 2 + b$.

    6. If $y = z - 3$, and $z - 3 = x$, then $y = x$.

    7. If $4x = 10$, then $4x - 3 = 10 - 3$.

    8. If $\dfrac{x}{3} = 2$, then $3 \cdot \dfrac{x}{3} = 3 \cdot 2$.

Give the degree of each term.

9. $3x^2$ **10.** 9 **11.** $-8xy^3$

12. $4x^3$ **13.** $10x$ **14.** $3y^2z^4$

Simplify each expression. If an expression cannot be simplified, so state.

15. $5m + 9m + 8 + 4$ **16.** $8x^2 - 6x + 7$

17. $5(r - 3) + 6r - 2r + 1$ **18.** $-(7m - 12) - 2(4m + 7) - 3m$

19. $\dfrac{2}{3}(-6x + 9) - \dfrac{1}{2}(4x^2 + 6x)$

Solve each equation. If an equation has no solution, so state.

20. $5 + 3x = 5x - 1$ **21.** $x + 5 = x - 3$ **22.** $2(x + 1) = 3x - 4$

23. $2(x - 6) - 3(2x - 2) = 0$ **24.** $7(2t + 3) = -(4 + t)$ **25.** $2(x + 3) - 3[2(x - 3) + 4] = 0$

26. $\dfrac{s}{4} + 1 = \dfrac{s}{3}$ **27.** $\dfrac{x + 5}{2} = \dfrac{x + 3}{3}$ **28.** $\dfrac{7x - 3}{7} - \dfrac{5x + 7}{5} = 1$

Answers to Exercise Set 2.1

  1. Reflexive property   **2.** Transitive property   **3.** Symmetric property

  4. Multiplication property   **5.** Addition property   **6.** Transitive property

  7. Addition property   **8.** Multiplication property   **9.** 2

10. 0   **11.** 4   **12.** 3

13. 1   **14.** 6   **15.** $14m + 12$

16. Cannot be simplified   **17.** $9r - 14$ **18.** $-18m - 2$

19. $-2x^2 - 7x + 6$ **20.** 3   **21.** No solution

22. 6   **23.** $-\dfrac{3}{2}$ **24.** $-\dfrac{5}{3}$

25. 3   **26.** 12   **27.** -9

28. No solution

2.2 Problem Solving and Using Formulas

Summary

Guidelines for Problem Solving

1. **Understand the problem.**

   • Read the problem carefully at least twice. In the first reading, get a general overview of the problem. In the second reading, determine (a) exactly what you are being asked to find and (b) what information the problem provides.

   • If possible, make a sketch to illustrate the problem. Label the information given.

   • Will listing the information in a table help in solving the problem?

2. **Translate the problem into mathematical language.**

   • This will generally involve expressing the problem algebraically.

   • Sometimes this involves selecting a particular formula to use, whereas other times it is a matter of generating your own equation. It may be necessary to check other sources for the appropriate formula to use.

3. **Carry out the mathematical calculations necessary to solve the problem.**

4. **Check the answer obtained in step 3.**

   • Ask yourself: "Does the answer make sense?" "Is the answer reasonable?" If the answer is not reasonable, recheck your method for solving the problem and your calculations.

   • Check the solution in the original problem if possible.

5. **Answer the question.** Make sure you have answered the question asked. State the answer clearly.

Example 1
Frank borrows $1,000 from a bank which charges simple interest at a rate of 8%. How much will Frank owe in 6 years if no payments are made in the meantime.

Solution
This is a simple interest problem where the formula $i = prt$ is used. Substituting $p = 1000$, $r = 0.08$, and $t = 6$ produces
$i = prt$
$\quad = (1000)(0.08)(6)$
$\quad = \$480$
The interest is $480 and the amount owed to the bank is $1,000 + \$480 = \$1,480$.

Example 2
Tom is building a patio and must order concrete from the local store. The patio is to be 6 feet by 7 feet with a depth of 4 inches. How many cubic feet of cement should he order?

Solution
We need to find the volume of the patio (cement). Volume is length 3 width 3 height or $V = lwh$.
Use 6 for l, 7 for w, and $\dfrac{4}{12} = \dfrac{1}{3}$ for h. Remember, the height is 4 inches which must be converted to feet by dividing by 12. Substitute these values
$V = lwh$
$\quad = (6)(7)\left(\dfrac{1}{3}\right)$
$\quad = 14$ cubic feet
Tom should order 14 cubic feet of cement.

Example 3
Sally invested $3000 in a savings certificate paying 8% compounded quarterly. How much money will be in the account at the end of 20 years.

Solution
Use the formula $A = p\left(1 + \dfrac{r}{n}\right)^{nt}$ with $p = 3000$, $r = 0.08$, $n = 4$, and $t = 20$. Then
$A = p\left(1 + \dfrac{r}{n}\right)^{nt}$
$\quad = 3000\left(1 + \dfrac{0.08}{4}\right)^{4 \cdot 20}$
$\quad = 3000(1 + 0.02)^{80}$
$\quad = 3000(1.02)^{80}$
$\quad \approx 14,626.32$
In 20 years, Sally can expect to have $14,626.32 in her savings account.

Summary

> **To evaluate a formula** means to find the value of one of the variables when you are given the values of the other variables.
>
> To evaluate a formula, follow the order of operations presented in Section 1.4.

Example 4
Consider the formula $P = 2l + 2w$. Find P when $l = 6$ and $w = 3$.

Solution
$$P = 2l + 2w$$
$$= 2(6) + 2(3)$$
$$= 12 + 6$$
$$= 18$$

Example 5
Consider the formula $A = \frac{1}{2}h(a + b)$. Find A when $h = 8$, $a = 3$, and $b = 11$.

Solution
$$A = \frac{1}{2}h(a + b)$$
$$= \frac{1}{2}(8)(3 + 11)$$
$$= \frac{1}{2}(8)(14)$$
$$= 4 \cdot 14$$
$$= 56$$

Summary

> **Literal Equations** are equations that have more than one letter.
>
> **Formulas** are literal equations that are used to represent a scientific or real-life principle in mathematical terms.
>
> To solve for a given variable in a formula or equation, it is necessary to get that variable all by itself on one side of the equal sign.

Summary

To Solve for a Variable in a Formula or Equation

1. If the formula contains a fraction or fractions, multiply all terms by the least common denominator to remove all fractions.

2. Use the distributive property, if necessary, to remove parentheses.

3. Collect all terms containing the variable that you are solving for on one side of the equation and all terms not containing that variable on the other side of the equation.

4. If there is more than one term containing the variable, and the terms cannot be combined, use the distributive property to rewrite the terms as a product of two expressions where the variable for which you are solving is one of the factors. (This process is called factoring out the variable.)

5. Isolate the variable for which you are solving by dividing both sides of the equation factor that multiplies the variable.

Example 6
Solve $4x + 3y = 12$ for y.

Solution
$$4x + 3y = 12$$
$$3y = 12 - 4x$$
$$y = \frac{12 - 4x}{3} \text{ or } 4 - \frac{4}{3}x$$

Example 7
Solve $s = \dfrac{a - rk}{k - x}$ for r.

Solution
$$s = \frac{a - rk}{k - x}$$
$$s(k - x) = a - rk$$
$$sk - sx = a - rk$$
$$sk - sx - a = -rk$$
$$\frac{sk - sx - a}{-k} = r$$
$$\frac{-sk + sx + a}{k} = r$$

Example 8
Solve $2xy + 3xz = z$ for z.

Solution
$$2xy + 3xz = z$$
$$2xy = z - 3xz$$
$$2xy = z(1 - 3x)$$
$$\frac{2xy}{1 - 3x} = z$$

Exercise Set 2.2

Evaluate the formulas for the value given. Round answers to the nearest hundredth.

1. $C = 2\pi r$, $\pi = 3.14$, $r = 8$

2. $A = \pi r^2$, $\pi = 3.14$, $r = 8$

3. $V = lwh$, $l = 8$, $w = 2$, $h = .5$

4. $V = \frac{4}{3}\pi r^3$, $\pi = 3.14$, $r = 4$

5. $C = \frac{5}{9}(F - 32)$, $F = 80$

Solve for the variable indicated.

6. $A = lw$, for l

7. $V = \frac{1}{3}Bh$, for B

8. $I = Prt$, for t

9. $C = \frac{5}{9}(F - 32)$, for F

10. $P = 2l + 2w$, for l

11. $S = \frac{a}{1 - r}$, for a

12. $S^2 = 1 - \frac{a}{r}$, for r

13. $9x = 3y + bx + 2$, for x

14. $\frac{x + 2}{7} = 9y - 3$, for x

15. $\frac{6a}{x} - \frac{y}{3} = \frac{2}{3x}$, for x

16. $500 is invested into a savings account earning 8% interest compounded quarterly. Find the amount in the account at the end of 10 years.

17. Tom wants to form a rectangular garden with 60 feet of fence where the width must be 12 feet. What is the length?

Answers to Exercise Set 2.2

1. 50.24

2. 200.96

3. 8

4. 267.95

5. 26.67

6. $l = \dfrac{A}{w}$

7. $B = \dfrac{3V}{h}$

8. $t = \dfrac{I}{Pr}$

9. $F = \dfrac{9C + 160}{5}$

10. $l = \dfrac{P - 2w}{2}$

11. $a = S - Sr$

12. $r = \dfrac{a}{1 - s^2}$

13. $x = \dfrac{3y + 2}{9 - b}$

14. $x = 63y - 23$

15. $x = \dfrac{18a - 2}{y}$

16. $1,104.02

17. 18 feet

2.3 Applications of Algebra

Summary

Problem-Solving Procedure for Solving Application Problems

1. **Understand the problem.** Identify the quantity or quantities you are being asked to find.

2. **Translate the problem into mathematical language** (express the problem as an equation).

   a. Choose a variable to represent one quantity, and write down exactly what it represents. Represent any other quantity to be found in terms of this variable.

   b. Using the information from step **a**, write an equation that represents the word problem.

3. **Carry out the mathematical calculations** (solve the equation).

4. **Check the answer** (using the original wording of the problem).

5. **Answer the question asked.**

Example 1
If twice a number is added to 11 the result is 49. Find the number.

Solution
(Step 1) We are asked to find an unknown variable.
(Step 2) Let x = the unknown number.
(Step 2) $2x + 11 = 49$
(Step 3) $2x + 11 = 49$

$$2x = 38$$

$$x = 19$$

(Step 5) The number is 19.
(Step 4) Twice a number added to 11 is 49.

$$2(19) + 11 = 49$$

$$38 + 11 = 49$$

$$49 = 49 \text{ True}$$

Example 2
Find two consecutive integers if the sum of three times the larger and the smaller is 39.

Solution
(Step 1) We are asked to find two consecutive integers.
(Step 2) Let x = the smaller number
          Let $x + 1$ = the larger number
(Step 2) $3(x + 1) + x = 39$
(Step 3) $3(x + 1) + x = 39$

$$3x + 3 + x = 39$$

$$4x + 3 = 39$$

$$4x = 36$$

$$x = 9$$

(Step 5) The smaller number is 9. The larger number is $9 + 1 = 10$.
(Step 4) Three times the larger added to the smaller is 39.

$$3(10) + 9 = 39$$

$$30 + 9 = 39$$

$$39 = 39 \text{ True}$$

Example 3
The sum of the angles of a triangle is 180°. Find the three angles of a triangle if one angle is 30° more than the smallest angle and the third angle is triple the smallest angle.

Solution
We are asked to find three angles of a triangle.
Let x = the smallest angle
Let $x + 30$ = the second angle
Let $3x$ = the third angle

$$x + x + 30 + 3x = 180$$

$$\begin{aligned} x + x + 30 + 3x &= 180 \\ 5x + 30 &= 180 \\ 5x &= 150 \\ x &= 30 \end{aligned}$$

The smallest angle is 30°, the second angle is $30 + 30 = 60°$, the third angle is $3(30) = 90°$.
One angle plus 30° plus that angle plus three times that angle is 180°.

$$\begin{aligned} 30 + 30 + 30 + 3(30) &= 180 \\ 90 + 3(30) &= 180 \\ 90 + 90 &= 180 \\ 180 &= 180 \text{ True} \end{aligned}$$

Example 4
The sale price of an item is $28.00. If this reflects a 20% reduction from the regular price, find the regular price.

Solution
We are asked to find the regular price of the item.
Let x = the regular price of the item.

$$x - 0.20x = 28.00$$

$$\begin{aligned} x - 0.20x &= 28.00 \\ 0.80x &= 28.00 \\ x &= 35.00 \end{aligned}$$

The regular price of the item is $35.00.
The regular price minus 20% of the regular price is the sale price.

$$\begin{aligned} 35 - 0.20(35) &= 28 \\ 35 - 7 &= 28 \\ 28 &= 28 \text{ True} \end{aligned}$$

Exercise Set 2.3

a. Write an equation that can be used to solve the problem and
b. Find the solution to the problem.

1. One number is 5 less than twice a second number. If the sum of the numbers is 19, find the two numbers.

2. A number decreased by 30% is 140. Find the number.

3. Find two consecutive integers if the sum of twice the first and three times the second is 43.

4. Find two consecutive odd integers when the sum of the first and 6 less than the second is 26.

5. The sum of the angles of a triangle is 180°. Find the three angles if the second angle is 10 degrees more than the first angle and the third angle is 10 degrees more than twice the first angle.

6. The perimeter of a rectangle is 36 feet. If the length is three feet longer than twice the width, find the length and width of the rectangle.

7. The sale price of an item is $14.45, which reflects a 15% reduction in the regular price. Find the regular price of the item.

8. An item is marked $24.00, which reflects a 20% profit on the cost of the item. Find the cost of the item.

Answers to Exercise Set 2.3

1. **a.** $x + (2x - 5) = 19$ **b.** The first is 8, the second is 11.

2. **a.** $x - 0.30x = 140$ **b.** The number is 200.

3. **a.** $2x + 3(x + 1) = 43$ **b.** The first is 8, the second is 9.

4. **a.** $x + (x + 2 - 6) = 26$ **b.** The first is 15, the second is 17.

5. **a.** $x + (x + 10) + (2x + 10) = 180$

   b. The angles are 40°, 50°, and 90°.

6. **a.** $2x + 2(2x + 3) = 36$ **b.** The width is 5 ft, the length is 13 ft.

7. **a.** $x - 0.15x = 14.45$ **b.** The regular price is $17.00.

8. **a.** $x + 0.20x = 24.00$ **b.** The cost of the item is $20.00.

2.4 Additional Application Problems

Summary

> **amount = rate · time**

Example 1

A pipe will fill a container at the rate of 4 gallons per minute. If the container holds 180 gallons of water, how long will it take the pipe to fill the container?

Solution

Use amount = rate · time

$$180 = 4 \cdot x$$
$$45 = x$$

It will take 45 minutes.

Summary

> **Distance Formula**
>
> distance = rate · time

Example 2

Two cars leave at the same time traveling in opposite directions. One car travels at 50 mph and the second car at 60 mph. In how many hours will the cars be 385 miles apart?

Solution

Car	Rate	Time	Distance
1	50	t	$50t$
2	60	t	$60t$

Distance of car 1 + distance of car 2 = 385

$$50t + 60t = 385$$
$$110t = 385$$
$$t = 3.5$$

In 3.5 hours the cars will be 385 miles apart.

Example 3

A car leaves a town at 1 P.M. traveling due north at 45 mph. A second car leaves the same town at 3 P.M. and travels due south at 55 mph. At what time will the cars be 390 miles apart?

Solution

Car	Rate	Time	Distance
1	45	t	$45t$
2	55	$t - 2$	$55(t - 2)$

Distance of car 1 + distance of car 2 = 390

$$45t + 55(t - 2) = 390$$
$$45t + 55t - 110 = 390$$
$$100t - 110 = 390$$
$$100t = 500$$
$$t = 5$$

So, 5 hours from 1 P.M. or 6 P.M.

Summary

Any problem in which two or more quantities are combined to produce a second quantity or a single quantity is separated into two or more different quantities may be considered a **mixture** problem. We will again use a table to organize the information.

Example 4

A chemist must mix 12 liters of a 40% solution of mixture which is 50% potassium chloride. How much of the 70% solution should be used?

Solution

Solution	Strength of Solution	Number of Liters	Amount of Potassium Chloride
1	0.40	12	0.40(12)
2	0.70	x	0.70(x)
Mixture	0.50	$x + 12$	0.50($x + 12$)

Amount of 40% solution + Amount of 70% solution = Amount of 50% solution

$$0.40(12) + 0.70x = 0.50(x + 12)$$
$$4.8 + 0.7x = 0.5x + 6$$
$$48 + 7x = 5x + 60$$
$$2x = 12$$
$$x = 6$$

So, 6 liters of the 70% solution should be added.

Exercise Set 2.4

Solve the problem.

1. A patient is to receive 1400 cubic centimeters of intravenous fluid over a period of 4 hours. What should the intravenous flow rate be?

2. A pipe can fill a swimming pool in 30 hours. If the flow rate of the pipe is 5 gallons per minute, how many gallons does the pool contain?

3. Two trains leave from the same station traveling in opposite directions. The rate of the first train is 55 mph and the rate of the second train is 60 mph. How long will it be before the trains are 345 miles apart?

4. A student can get to school in $\frac{1}{4}$ hour if she rides her bike. It takes $\frac{3}{4}$ hour if she walks. Her speed when walking is 10 mph slower than when riding. What is her speed when she rides?

5. How many liters of 10% alcohol solution must be mixed with 30 liters of a 50% solution to obtain a 20% solution?

6. A total of $60,000 is to be invested for one year, part at 15% and part at 8% simple interest. If they earned $7,600, how much was invested at each rate?

7. 20 liters of a solution is 30% acid. How much of a 70% acid solution must be mixed to obtain a solution that is 40% acid?

Answers to Exercise Set 2.4

1. 350 cubic centimeters per hour   **2.** 9000 gallons   **3.** 3 hours

4. 15 mph   **5.** 90 liters

6. $40,000 at 15%; $20,000 at 8%

7. $6\frac{2}{3}$ liters

2.5 Solving Linear Inequalities

Summary

Properties Used to Solve Inequalities

1. If $a > b$, then $a + c > b + c$.

2. If $a > b$, then $a - c > b - c$.

3. If $a > b$ and $c > 0$, then $ac > bc$.

4. If $a > b$ and $c > 0$, then $\dfrac{a}{c} > \dfrac{b}{c}$.

5. If $a > b$ and $c < 0$, then $ac < bc$.

6. If $a > b$ and $c < 0$, then $\dfrac{a}{c} < \dfrac{b}{c}$.

Example 1
Solve the inequality $2x - 7 \le 1$ and graph on a number line.

Solution

$$2x - 7 \le 1$$
$$2x - 7 + 7 \le 1 + 7$$
$$2x \le 8$$
$$x \le 4$$

Summary

The solution set of an inequality graphed on the number line and written in interval notation.

Inequality	Graph	Interval Notation
$x > 5$		$(5, \infty)$
$x \geq 5$		$[5, \infty)$
$x < 5$		$(-\infty, 5)$
$x \leq 5$		$(-\infty, 5]$
$5 \leq x < 7$		$[5, 7)$
$5 \leq x \leq 7$		$[5, 7]$
$5 < x < 7$		$(5, 7)$

Example 2
Solve the inequality $2x + 8 \leq 4(x - 3)$. Give the solution on a graph and in interval notation.

Solution
$$2x + 8 \leq 4(x - 3)$$
$$2x + 8 \leq 4x - 12$$
$$-2x + 8 \leq -12$$
$$-2x \leq -20$$
$$x \geq 10$$

Graph:

Interval notation: $[10, \infty)$

Example 3
A box contains twice as many dimes as nickels and contains at least 15 coins. At least how many nickels does it have?

Solution
Let x = number of nickels
  $2x$ = number of dimes
 Number of nickels + Number of dimes ≥ 15
$$x + 2x \geq 15$$
$$3x \geq 15$$
$$x \geq 5$$
It must contain at least 5 nickels.

Summary

A **compound inequality** is formed by joining the two inequalities with the word **and** or **or**.

To find the solution set of an inequality containing the word **and**, take the **intersection** of the solution sets of the two inequalities.

To find the solution set of an inequality containing the word **or**, take the **union** of the solution sets of the two inequalities.

Example 4
Solve $3x - 4 > 2$ and $2x - 3 \leq 5$.

Solution
Solve each inequality separately.

$3x - 4 > 2$	$2x - 3 \leq 5$
$3x > 6$	$2x \leq 8$
$x > 2$	$x \leq 4$

The solution is the intersection of $x > 2$ and $x \leq 4$ which is $2 < x \leq 4$.

Example 5
Solve $4x - 2 > 6$ or $2x + 5 < -3$.

Solution
Solve each inequality separately.

$4x - 2 > 6$	$2x + 5 < -3$
$4x > 8$	$2x < -8$
$x > 2$	$x < -4$

The solution is the union of $x > 2$ or $x < -4$ which is $x > 2$ or $x < -4$. Interval notation: $(-\infty, -4) \cup (2, \infty)$

Summary

A compound inequality using the word *and* can usually be written in a shorter form. For example, $a < x$ *and* $x < b$ can be written as $a < x < b$. When solving an inequality in this form, whatever we do to one part we must do to all three parts.

Example 6
Solve the inequality $-4 \leq 2(x - 3) \leq 2$.

Solution
$$-4 \leq 2(x - 3) \leq 2$$
$$-4 \leq 2x - 6 \leq 2$$
$$2 \leq 2x \leq 8$$
$$1 \leq x \leq 4$$
Graph:
         1   4

Interval notation: $[1, 4]$

Exercise Set 2.5

Express each inequality **a.** using a number line **b.** in interval notation and **c.** as a solution set.

  1. $x \geq -2$

  2. $x < \dfrac{2}{3}$

  3. $-1 < x \leq 0$

  4. $x > 6$

  5. $1 \leq x \leq \dfrac{5}{4}$

Solve the inequality and graph the solution on a number line.

  6. $x + 7 > 10$

  7. $5 - x > 1$

  8. $6x + 3 \leq 2x - 7$

  9. $5(x + 1) < 2(1 - x)$

  10. $3 \leq 2x + 1 \leq 5$

  11. $2x > 6$ or $x - 1 < -2$

Solve the inequality and give the solution in interval notation.

  12. $2x \leq 1$

  13. $-6x < 12$

  14. $x - 7 < 5x + 4$

  15. $12x + 17 \leq 11 - 3x$

  16. $-10 \leq 5x + 5 < 5$

  17. To receive a grade of C, a student must have an average greater than or equal to 70 and less than 80. If a student has scores of 65, 75, 81, 63, 60 on 5 tests, what score must be made on the 6th test to receive a grade of C?

Answers to Exercise Set 2.5

  1. a.
      -2

  b. $[-2, \infty)$

  c. $\{x | x \geq -2\}$

  2. a.
      $\dfrac{2}{3}$

  b. $\left(-\infty, \dfrac{2}{3}\right)$

  c. $\left\{x | x < \dfrac{2}{3}\right\}$

  3. a.
      -1 0

  b. $(-1, 0]$

  c. $\{x | -1 < x \leq 0\}$

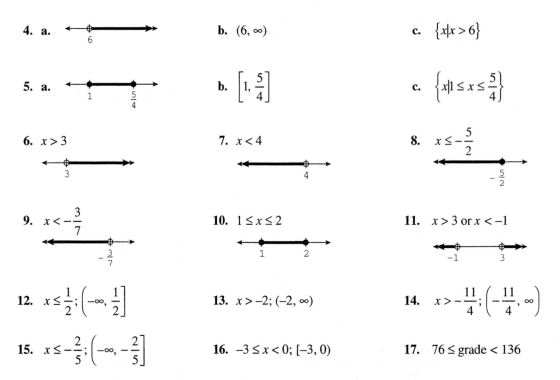

4. a. (number line with open circle at 6, shaded right)   **b.** $(6, \infty)$ **c.** $\{x|x > 6\}$

5. a. (number line with closed circles at 1 and $\frac{5}{4}$, shaded between)   **b.** $\left[1, \frac{5}{4}\right]$ **c.** $\left\{x|1 \le x \le \frac{5}{4}\right\}$

6. $x > 3$

(number line with open circle at 3, shaded right)

7. $x < 4$

(number line with open circle at 4, shaded left)

8. $x \le -\frac{5}{2}$

(number line with closed circle at $-\frac{5}{2}$, shaded left)

9. $x < -\frac{3}{7}$

(number line with open circle at $-\frac{3}{7}$, shaded left)

10. $1 \le x \le 2$

(number line with closed circles at 1 and 2, shaded between)

11. $x > 3$ or $x < -1$

(number line with open circles at -1 and 3, shaded outward)

12. $x \le \frac{1}{2}; \left(-\infty, \frac{1}{2}\right]$

13. $x > -2; (-2, \infty)$

14. $x > -\frac{11}{4}; \left(-\frac{11}{4}, \infty\right)$

15. $x \le -\frac{2}{5}; \left(-\infty, -\frac{2}{5}\right]$

16. $-3 \le x < 0; [-3, 0)$

17. $76 \le$ grade < 136

2.6 Solving Equations and Inequalities Containing Absolute Values

Summary

Procedures for Solving Equations and Inequalities Containing Absolute Values

For $a > 0$

   1. If $|x| = a$, then $x = a$ or $x = -a$.

   2. If $|x| < a$, then $-a < x < a$.

   3. If $|x| > a$, then $x < -a$ or $x > a$.

   4. If $|x| = |y|$, then $x = y$ or $x = -y$.

Example 1
Solve the equation.
$$|4x - 1| = 11$$

Solution
$$4x - 1 = 11 \quad \text{or} \quad 4x - 1 = -11$$
$$4x = 12 \quad \text{or} \quad 4x = -10$$
$$x = 3 \quad \text{or} \quad x = -\frac{5}{2}$$

Example 2
Solve the equation.
$$|2x + 3| - 2 = 9$$

Solution
First isolate the absolute value.
$$|2x + 3| - 2 = 9$$
$$|2x + 3| = 11$$
$$2x + 3 = 11 \quad \text{or} \quad 2x + 3 = -11$$
$$2x = 8 \quad \text{or} \quad 2x = -14$$
$$x = 4 \quad \text{or} \quad x = -7$$

Example 3
Solve the inequality.
$$|2x - 5| + 3 \le 12$$

Solution
Again, isolate the absolute value.
$$|2x + 5| + 3 \le 12$$
$$|2x + 5| \le 9$$
$$-9 \le 2x - 5 \le 9$$
$$-4 \le 2x \le 14$$
$$-2 \le x \le 7$$

Example 4
Solve the inequality.
$$|3x + 2| > 10$$

Solution
$$3x + 2 > 10 \quad \text{or} \quad 3x + 2 < -10$$
$$3x > 8 \qquad\qquad 3x < -12$$
$$x > \frac{8}{3} \qquad\qquad x < -4$$

Example 5
Solve the equation.
$|2x+3|=|6x-11|$

Solution
$|2x+3|=|6x-11|$

$2x+3=6x-11$ or $2x+3=-(6x-11)$
$-4x+3=-11$ or $2x+3=-6x+11$
$-4x=-14$ or $8x=8$
$x=\dfrac{7}{2}$ $x=1$

Note:
If $|x|>0$, the solution is all real numbers except $x=0$.
If $|x|<0$, then there is no solution.
If $|x|\ge 0$, the solution is all real numbers.
If $|x|\le 0$, the solution is $x=0$.

Example 6
Solve $|3x+2|\le 0$.

Solution
$|3x+2|\le 0$
$3x+2=0$
$x=-\dfrac{2}{3}$

Exercise Set 2.6

Solve the equation.

1. $|y+3|=1$
2. $|2x+7|=3$
3. $|4x+5|-4=4$

4. $|2s|=|s+3|$
5. $|2x+5|=|7-2x|$

Solve the inequality.

6. $|2x+5|>7$
7. $|2x-9|-1\le 0$
8. $|5x-8|>9$

9. $|5-2z|-3<0$
10. $\left|\dfrac{2x-1}{3}\right|\le 4$
11. $\left|2x-\dfrac{1}{3}\right|<2$

12. $|x+1|\ge 0$

Answers to Exercise Set 2.6

1. $-2, -4$

2. $-5, -2$

3. $-\dfrac{13}{4}, \dfrac{3}{4}$

4. $-1, 3$

5. $\dfrac{1}{2}$

6. $x < -6$ or $x > 1$

7. $4 \le x \le 5$

8. $x < -\dfrac{1}{5}$ or $x > \dfrac{17}{5}$

9. $1 < z < 4$

10. $-\dfrac{11}{2} \le x \le \dfrac{13}{2}$

11. $-\dfrac{5}{6} < x < \dfrac{7}{6}$

12. all real numbers

Chapter 2 Practice Test

1. State the degree of the term $4x^2 y^3$.

2. Solve the equation: $2(x - 6) - 3(2x - 2) = 0$

3. Solve the equation: $\dfrac{x}{3} - 4 = \dfrac{x}{2} + 1$

4. Solve the equation: $\dfrac{2x + 1}{2} = \dfrac{1}{3} + \dfrac{x - 3}{4}$

5. Find the value of s if $s = a + (n - 1)d$ and $a = 6$, $n = 5$, and $d = -4$.

6. Solve for x in the equation $2x = 4y + xy$.

7. Solve for d in the equation $s = a + (n - 1)d$.

For each problem, write an equation that can be used to solve the problem. Solve thee quation and answer the question asked.

8. Find two consecutive integers such that twice the first plus the second is 61.

9. The sale price of an item is $15.00 which reflects a 25% reduction in the regular price. Determine the regular price.

10. Two planes fly from the same point at the same time in opposite directions. The rate of the first plane is 450 mph and the rate of the second plane is 350 mph. How many hours until they are 2800 miles apart?

11. How many liters of a 16% salt solution must be added to 12 liters of a 24% solution to obtain a 22% salt solution?

12. A total of $40,000 is to be invested. Part of the money is placed in a savings account paying 6% simple interest. The rest of the money is placed in a savings account paying 10% simple interest. If the total interest earned after one year is to be $3600, find the amount to be invested in each account.

13. Solve the inequality $\dfrac{3-4x}{2} \le 6$ and graph the solution on the number line.

14. Solve the inequality $-2 \le 2(x+3) \le 6$ and write the solution in interval notation.

Find the solution to the following equations.

15. $|3x-2| = 8$ 16. $|4x+2| = |x-6|$

Find the solution to the following inequalities.

17. $\left|\dfrac{3x+1}{2}\right| \le \dfrac{2}{3}$ 18. $|5x+2| - 1 > 10$

Answers to Chapter 2 Practice Test

1. 5   2. $-\dfrac{3}{2}$ 3. -30

4. $-\dfrac{11}{9}$ 5. $s = -10$ 6. $x = \dfrac{4y}{2-y}$

7. $d = \dfrac{s-a}{n-1}$

8. $2x + x + 1 = 61$
   The 1st is 20.
   The 2nd is 21.

9. $x - 0.25x = 15$
   Regular price is \$20.

10. $450t + 350t = 2800$
    The time is 3.5 hours.

11. $0.16x + (0.24)(12) = 0.22(x+12)$
    4 liters must be added.

12. $0.06x + 0.10(40,000 - x) = 3600$
    \$10,000 at 6%
    \$30,000 at 10%

13. $x \ge -\dfrac{9}{4}$

14. $-4 \le x \le 0;\ [-4, 0]$ 15. $\dfrac{10}{3}, -2$ 16. $-\dfrac{8}{3}, \dfrac{4}{5}$

17. $-\dfrac{7}{9} \le x \le \dfrac{1}{9}$ **18.** $x > \dfrac{9}{5}$ or $x < -\dfrac{13}{5}$

CHAPTER 2 SUMMARY

IMPORTANT FACTS

Properties of Equality:

- Reflexive property: $a = a$
- Symmetric property: If $a = b$, then $b = a$.
- Transitive property: If $a = b$ and $b = c$, then $a = c$.
- Addition property of equality: If $a = b$, then $a + c = b + c$
- Multiplication property of equality: If $a = b$, then $ac = bc$.

To Solve Linear Equations

1. Clear fractions.
2. Simplify each side separately.
3. Isolate the variable term on one side.
4. Solve for the variable.
5. Check the solution.

Formulas

- *Distance Formula*: distance = rate · time ($d = rt$)
- *Simple Interest Formula*: interest = principal · rate · time ($i = prt$)

Angle Measures

- *Complementary Angles*: Complementary angles are two angles whose sum measures $90°$.
- *Supplementary Angles*: Supplementary angles are two angles whose sum measures $180°$.

Problem-Solving Procedure

1. Understand the problem.
2. Translate the problem into mathematical language.
3. Carry out the mathematical calculations necessary to solve the problem.
4. Check the answer obtained in step 3.
5. Answer the question.

Properties Used to Solve Inequalities

- If $a > b$, then $a + c > b + c$
- If $a > b$, then $a - c > b - c$
- If $a > b$ and $c > 0$, then $ac > bc$
- If $a > b$ and $c > 0$, then $\dfrac{a}{c} > \dfrac{b}{c}$
- If $a > b$ and $c < 0$, then $ac < bc$
- If $a > b$ and $c < 0$, then $\dfrac{a}{c} < \dfrac{b}{c}$

Absolute Value, for $a > 0$

- If $|x| = a$, then $x = a$ or $x = -a$
- If $|x| < a$, then $-a < x < a$
- If $|x| > a$, then $x < -a$ or $x > a$
- If $|x| = |y|$, then $x = y$ or $x = -y$

HELPFUL HINTS

- The equation $\dfrac{1}{3}(x + 7) = \dfrac{1}{4}x$ may also be written as $\dfrac{x+7}{3} = \dfrac{x}{4}$
- As you read through the examples in this chapter, think about how they can be applied to other, similar problems. For instance, when you know that 'the diameter, d, decreased by 7 inches, can be represented by $d - 7$', you can apply this to a similar problem such as 'the height, h, decreased by 5 feet, can be represented as $h - 5$'.

- When asked to find a percent, you are being asked to find the percent of some quantity. Therefore, when a percent is listed, it is **always** multiplied by a number or a variable.

- Suppose you read the following sentence in a application problem: "A 16-inch string is cut into two pieces." You know that you should let the length of the first piece be represented by x. But you may not be sure whether you should let the length of the second piece be represented by $x - 16$ or by $16 - x$. Plugging in specific numbers may help you decide. For example:

If the First Piece Is....	Then the Second Piece Is....
6 in	10 in = 16 in – 6 in
11 in	5 in = 16 in – 11 in

    From this exercise, you can see that if the first piece is x inches, then the second piece is $16 - x$ inches.

- Here are some suggestions to help you out with application problems.

    1. Make an appointment to see your instructor.
    2. View the videotapes that go with the chapter.
    3. Use the Student Study Guide.
    4. Take advantage of any free tutoring available at your college.
    5. Form a study group with classmates.
    6. Use the Student Solutions Manual if you get stuck on an exercise.
    7. Visit the Prentice Hall—Allen Angel website at prenhall.com/angel and study the material that relates to this chapter.
    8. Use Math Pro if it is available.
    9. Use the Prentice Hall Mathematics Tutor, if available.
    10. Remember, the more you practice, the better you will become.

- Make sure to reverse the direction of the inequality symbol when multiplying or dividing both sides of an inequality by a negative number. For example,

Inequality	Direction of Inequality Symbol
$-4x > 8$	$\dfrac{-4x}{-4} < \dfrac{8}{-4}$

- Generally, when writing a solution to an inequality, we write the variable on the left. For example, $6 < x$ means $x > 6$. Notice that the inequality symbol points to the 6 in both cases.

- Be very careful when writing the solution to a compound inequality. Both inequality symbols should point to the smaller number. For example, $3 > x > -4$ can also be written as $-4 < x < 3$.

- There are various ways to write the solution for an inequality. Be sure to indicate the solution in the form requested by your professor, such as: Inequality, Number Line, Interval Notation, or Solution Set.

- When solving equations and inequalities containing absolute value, recognizing the form of the problem will be helpful in determining the solution. In the examples below, a, b, and c are real numbers where $a \neq 0$ and $c > 0$:

Form	**Solution**
$|ax + b| = c$	Two distinct numbers, p and q
$|ax + b| < c$	The set of numbers between two numbers, $p < x < q$
$|ax + b| > c$	The set of numbers less than one number or greater than a second number, $x < p$ or $x > q$

Chapter 3

3.1 Graphs

Summary

Cartesian Coordinate System

1. The **Cartesian coordinate system** consists of two axes (number lines) which meet at right angles at a point called the **origin**.

2. To graph a point, its *x*-coordinate and *y*-coordinate must be known.

3. An **ordered pair** (x, y) is used to give the coordinates of a point. The *x*-coordinate is always listed first.

Example 1
Plot the following ordered pairs: **a.** $(-2, 3)$ **b.** $(4, 0)$ **c.** $(0, -3)$ **d.** $(5, 8)$

Solution

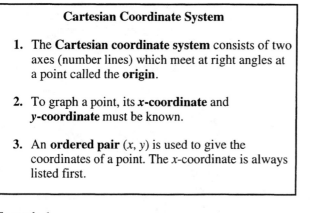

Summary

A **graph** is an illustration of the set of points whose coordinates satisfy the equation. Sometimes when drawing a graph, we list a few points that satisfy the equation in a table and then plot the points. We then draw a line through the points to obtain the graph.

Example 2

Graph $y = \dfrac{1}{2}x + 1$.

Solution
Construct a table, plot the points, and draw the graph.

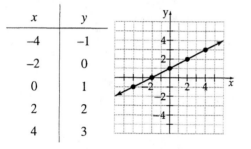

x	y
−4	−1
−2	0
0	1
2	2
4	3

Example 3
Graph $y = x^2 - 1$.

Solution
Construct a table, plot the points, and draw the graph.

x	y
−3	8
−2	3
−1	0
0	−1
1	0
2	3
3	8

Example 4
Graph $y = |x| - 2$.

Solution
Construct a table, plot the points, and draw the graph.

x	y
-4	2
-3	1
-2	0
-1	-1
0	-2
1	-1
2	0
3	1
4	2

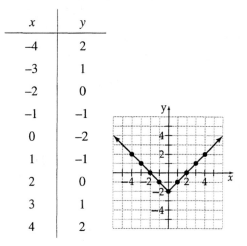

Exercise Set 3.1

1. Plot the following points.

$A(3, 2)$ $B(-2, 4)$ $C(-4, -1)$

$D(5, -2)$ $E(-3, 0)$

2. Graph the following.

    a. $y = 2x + 1$ **b.** $y = \dfrac{1}{3}x$ **c.** $y = x^2 + 1$

    d. $y = \dfrac{2}{x}$ **e.** $y = |x| + 3$

Answers to Exercise Set 3.1

1.

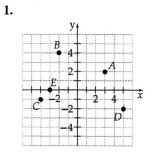

2. a.   **b.**   **c.**

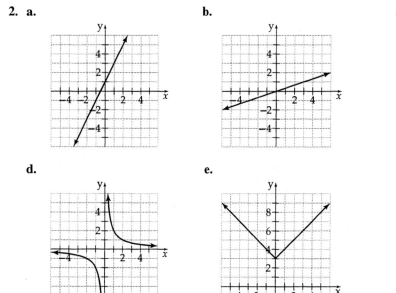

d.   **e.**

3.2 Functions

Summary

Relations
1. A **relation** is any set of ordered pairs.
2. A **relation** may be represented by:
a. set of ordered pairs
b. table of values
c. graph
d. rule
e. an equation
3. The **domain** of a relation is the set of values that can be used for the **independent variable.**
4. The **range** of a relation is the set of values that represent the **dependent variable**.

Example 1
Each of the following represents the same relation.

1. $((1, 3), (2, 5), (3, 7), (4, 9), (5, 11))$

2. Table of values:

x	1	2	3	4	5
y	3	5	7	9	11

3. Graph:

4. Rule: For each natural number from 1 to 5 inclusive, double it and add 1 to obtain the corresponding y-value.

5. Equation: $y = 2x + 1$ for $1 \le x \le 5, x \in N$.

The domain of this relation is the set $\{1, 2, 3, 4, 5\}$ and the range is the set $\{3, 5, 7, 9, 11\}$

Example 2
Postage stamps currently cost $.32. The cost C of n postage stamps is given by the rule $C = 0.32n$. This is an example of a relation. What is its domain and range?

Solution
The domain is the set of possible input values of this relation. Since n represents the number of stamps that can be purchased, $n \ge 0, n \in W$, (whole numbers). We call n the **independent variable** since it can be any whole number we choose. Once n is chosen, however, then the cost of n stamps, C, is uniquely determined. We say the variable C is the **dependent variable** since C depends upon the number of stamps purchased.

Summary

Functions

A **function** is a correspondence between a first set of elements, the domain, and a second set of elements, the range, such that each element of the domain corresponds to exactly one element in the range.

Example 3
Determine whether the figure represents a function or does not represent a function:

a.

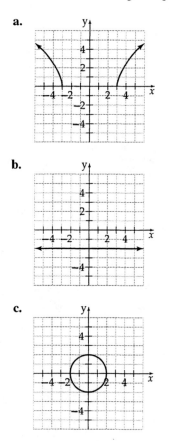

b.

c.

Solution

　　　a is a function, **b** is a function, **c** not a function

Example 4

a. State the domain and range of the function graphed below.

b. Use the graph to determine $f(0)$, $f(-2)$ and $f(2)$.

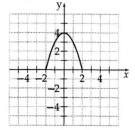

Solution

    a. The domain is $\{x|-2 \le x \le 2\}$. The range is $\{y|0 \le y \le 4\}$.

    b. From the graph, $f(0)$ is the y-value when x is zero. So, $f(0) = 4, f(2) = f(-2) = 0$.

Example 5
Evaluate the function indicated at $x = -2$:

    a. $f(x) = \sqrt[3]{-x^2 + 4x - 1}$ **b.** $g(x) = |2x - 9|$ **c.** $h(x) = -2x^2 + 3x$

Solution

    a. $f(x) = \sqrt[3]{-x^2 + 4x - 1}$

         $f(-2) = \sqrt[3]{-(-2)^2 + 4(-2) - 1}$

             $= \sqrt[3]{-(4) + (-8) - 1}$

             $= \sqrt[3]{-13}$

    b. $g(x) = |2x - 9|$

         $g(-2) = |2(-2) - 9|$

             $= |-4 - 9|$

             $= |-13|$

             $= 13$

    c. $h(x) = -2x^2 + 3x$

         $h(-2) = -2(-2)^2 + 3(-2)$

             $= -2(4) + (-6)$

             $= -14$

Example 6
A box in the shape of a rectangular solid is to have a length which is twice the width. The height of the box is to be 2 inches. Find a function, $V(x)$, which expresses the volume of the box as a function of its width, x, in cubic inches. Then find (if possible), $V(4)$, $V(3)$, $V(0)$ and $V(-2)$ and interpret the results.

Solution
The volume of the box can be found using the formula: $V = l \cdot w \cdot h$.
If $w = x$, then $l = 2x$. We are given that $h = 2$. Thus, $V(x) = (2x) \cdot x \cdot 2 = 4x^2$. $V(4)$ represents the volume of the box if the width is 4 inches.
$V(4) = 4(4)^2 = 4(16) = 64$ cubic inches
$V(3) = 4(3)^2 = 36$ cubic inches
$V(0) = 4(0)^2 = 0$
(The volume of the box is zero cubic inches if the width of the box is zero).
Finally, $V(-2)$ represents the volume of the box when the width is -2 inches.
Since a dimension cannot be negative, $V(-2)$ does not make sense. The domain of $V(x)$ is $\{x|x \ge 0\}$.

Exercise Set 3.2

Determine which of the relations are functions. Give the domain and range of each relation or function. For exercises 4–10 state the domain and range based upon the graph. When arrows are used, the graph extends in that direction.

1. {(1, 1), (2, 4), (3, 9), (4, 16)}

2. {(−1, 1), (−1, 4), (4, 8), (6, 9), (7, 10)}

3. {(−2, 3), (−1, 3), (0, 3), (4, 3), (8, 3)}

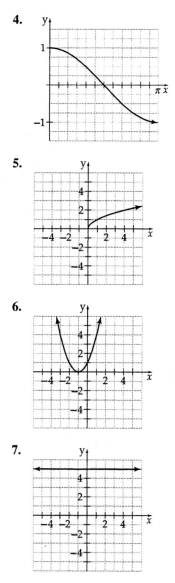

4.

5.

6.

7.

8.

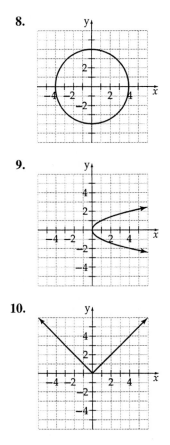

9.

10.

Evaluate the functions at the values indicated.

11. $f(x) = -2x^2 + 3x$ **a.** $f(-4)$ **b.** $f(2)$

12. $h(x) = 5 - 7x$ **a.** $h(0)$ **b.** $h(5)$

13. $g(x) = -\dfrac{3}{4}x + \dfrac{5}{6}$ **a.** $g(-4)$ **b.** $g(8)$

14. $f(x) = -x^3 - x^2 + 6x - 5$ **a.** $f(-1)$ **b.** $f(-2)$

15. $g(x) = \sqrt{-3x^2 + 5}$ **a.** $g(-3)$ **b.** $g(0)$

16. $h(x) = \dfrac{3x^2 + 4x}{-2x + 5}$ **a.** $h(4)$ **b.** $h(-3)$

17. $g(x) = |-3x + 7|$ **a.** $g(-3)$ **b.** $g(9)$

18. $f(x) = \dfrac{1}{2}x^3 + 3x$ **a.** $f\left(\dfrac{1}{2}\right)$ **b.** $f\left(-\dfrac{2}{3}\right)$

19.   The height of a rock thrown from ground level at a speed of 80 feet per second is given by the function $h(t) = -16t^2 + 80t$. Find and interpret $h(0)$, $h(2.5)$ and $h(5)$.

20.   A peach orchard near Macon, Georgia has 20 peach trees per acre. Each tree currently produces, on the average, 300 peaches. For each additional tree planted beyond 20, the average number of peaches per tree will be reduced by 10.
The function $Y(x) = (20 + x) \cdot (300 - 10x)$ gives the total yield of peaches for the peach orchard. Find and interpret $Y(0)$, $Y(5)$, and give the largest possible value of x.

Answers to Exercise Set 3.2

1. A function; Domain = {1, 2, 3, 4}; Range = {1, 4, 9, 16}

2. Not a function; Domain = {−1, 4, 6, 7}; Range = {1, 4, 8, 9, 10}

3. A function; Domain = {−2, −1, 0, 4, 8}; Range = {3}

4. A function; Domain = $\left\{x \mid x \text{ is a real number}\right\}$; Range = $\left\{y \mid -1 \le y \le 1\right\}$

5. A function; Domain = $\left\{x \mid x \ge 0\right\}$; Range = $\left\{y \mid y \ge 0\right\}$

6. A function; Domain = $\left\{x \mid x \text{ is a real number}\right\}$; Range = $\left\{y \mid y \ge 0\right\}$

7. A function; Domain = $\left\{x \mid x \text{ is a real number}\right\}$; Range = {5}

8. Not a function; Domain = $\left\{x \mid -4 \le x \le 4\right\}$; Range = $\left\{y \mid -4 \le y \le 4\right\}$

9. Not a function; Domain = $\left\{x \mid x \ge 0\right\}$; Range = $\left\{y \mid y \text{ is real number}\right\}$

10. A function; Domain = $\left\{x \mid x \text{ is a real number}\right\}$; Range = $\left\{y \mid y \ge 0\right\}$

11. a. $f(-4) = -44$ **b.** $f(2) = -2$

12. a. $h(0) = 5$ **b.** $h(5) = -30$

13. a. $g(-4) = \dfrac{23}{6}$ **b.** $g(8) = -\dfrac{31}{6}$

14. a. $f(-1) = -11$ **b.** $f(-2) = -13$

15. a. $g(-3)$ is not a real number.   **b.** $g(0) = \sqrt{5}$

16. **a.** $h(4) = -\dfrac{64}{3}$ **b.** $h(-3) = \dfrac{15}{11}$

17. **a.** $g(-3) = 16$ **b.** $g(9) = 20$

18. **a.** $f\left(\dfrac{1}{2}\right) = \dfrac{25}{16}$ **b.** $f\left(-\dfrac{2}{3}\right) = -\dfrac{58}{27}$

19. $h(0) = 0$; the height of the ball initially is zero feet.
$h(2.5) = 100$; the ball is 100 feet high after 2.5 seconds.
$h(5) = 0$; the ball hits the ground after 5 seconds.

20. $Y(0) = 6000$; this is the yield of peaches if no additional trees are planted. $Y(5) = 6,250$; this is the yield if 5 additional trees are planted. The largest value of x is 30 since the term $(300 - 10x)$ must be nonnegative.

3.3 Linear Functions: Graphs and Applications

Summary

Linear Equations

1. The **standard form of a linear equation** is given by: $ax + by = c$, where a and b are not both equal to zero.

2. A **graph** of an equation is an illustration of the set of points whose coordinates satisfy the equation.

3. The graphs of all linear equations are **lines**. For that reason, it is only required to find and plot **two ordered pairs** that satisfy the equation. It is a good idea to find and plot a **third** point as a check.

Example 1
Graph $y = 2x + 5$

Solution
Pick three arbitrary values of x, substitute into the equation and determine the three corresponding y-values:

	$y = 2x + 5$	ordered pair
$x = 0$	$y = 2(0) + 5 = 5$	$(0, 5)$
$x = 2$	$y = 2(2) + 5 = 9$	$(2, 9)$
$x = -4$	$y = 2(-4) + 5 = -3$	$(-4, -3)$

Plot the three ordered pairs on a grid and connect them with a straight line:

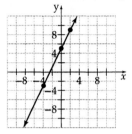

Example 2
Graph $-4x + 2y = -8$.

Solution
First, solve the equation for y:
$$-4x + 2y = -8$$
$$2y = 4x - 8$$
$$y = 2x - 4$$

Choose three arbitrary values of x, substitute these values into the equation and solve the resulting equation for y. It is a good idea to always choose at least one negative value for x.

	$y = 2x - 4$	ordered pair
$x = 0$	$y = 2(0) - 4 = -4$	$(0, -4)$
$x = -2$	$y = 2(-2) - 4 = -8$	$(-2, -8)$
$x = 3$	$y = 2(3) - 4 = 2$	$(3, 2)$

Plot the three ordered pairs and connect the points with a straight line:

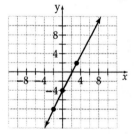

Example 3

Graph $\dfrac{1}{6}x - \dfrac{3}{4}y = \dfrac{3}{2}$

Solution

This equation, like the two previous examples, is a linear equation since it is of the form $ax + by = c$. Therefore, the graph of this equation is also a line.

First, multiply each side of the equation by the LCD of 12 to eliminate all fractions:

$$12\left(\frac{1}{6}x - \frac{3}{4}y\right) = 12 \cdot \frac{3}{2}$$

$$12\left(\frac{1}{6}x\right) - 12\left(\frac{3}{4}y\right) = \frac{12}{1} \cdot \frac{3}{2}$$

$$2x - 9y = 18$$

Now, solve the equation $2x - 9y = 18$ for y:

$$2x - 9y = 18$$
$$-9y = -2x + 18$$
$$y = \frac{2}{9}x - 2$$

Choose three arbitrary x-values and substitute these values into the equation to find three corresponding values of y. Choose x values which are multiplies of 9 to make the calculations easier.

$x = 9$ $\qquad y = \dfrac{2}{9}(9) - 2 = 0$ $\qquad$ (9, 0)

$x = -9$ $\qquad y = \dfrac{2}{9}(-9) - 2 = -4$ $\qquad$ (–9, –4)

$x = 18$ $\qquad y = \dfrac{2}{9}(18) - 2 = 2$ $\qquad$ (18, 2)

Plot the three points and connect them with a straight line:

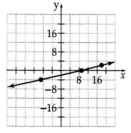

Summary

┌───┐

X- and *Y*-intercepts

1. The ***x*-intercept** is the point where the graph of an equation crosses the *x*-axis. It is found by letting $y = 0$ and solving the equation for x.

2. The ***y*-intercept** is the point where the graph of an equation crosses the *y*-axis. It is found by letting $x = 0$ and solving the equation for y.

3. The intercepts are convenient points to use when graphing linear equations.

└───┘

Example 4
Graph $4y = -5x + 20$ by plotting intercepts.

Solution
Find the *y*-intercept by letting $x = 0$:
$$4y = -5x + 20$$
$$4y = -5(0) + 20$$
$$4y = 20$$
$$y = 5$$
Thus, (0, 5) is the *y*-intercept:

Find the *x*-intercept by letting $y = 0$:
$$4y = -5x + 20$$
$$4(0) = -5x + 20$$
$$0 = -5x + 20$$
$$5x = 20$$
$$x = 4$$
Thus, (4, 0) is the *x*-intercept.

Plot (0, 5) and (4, 0) and draw the graph:

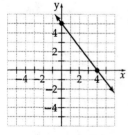

Summary

+---+
| **Special Cases** |
| |
| 1. The graph of $y = b$ will be a |
| horizontal line b units above or |
| below the x-axis, depending upon the |
| sign of b. |
| |
| 2. The graph of $x = a$ will be a |
| vertical line a units right or left |
| of the y-axis, depending upon the |
| sign of a. |
+---+

Example 5
Graph $y = -4$.

Solution
The equation can be rewritten as $0x + y = -4$.

For each x-value selected, y will **always be -4**. For instance, let $x = -2$. Then $0(-2) + y = -4$, or $y = -4$. Let $x = 3$. Then $0(3) + y = -4$, or $y = -4$. The graph will be a **horizontal** line 4 units **below** the x-axis.

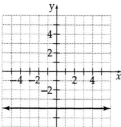

Example 6
Graph $x = 5$.

Solution
Rewrite the equation as $1x + 0y = 5$. In this case, no matter what the value of y is, x will **always be 5**. For example, if $y = -2$, then $1x = 0(-2) = 5$, or $x = 5$. This graph will be a **vertical** line 5 units to the **right** of the y-axis.

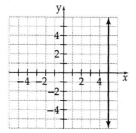

Here's an application problem involving a linear equation:

Example 7
A car's average speed is 55 miles per hour. Presently, the car is 30 miles from a certain city. Using the formula $d = rt$, (distance = rate 3 time), draw a graph of distance of the car (from the city) versus time (in hours).

Solution
Using $d = rt$, we have $D = 55t + 30$ where 30 represents the starting point from the city. It is of the form $y = 55t + 30$, which can be written in the form $ax + by = c$. Thus, the graph of this equation will be a line.

Pick two arbitrary values of t, such as $t = 1$ and $t = 2$ and substitute the values into the equation to solve for d:

If $t = 1$, then $d = 55(1) + 30 = 85$
If $t = 2$, then $d = 55(2) + 30 = 140$

Plot (1, 85) and (2, 140) and draw a line connecting these points. Note: You will have to adjust the vertical scale on the y-axis to sketch a complete graph. Each tick mark on the vertical scale could represent 10 or 15 miles. Thus, you would need about 10 to 15 tick marks on the vertical scale to be able to plot the y-value of 140.

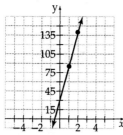

Exercise Set 3.3

Graph each equation by solving for y (if the equation is not already in that form), selecting 3 values of x and finding the corresponding values of y.

1. $y = -3$

2. $x = 4$

3. $2x + y = 4$

4. $-3x + 2y = 6$

5. $y = -\frac{2}{3}x + 1$

6. $4x - y = 3$

7. $\frac{1}{2}x + \frac{3}{4}y = 1$

8. $\frac{2}{3}x - \frac{1}{5}y = 1$

Graph using intercepts.

9. $-5x + 2y = 10$

10. $\frac{1}{6}x - \frac{1}{2}y = -1$

11. $-2x + 7y = 14$

12. A mechanic's bill is $40.00 per hour labor in addition to $150.00 for parts on a certain job. Draw a graph of the mechanic's bill (y) versus number of hours worked (x) from $0 \le x \le 10$.

13. The total cost to produce an item sold by a company consists of fixed costs of $80.00 plus a cost of $45.00 for each item produced.

    a. Draw a graph of the cost versus number of items produced from 0 to 15 items.

     b.   Approximately how many items can be produced at a cost of $700.00?

     c.   Find the cost of producing 9 items.

Answers to Exercise Set 3.3

1.   **2.**

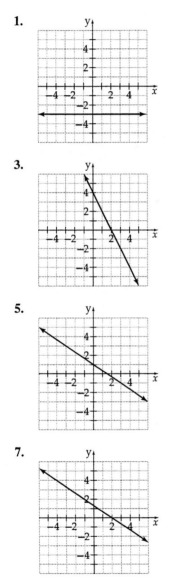

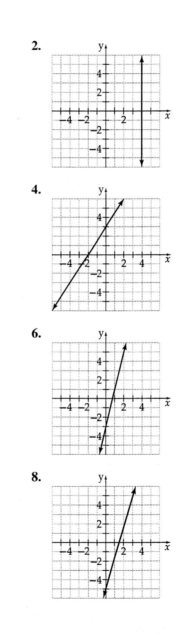

9.

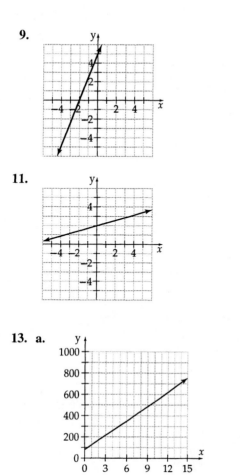

10.

11.

12.

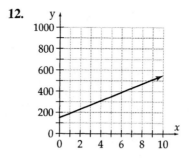

13. a.

b. 13 items

c. Cost equals $485.00.

3.4 The Slope-Intercept Form of a Linear Equation

Summary

Slope

1. The **slope** of a line is a ratio of the vertical change to the horizontal change between **any two points** on the line.

2. The **slope** of the line through $P(x_1, y_1)$ and $Q(x_2, y_2)$ is given by
$$m = \frac{\text{change in } y}{\text{change in } x} = \frac{y_2 - y_1}{x_2 - y_1} = \frac{\Delta y}{\Delta x}$$
provided that $x_1 \neq x_2$.

Example 1
Find the slope of the line containing $P(-2, 5)$ and $Q(4, 7)$.

Solution
Use the formula $m = \dfrac{y_2 - y_1}{x_2 - x_1}$.

$$m = \frac{7-5}{4-(-2)} = \frac{2}{6} = \frac{1}{3}$$

Summary

Positive and Negative Slopes Zero and Undefined Slopes

1. The slope of **any horizontal line** is zero.

2. The slope of **any vertical line** is undefined.

3. A line that rises going from left to right has a **positive slope.**

4. A line that falls going from left to right has a **negative slope**.

Example 2
The table below give an individual's salary in a given year:

Year:	Salary:
1973	$9,000
1983	$19,000
1987	$36,000
1990	$43,000
1995	$50,000

The table can be thought of as ordered pairs in which the first coordinate is the year and the second coordinate is the salary.

Find the slope of the line segments between

    a. 1973 and 1983 and

    b. between 1987 and 1995.

Solution

    a. $m = \dfrac{\text{vertical change}}{\text{horizontal change}} = \dfrac{19,000 - 9000}{1983 - 1973} = \dfrac{10,000}{10} = 1000$

    Interpretation: The slope of 1000 represents the yearly average change in annual salary over the ten year period from 1973 to 1983.

    b. $m = \dfrac{\text{vertical change}}{\text{horizontal change}} = \dfrac{50,000 - 36,000}{1995 - 1987} = \dfrac{14,000}{8} = 1750$

    This can be interpreted as an increase of $1750 in income per year over the 8-year period from 1987 to 1995.

Summary

Slope-Intercept Form of a Linear Equation

$y = mx + b$ where m is the **slope** and b is the **y-intercept.**

Example 3
Write the equation $-2x + 4y = 8$ in slope-intercept form. State the slope and the y-intercept.

Solution
First solve for y: $-2x + 4y = 8$

$$4y = 2x + 8$$

$$y = \frac{1}{2}x + 2$$

To graph the line, start at the point (0, 2), (*y*-intercept) and move vertically upward 1 unit and horizontally to the right 2 units to obtain a second point, (2, 3). Repeat this procedure to obtain a third point (4, 4). Plot all three points and connect them with a straight line.

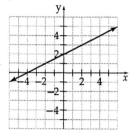

Exercise Set 3.4

Find the slope of the line through the given points. If the slope is undefined, then so state.

  1. (3, 5) and (9, 7)   **2.** (–3, 2) and (4, 16)

  3. (6, –2) and (–1, –2)   **4.** (–3, 5) and (–3, 10)

  5. (–5, –11) and (4, –3)

Solve for *x* if the line through the given points is to have the given slope.

  6. (1, 0), (5, *x*); slope is –3   **7.** (–4, –1), (*x*, 2); slope $= -\dfrac{3}{5}$

  8. Find the slope of the line in each figure below:

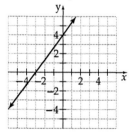

Write each equation in slope-intercept form and indicate the slope and the *y*-intercept. Then, use the *y*-intercept and slope to draw the graph of the linear equation.

  9. $3x - y = -2$ **10.** $60x = 30y + 60$ **11.** $-2x - 9y = 18$

Answers to Exercise Set 3.4

  1. $\dfrac{1}{3}$ **2.** 2   **3.** 0

  4. Slope is undefined.   **5.** $\dfrac{8}{9}$ **6.** $x = -12$

7. $x = -9$ **8.** $m = \dfrac{4}{3}$

9. $y = 3x + 2$, $m = 3$, y-intercept $(0, 2)$

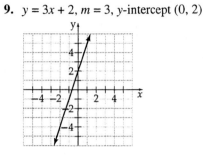

10. $y = 2x - 2$; $m = 2$, y-intercept $(0, -2)$

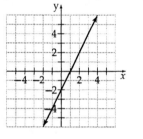

11. $y = -\dfrac{2}{9}x - 2$; $m = -\dfrac{2}{9}$; $b = -2$

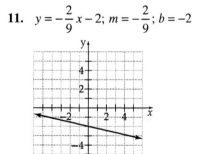

3.5   The Point-Slope Form of a Linear Equation

Summary

Point-Slope Form of a Linear Equation
$y - y_1 = m(x - x_1)$, where m is the slope and (x_1, y_1) is a specific point on the line and (x, y) is another arbitrary point on the line.

Example 1
Find the equation of a line, in slope-intercept form, whose slope is –4 which passes through $P(-2, 5)$.

Solution
Let $Q(x, y)$ be **any arbitrary** point on the line and $P(-2, 5)$ be a specific point. Use the point-slope form for the equation of a line:
$$y - y_1 = m(x - x_1)$$
$$y - 5 = -4(x - (-2))$$
$$y - 5 = -4(x + 2)$$
$$y - 5 = -4x - 8$$
$$y = -4x - 3$$

Example 2
Find the slope intercept form of the equation of a line which passes through $P(-2, 7)$ and $Q(4, -9)$.

Solution

First, find the slope of the line using the slope formula: $m = \dfrac{y_2 - y_1}{x_2 - x_1} = \dfrac{-9 - 7}{4 - (-2)} = \dfrac{-16}{6} = -\dfrac{8}{3}$

Now, use the point slope formula and choose either P or Q as (x_1, y_1). P will be used in our example:
$$y - y_1 = m(x - x_1)$$
$$y - 7 = -\frac{8}{3}(x - (-2))$$
$$y - 7 = -\frac{8}{3}(x + 2)$$
$$y - 7 = -\frac{8}{3}x + \frac{-16}{3}$$
$$y = -\frac{8}{3}x - \frac{16}{3} + \frac{21}{3}$$
$$y = -\frac{8}{3}x + \frac{5}{3}$$

Summary

Parallel and Perpendicular Lines

1. Two lines are **parallel** if and only if their slopes are the same.

2. Two lines are **perpendicular** if and only if the product of their slopes is negative one. This means that their slopes are negative reciprocals of each other.

Example 3
Determine if the two lines are parallel, perpendicular or neither.

    a. L_1: (3, 5), (4, 7); L_2: (8, 7), (10, 6)

    b. L_1: (7, 10), (11, 13); L_2: (8, 11), (12, 14)

Solution

    a. The slope of L_1 is $\dfrac{7-5}{4-3} = 2$. The slope of L_2 is $\dfrac{6-7}{10-8} = -\dfrac{1}{2}$. Since $2 \cdot -\dfrac{1}{2} = -1$, the lines are perpendicular.

    b. The slope of L_1 is $m = \dfrac{13-10}{11-7} = \dfrac{3}{4}$. The slope of L_2 is $m = \dfrac{14-11}{12-8} = \dfrac{3}{4}$. Since the slopes are equal, the lines are parallel.

Example 4
Determine if the graphs of the equations are parallel or perpendicular lines.
$-2x + 3y = 6$
$6x - 9y = 8$

Solution
Solve each equation for y and note the coefficient of the x term. This coefficient will be the slope of the line.
$-2x + 3y = 6$
$3y = 2x + 6$
$y = \dfrac{2}{3}x + 2$

Thus, the slope of the first line is $\dfrac{2}{3}$.

$6x - 9y = 8$
$-9y = -6x + 8$
$y = \dfrac{-6x}{-9} + \dfrac{8}{-9}$
$y = \dfrac{2}{3}x - \dfrac{8}{9}$

Thus, the slope of the second line is $\dfrac{2}{3}$.

Since the slopes are the same, the lines are parallel.

Example 5
Consider the equation $3x - 5y = 15$. Determine the equation of the line which has a y-intercept of 6 and is

    a. parallel to the given line and

    b. perpendicular to the given line.

Solution
Solve $3x - 5y = 15$ for y to find the slope.

$$3x - 5y = 15$$
$$-5y = -3x + 15$$
$$y = \frac{3}{5}x - 3$$

Thus, the slope of the line is $\frac{3}{5}$.

    a. The slope of the parallel line is also $\frac{3}{5}$.

       use the point slope formula with the given point $P(0, 6)$, (y-intercept) and the slope of $\frac{3}{5}$.

$$y - y_1 = m(x - x_1)$$
$$y - 6 = \frac{3}{5}(x - 0)$$
$$y - 6 = \frac{3}{5}x$$
$$y = \frac{3}{5}x + 6$$

    b. Again, use the point-slope formula with the given point $(0, 6)$ but this time use a slope of $-\frac{5}{3}$, since $-\frac{5}{3}$ is the negative reciprocal of $\frac{3}{5}$.

$$y - y_1 = m(x - x_1)$$
$$y - 6 = -\frac{5}{3}(x - 0)$$
$$y - 6 = -\frac{5}{3}x$$
$$y = -\frac{5}{3}x + 6$$

Exercise Set 3.5

Two points on L_1 and two points on L_2 are given. Determine if L_1 is parallel to, perpendicular to, or neither parallel nor perpendicular to L_2.

1. L_1: (9, –5) and (4, 6); L_2: (3, –2) and (–2, –5)

2. L_1: (4, 7) and (6, 12); L_2: (–3, –3) and (–1, 2)

3. L_1: (7, 10) and (11, 13); L_2: (8, 11) and (12, 14)

Determine if the given lines are parallel, perpendicular or neither:

4. $-2x + y = 7$ and $-4x + 2y = 10$

5. $y = -\dfrac{3}{4}x + 7$ and $y = \dfrac{4}{3}x - 5$

6. $x - 3y = -9$ and $y = 3x + 6$

Write the equation of the line in point-slope form given the following properties of the line:

7. line has slope –3 and passes through (–2, 4)

8. line passes through (–2, 5) and (3, –7)

9. line passes through (–1, 8) and (7, 16)

10. through (2, 5) and parallel to the line with x-intercept and y-intercept 3.

11. Through (0, 0) and perpendicular to the line whose equation is $\dfrac{1}{5}x - \dfrac{2}{7}y = 1$

12. An office machine was purchased in 1980 at a cost of $100,000. In the year 2000, the machine will have a market value of 0 dollars. Assuming that the relationship between the value of the machine (V) and the time (t) in years is linear, find an equation of the line depicting value versus time. Use this equation to find the value of the machine in 1995.

Answers to Exercise Set 3.5

1. Neither	2. Parallel	3. Parallel
4. Parallel	5. Perpendicular	6. Neither
7. $y = -3x + 2$	8. $y = -\dfrac{12}{5}x + \dfrac{1}{5}$	9. $y = x + 9$
10. $y = -x + 7$	11. $y = -\dfrac{10}{7}x$	12. $V = -5000t + 100,000$ At $t = 15$, then $V = 25,000$

3.6 The Algebra of Functions

Summary

Algebra of Functions
If $f(x)$ represents one function and $g(x)$ represents a second function, then the following operations on functions may be performed:
Sum of functions: $(f + g)(x) = f(x) + g(x)$
Difference of functions: $(f - g)(x) = f(x) - g(x)$
Product of functions: $(f \cdot g)(x) = f(x) \cdot g(x)$
Quotient of functions: $\left(\dfrac{f}{g}\right)(x) = \dfrac{f(x)}{g(x)}$
$g(x) \neq 0$

Example 1

Let $f(x) = 2x^2 + 3x - 1$; $g(x) = 3x - 2$. Find the following:

   a. $(f + g)(x)$ **b.** $(f - g)(x)$ **c.** $(g - f)(x)$

   d. $(f \cdot g)(x)$ **e.** $(f + g)(2)$ **f.** $\left(\dfrac{f}{g}\right)\left(\dfrac{2}{3}\right)$

Solution

   a. $(f + g)(x) = f(x) + g(x)$
$$= 2x^2 + 3x - 1 + (3x - 2)$$
$$= 2x^2 + 6x - 3$$

   b. $(f - g)(x) = f(x) - g(x)$
$$= 2x^2 + 3x - 1 - (3x - 2)$$
$$= 2x^2 + 3x - 1 - 3x + 2$$
$$= 2x^2 + 1$$

   c. $(g - f)(x) = g(x) - f(x)$
$$= 3x - 2 - (2x^2 + 3x - 1)$$
$$= 3x - 2 - 2x^2 - 3x + 1$$
$$= -2x^2 - 1$$

d. $(f \cdot g)(x) = f(x) \cdot g(x)$

$$= (2x^2 + 3x - 1)(3x - 2)$$
$$= 6x^3 - 4x^2 + 9x^2 - 6x - 3x + 2$$
$$= 6x^3 + 5x^2 - 9x + 2$$

e. $(f + g)(2) = f(2) + g(2)$

$$= 2(2)^2 + 3(2) - 1 + (3(2) - 2)$$
$$= 8 + 6 - 1 + 4$$
$$= 17$$

f. $\left(\dfrac{f}{g}\right)\left(\dfrac{2}{3}\right) = \dfrac{f\left(\frac{2}{3}\right)}{g\left(\frac{2}{3}\right)} = \dfrac{2\left(\frac{2}{3}\right)^2 + 3\left(\frac{2}{3}\right) - 1}{3\left(\frac{2}{3}\right) - 2} = \dfrac{\frac{17}{9}}{0}$

Since division by 0 is not permitted, the expression $\left(\dfrac{f}{g}\right)\left(\dfrac{2}{3}\right)$ is not defined.

Example 2
Using the graphs of $f(x)$ and $g(x)$, find

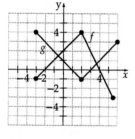

a. $(f + g)(1)$ **b.** $(f - g)(5)$ **c.** $(f \cdot g)(5)$

Solution

a. $(f + g)(1) = f(1) + g(1)$ **b.** $(f - g)(5) = f(5) - g(5)$ **c.** $(f \cdot g)(5) = f(5) \cdot g(5)$
$\qquad\qquad = 3 + 0$ $= (-2) - 2$ $= (-2)(2)$
$\qquad\qquad = 3$ $= -4$ $= -4$

Exercise Set 3.6

For exercises 1–3, use $f(x)$ and $g(x)$ to find

a. $(f + g)(x)$ **b.** $(f - g)(x)$ **c.** $(f \cdot g)(x)$

d. $\left(\dfrac{f}{g}\right)(x)$

1. $f(x) = 3x$ and $g(x) = x^2$

2. $f(x) = 5x - 2$ and $g(x) = x^2 - 3x + 1$

3. $f(x) = 2x^2 - x + 5$ and $g(x) = 3x + 7$

Given $f(x) = x^2 - 4x + 5$ and $g(x) = 2x - 3$, find

4. $(f \cdot g)(3)$ **5.** $(f - g)(2)$

Given $f(x) = 2x^2 - 3x + 2$ and $g(x) = 5x - 2$, find

6. $(f + g)(-1)$ **7.** $\left(\dfrac{f}{g}\right)(1)$

Answers to Exercise Set 3.6

1. a. $3x + x^2$ **b.** $3x - x^2$ **c.** $3x^3$ **d.** $\dfrac{3}{x}$

2. a. $x^2 + 2x - 1$ **b.** $-x^2 + 8x - 3$ **c.** $5x^3 - 17x^2 + 11x - 2$ **d.** $\dfrac{5x - 2}{x^2 - 3x + 1}$

3. a. $2x^2 + 2x + 12$ **b.** $2x^2 - 4x - 2$ **c.** $6x^3 + 11x^2 + 8x + 35$ **d.** $\dfrac{2x^2 - x + 5}{3x + 7}$

4. 6   **5.** 0   **6.** 0   **7.** $\dfrac{1}{3}$

3.7 Graphing Linear Inequalities

Summary

To graph a linear inequality in two variables

1. Replace the inequality symbol with an equals (=) sign.

2. Draw the graph of the linear function in step 1. If the original inequality has the symbol ≤ or ≥, the line drawn should be solid. Otherwise the line should be dashed. The graph of the line separates the coordinate plane into two half-planes, one above the line and one below the line.

3. Select **any** point not on the line (usually the origin, (0, 0) is a good choice unless it lies on the line) and determine whether its coordinates satisfy the **original inequality**. If so, shade the half-plane on the side of the line containing this point. If the point does not satisfy the inequality, shade the half-plane on the side of the line not containing this point.

Example 1
Graph $y \geq -3x + 2$.

Solution

1. Replace the inequality symbol with the equals sign: $y = -3x + 2$

2. Graph the line $y = -3x + 2$. This line has a slope of -3 and y-intercept of $(0, 2)$. The line should be solid since the original inequality contained the symbol $\geq$.

    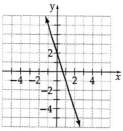

3. Choose the point $(0, 0)$ and determine if it satisfies the original inequality: $0 \geq -3(0) + 2$ is false, so the half-plane not containing the origin is shaded. Thus, the region above the line is shaded.

    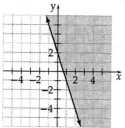

Example 2
Graph $-3x + 4y < 12$.

Solution

1. Replace the inequality symbol with an equals sign.
    $-3x + 4y = 12$

2. Graph the line $-3x + 4y = 12$ using the intercept method since the coefficients of both x and y are factors of 12. If $x = 0$, then $y = 3$, so $(0, 3)$ is the y-intercept. If $y = 0$, then $x = -4$, $(-4, 0)$ is the x-intercept. The line drawn should be dotted since original inequality contains the symbol $>$.

    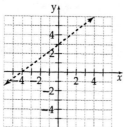

3. Select the point (0, 0) (not on the line) and determine whether or not it satisfies the original inequality: $-3(0) + 4(0) < 12$ is true. Thus, shade the half-plane containing the origin. This is the half-plane below the line.

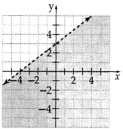

Example 3
Graph $x \geq -5$.

Solution

1. Graph the line $x = -5$. This is a vertical line 5 units to the left of the y-axis. This line should be solid since the original inequality contains the symbol $\geq$.

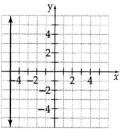

2. Since the point (0, 0) does not lie on the line, substitute this point into the original inequality and determine whether it satisfies the original inequality: $0 \geq -5$ is true.

3. Shade the half-plane to the right of the line $x = -5$.

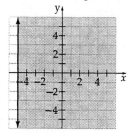

Exercise Set 3.7

Graph each inequality.

1. $x > -2$ 2. $y \leq -3$ 3. $y < -3x + 1$

4. $y \geq \dfrac{2}{3}x + 2$ **5.** $-4x + 5y < 20$ **6.** $-3x + y > 4$

7. $\dfrac{1}{4}x - \dfrac{2}{3}y \leq 2$ **8.** $\dfrac{1}{4}y \geq \dfrac{5}{12}x + \dfrac{3}{4}$ **9.** $-2x + 3y \geq 6$

10. $y \leq \dfrac{3}{4}x$ **11.** $y > -2x$ **12.** $x \geq 0$

13. $y \geq 0$ **14.** $x > y$

Answers to Exercise Set 3.7

1.
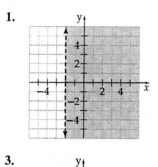

2.
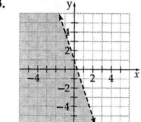

3.
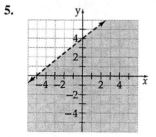

4.
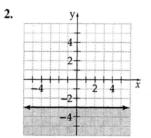

5.
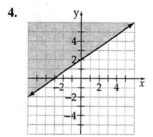

6.
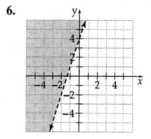

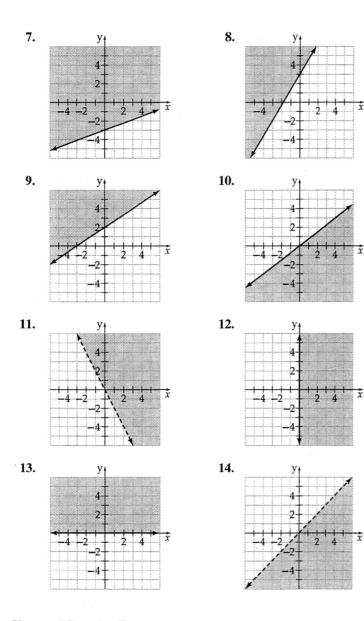

Chapter 3 Practice Test

1. Are the lines $2x + 3y = 5$ and $2x - 3y = 7$ parallel?

2. Find the slope and *y*-intercept of $-3x + 6y = 18$.

3. Write the equation of a line passing through the points $(-2, 3)$ and $(5, 10)$.

4. Write the equation of a line through $(0, 3)$ and perpendicular to the line $-3x + 5y = 10$.

5. Graph $y = -\dfrac{3}{5}x + 1$.

6. Graph $-4x + 2y = 8$, using x- and y-intercepts.

7. The distance that an automobile is from a certain city is estimated by the function $d(t) = 100 + 55t$ where t is in hours and d is in miles.

    a.   Graph $d(t)$ for $0 \le t \le 10$.

    b.   Find $d(0)$, $d(5)$ and interpret the results.

    c.   For $0 \le t \le 10$, find the range of this function.

8. For $f(x) = -3x^2 + 4x - 2$, find

    a. $f(-2)$ **b.** $f\left(\dfrac{2}{3}\right)$

9. Graph $f(x) = 5$.

10. Graph $y \le -3x + 2$.

For problems 11–12, find the domain and range of each relation and determine if the relation is a function.

11. $\{(3, 4), (-2, 6), (5, 8), (-2, 5)\}$

12.

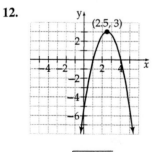

13. $f(x) = \sqrt{x^2 + 16}$, find

    a. $f(2)$ **b.** $f(-3)$ **c.** $f(0)$

Answers to Chapter 3 Practice Test

  1. No

  2. Slope is $\dfrac{1}{2}$; y-intercept $(0, 3)$

  3. $y = x + 5$

4. $y = -\dfrac{5}{3}x + 3$

5.

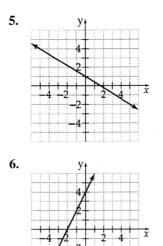

6.

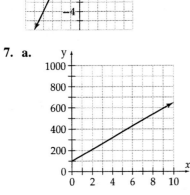

7. a.

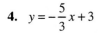

b. $d(0) = 100$; $d(5) = 375$
Interpretation: $d(0) = 100$ means that after $t = 0$ hours, the car is 100 miles from the city.
$d(5) = 375$ means that after 5 hours, the car is 375 miles from this certain city.

c. The range is $\{y \mid 0 \le y \le 650\}$.

8. a. $f(-2) = -22$ **b.** $f\left(\dfrac{2}{3}\right) = -\dfrac{2}{3}$

9.

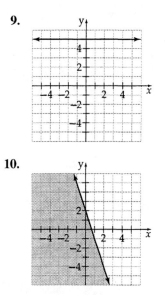

10.

11. Domain = $\{-2, 3, 5\}$; range = $\{4, 5, 6, 8\}$; not a function

12. Domain = $\{x | x \text{ is a real number}\}$; range = $\{y | y \leq 3\}$, a function

13. a. $f(2) = \sqrt{20} = 2\sqrt{5}$ **b.** $f(-3) = 5$ **c.** $f(0) = 4$

CHAPTER 3 SUMMARY

IMPORTANT FACTS

Graphic Equations: $x = a$ and $y = b$

- The graph of an equation in the form $y = b$ is a horizontal line for any real number b.

- The graph of an equation in the form $x = a$ will always be a vertical line for any real number a.

Slope of a Line

$$m = \frac{\Delta y}{\Delta x} = \frac{y_2 - y_1}{x_2 - x_1}$$

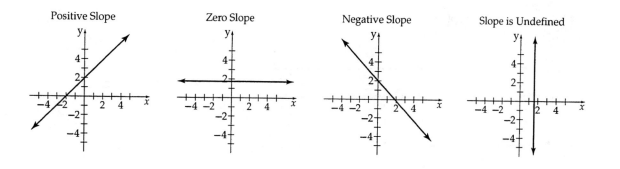

Operations on Functions

- Sum of functions: $(f + g)(x) = f(x) + g(x)$

- Difference of functions: $(f - g)(x) = f(x) - g(x)$

- Product of functions: $(f \cdot g)(x) = f(x) \cdot g(x)$

- Quotient of functions: $(f / g)(x) = \dfrac{f(x)}{g(x)} \cdot g(x) \neq 0$

HELPFUL HINTS

- The following are some suggestions to improve the quality of the graphs you produce when plotting points and drawing graphs using the Cartesian coordinate system:

  - Use graph paper to draw your graphs when doing your homework in order to help maintain a consistent scale throughout your graph.

  - Use a ruler or straightedge in order to draw accurate and clear axes and lines.

  - If you do not use graph paper, use a ruler to make a consistent scale on your axes. Otherwise, your graph will not be accurate.

  - Use a pencil instead of a pen so that you can quickly erase and fix a mistake instead of having to start over.

  - Do all the homework problems you are assigned. You must practice to improve your graphing skills.

- Linear equations that are not solved for y can be written using function notation by solving the equation for y, then replacing y with $f(x)$. For example, the equation $8x + 2y = 6$ becomes $y = -4x + 3$ and then can be written as $f(x) = -4x + 3$.

- When asked for the slope of a horizontal line, your answer shold be "the slope is 0". When asked for the slope of a vertical line, your answer should be "the slope is undefined". Do not answer "no slope" because this may be interpreted differently by your instructor and considered a wrong answer.

- The following chart summarizes the three forms of linear equations and when each equation may be useful:

Equation Form	Uses of the Form
Standard form $ax + by = c$	When finding the intercepts of a graph In Chapter 4, Systems of Equations and Inequalities
Slope-intercept form $y = mx + b$	To find the slope and y-intercept of a line To find the equation of a line given its slope and y-intercept To determine if two lines are parallel or perpendicular To graph a linear equation
Point-slope form $y - y_1 = m(x - x_1)$	To find the equation of a line when given the slope of a line and a point on the line To find the equation of a line when given two points on a line

AVOIDING COMMON ERRORS

- When graphing nonlinear equations, make sure you plot enough points to get a true picture of the entire graph. When you plot a graph that contains a variable in the denominator, select values for the variable that are very close to the value that makes the denominator zero. For example, when graphing $y = \dfrac{1}{x-5}$, you should use the values of x close to 5, such as 4.9 and 5.1 or 4.99 and 5.01. Also, when graphing an equation such as $y = |x|$ or $y = x^2$, you should use positive and negative values for x.

Chapter 4

4.1 Solving Systems of Linear Equations in Two Variables

Summary

> A **solution to a system of equations** is an ordered pair or pairs that satisfy all equations in the system.

Example 1
Determine if the ordered pair (–2, 4) is a solution to the system of equations
$$y + x = 2$$
$$y = 3x + 10$$

Solution
Substitute $x = -2$ and $y = 4$ into both equations.

$y + x = 2$	$y = 3x + 10$
$4 + -2 = 2$	$4 = 3(-2) + 10$
$2 = 2$ True	$4 = -6 + 10$
	$4 = 4$ True

Therefore, (–2, 4) is a solution to the system of equations.

Summary

> **Types of Solutions for Systems of Linear Equations**
>
> A **consistent** system is one which has a solution. If it has exactly one solution, then the slope of the lines will be unequal.
>
> A consistent system which has an infinite number of solutions is called a **dependent** system. The slope and y-intercepts of the lines will be equivalent.
>
> An **inconsistent** system is one which does not have a solution. The slope of the lines are the same but the y-intercepts are different.

Example 2
Determine if the following system is consistent with a single solution, dependent, or inconsistent.
$$2x + 3y = 8$$
$$-5x - 6y = 12$$

Solution
Write each equation in slope-intercept form.

$2x + 3y = 8$ $-4x - 6y = 12$

$3y = -2x + 8$ $-6y = 4x + 12$

$y = -\dfrac{2}{3}x + \dfrac{8}{3}$ $y = -\dfrac{2}{3}x - 2$

Since the equations have the same slope, $-\dfrac{2}{3}$, but different *y*-intercepts, the system is inconsistent and has no solution.

Summary

Graphing the Solution

To solve a system of linear equations graphically, graph all equations in the system on the same axes. The solution to the system will be the ordered pair, (or pairs) common to all the lines, or the point of intersection of all lines in the system.

Example 3
Solve the following system of equations graphically.

$x + y = 13$

$x - y = 3$

Solution
Graph both equations on the same set of axes.

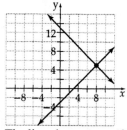

The lines intersect at (8, 5), so that is the solution.

Summary

To Solve a Linear System of Equations by Substitution

1. Solve for a variable in either equation. (If possible, solve for a variable with a numerical coefficient of 1 to avoid working with fractions.)

2. Substitute the expression found for the variable in step one into the other equation. This will result in an equation containing only one variable.

3. Solve the equation obtained in step two to find the value of this variable.

4. Substitute the value found in step three into the equation from step one. Solve the equation to find the remaining variable.

5. Check your solution in all equations in the system.

Example 4
Solve the following system of equations by substitution.
$$2x + y = 2$$
$$6x - 4y = -1$$

Solution
Solve $2x + y = 2$ for y.
$$2x + y = 2$$
$$y = 2 - 2x$$
Substitute $y = 2 - 2x$ in the equation $6x - 4y = -1$ and solve for x.
$$6x - 4y = -1$$
$$6x - 4(2 - 2x) = -1$$
$$6x - 8 + 8x = -1$$
$$14x - 8 = -1$$
$$14x = 7$$
$$x = \frac{1}{2}$$
Substitute $x = \frac{1}{2}$ into $y = 2 - 2x$ and solve for y.
$$y = 2 - 2x$$
$$y = 2 - 2\left(\frac{1}{2}\right)$$
$$y = 2 - 1$$
$$y = 1$$

The solution to the system is $\left(\frac{1}{2}, 1\right)$.

Example 5
Solve the following system of equations by substitution.

$3x + y = 5$
$9x + 3y = 15$

Solution
Solve $3x + y = 5$ for y.

$3x + y = 5$
$\qquad y = -3x + 5$

Substitute $y = -3x + 5$ in the equation $9x + 3y = 15$ and solve for x.

$\qquad 9x + 3y = 15$
$9x + 3(-3x + 5) = 15$
$\quad 9x - 9x + 15 = 15$
$\qquad\qquad\quad 15 = 15$

Since this is a true statement for all values of x, there is an infinite number of solutions and this must be a dependent system of equations. If you were to graph both equations from the system, the same line would be obtained.

Summary

To Solve a Linear System of Equations by the Addition (or Elimination) Method

1. If necessary, rewrite each equation in standard form. That is, the terms containing variables on the left side of the equal sign and the constant terms on the right side of the equal sign.

2. If necessary, multiply one or both equations by a constant(s) so that when the equations are added, the sum will contain only one variable.

3. Add the equations. This will result in a single equation containing only one variable.

4. Solve for the variable in the equation obtained in step three.

5. Substitute the value found in step four into either of the original equations. Solve that equation to find the value of the remaining variable.

6. Check your solution in all equations in the system.

Example 6
Solve the following system of equations using the addition method.

$2x + 5y = 11$
$\quad 3x = 15 - 7y$

Solution
First, write the second equation in standard form to obtain
$2x + 5y = 11$
$3x + 7y = 15$
Now, multiply the top equation by 3 and the bottom equation by –2.

$3(2x + 5y) = 3(11)$　　$\Rightarrow$　　$6x + 15y = 33$
$-2(3x + 7y) = -2(15)$　$\Rightarrow$　$\underline{-6x - 14y = -30}$
　　　　　　　　Add:　　　$y = 3$

Substitute $y = 3$ into $2x + 5y = 11$ and solve for x.
$2x + 5(3) = 11$
　$2x + 15 = 11$
　　　$2x = -4$
　　　　$x = -2$
So, the solution to the system is (–2, 3).
Check:

In the first equation,　　　　　　　In the second equation,
　　$2x + 5y = 11$　　　　　　　　　　$3x = 15 - 7y$
$2(-2) + 5(3) = 11$　　　　　　　　$3(-2) = 15 - 7(3)$
　　　$-4 + 15 = 11$　　　　　　　　　$-6 = 15 - 21$
　　　　　$11 = 11$　　　　　　　　　　$-6 = -6$
　　　　　True　　　　　　　　　　　　True

Exercise Set 4.1

Determine which, if any, of the ordered pairs or ordered triples satisfy the system of linear equations.

1. $x + 2y = 5$
   $2x - y = 0$

   a. (4, 8)　　　　　**b.** (1, 2)　　　　　**c.** (5, 0)

2. $2x - y = 7$
   $3x + y = 8$

   a. (6, 5)　　　　　**b.** (3, –1)　　　　**c.** (2, 2)

3. 　$x + y + z = 6$
   　$x + 2y + z = 9$
   　$2x + 2y - z = 6$

   a. (1, 2, 3)　　　　**b.** (3, 2, 1)　　　　**c.** (2, 1, 3)

Write each equation in slope-intercept form. Without graphing the equation, state whether the system of equations is consistent, inconsistent, or dependent. Also, indicate whether the system has exactly one solution, no solution or infinite number of solutions.

4. $2x + y = 6$　　　　5. $x + y = 4$　　　　6. $y = -3x + 4$
   　$y - x = 2$　　　　　　$2x = 8 - 2y$　　　　　$6x + 2y = 3$

Solve the following systems of equations graphically.

7. $x + y = 1$
   $x - y = 3$

8. $x - 2y = 0$
   $2x + y = 5$

Solve the following systems of equation by the substitution method.

9. $x - 2y = 4$
   $2x - y = 5$

10. $4x - 5y = -8$
    $2x + 3y = 7$

11. $\quad 2x - y = 4$
    $\quad 6x - 3y = 8$

Solve the following systems of equation using the addition method.

12. $\quad x - 2y = 1$
    $\quad 3x + 2y = 11$

13. $2x + 3y = 2$
    $\quad x + 5y = -6$

14. $5x + 3y = 1$
    $\quad 2x = 3 + 4y$

15. $\dfrac{1}{2}x + \dfrac{3}{4}y = \dfrac{7}{4}$
    $\dfrac{1}{3}x - \dfrac{1}{6}y = \dfrac{1}{2}$

Answers to Exercise Set 4.1

1. b

2. b

3. None

4. Consistent, one solution

5. Dependent, infinite number of solutions

6. Inconsistent, no solution

7.

8.

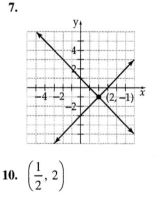

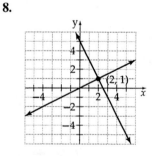

9. $(2, -1)$

10. $\left(\dfrac{1}{2}, 2\right)$

11. No solution

12. $(3, 1)$

13. $(4, -2)$

14. $\left(\dfrac{1}{2}, -\dfrac{1}{2}\right)$

15. $(2, 1)$

4.2 Solving Systems of Linear Equations in Three Variables

Summary

A third-order system consists of three equations and three unknowns. The substitution method or addition method introduced in Section 4.1 can be used to solve these systems.

Example 1
Solve the following system using the substitution method.
$$x + 2y + 3z = -2$$
$$y + z = -1$$
$$z = -2$$

Solution:
Substitute $z = -2$ into $y + z = -1$ and solve for y.
$$y + z = -1$$
$$y + (-2) = -1$$
$$y = 1$$
Now, substitute $y = 1$ and $z = -2$ into $x + 2y + 3z = -2$ and solve for x.
$$x + 2y + 3z = -2$$
$$x + 2(1) + 3(-2) = -2$$
$$x + 2 - 6 = -2$$
$$x = 2$$
So, the solution is the ordered triple (2, 1, –2).

Example 2
Solve the following system by the addition method.
$$x + 2y + z = 3 \quad (1)$$
$$x - 3y - z = 2 \quad (2)$$
$$x - 2y - 2z = -2 \quad (3)$$

Solution
In using the addition method, we choose two equations and attempt to eliminate a variable. Then choose another two equations and attempt to eliminate the same variable. The result will be two equations with two variables which then can be solved.
Here, add equations (1) and (2) to eliminate z.
$$x + 2y + z = 3$$
$$\underline{x - 3y - z = 2}$$
$$2x - y = 5 \ (4)$$
Multiply equation (1) by 2 and add to equation 3.
$$2(x + 2y + z) = 2(3) \Rightarrow 2x + 4y + 2z = 6$$
$$2x + 4y + 2z = 6$$
$$\underline{x - 2y - 2z = -2}$$
$$3x + 2y = 4 \ (5)$$
Multiply equation (4) by 2 and add to equation (5).
$$2(2x - y) = 2(5) \Rightarrow 4x - 2y = 10$$

$$4x - 2y = 10$$
$$\underline{3x + 2y = 4}$$
$$7x = 14$$
$$x = 2$$

Now substitute $x = 2$ into equation (4) and solve for y.

$$2x - y = 5$$
$$2(2) - y = 5$$
$$4 - y = 5$$
$$-y = 1$$
$$y = -1$$

Finally, substitute $x = 2$ and $y = -1$ into equation (1) and solve for z.

$$x + 2y + z = 3$$
$$2 + 2(-1) + z = 3$$
$$2 - 2 + z = 3$$
$$z = 3$$

So, the solution is ordered triple $(2, -1, 3)$.

Example 3
Solve the following system using the addition method.

$$x - y + 3z = 1 \quad (1)$$
$$-x + 2y - 2z = 1 \quad (2)$$
$$\underline{x - 3y + z = 2} \quad (3)$$

Solution
Add equations (1) and (2) to eliminate x.

$$x - y + 3z = 1$$
$$\underline{-x + 2y - 2z = 1}$$
$$y + z = 2 \quad (4)$$

Add equations (2) and (3) to eliminate x.

$$-x + 2y - 2z = 1$$
$$\underline{x - 3y + z = 2}$$
$$-y - z = 3 \quad (5)$$

Now, add equations (4) and (5).

$$y + z = 2$$
$$\underline{-y - z = 3}$$
$$0 = 5 \quad \text{Which is a false statement.}$$

Therefore, the system is inconsistent and has no solution.
Note: If we obtain the true statement $0 = 0$, then the system is dependent and has an infinite number of solutions.

Exercise Set 4.2

Solve by the substitution method.

1. $x = 3$
    $2x - y = 7$
    $x + y + 2z = 3$

2. $3x - 2y = 7$
    $y = -2$
    $2x + 4z = 6$

3. $4x = 8$
    $2x - y = 3$
    $x + y - z = 1$

Solve the using the addition method.

4. $x + y + 3z = 0$
    $2x - y + 2z = 1$
    $3x + y + z = 6$

5. $3x - 2y + 4z = 22$
    $x + y + z = 3$
    $2x - 2y - 3z = -1$

6. $2x + 2y - z = 1$
    $x + 2y - 3z = 4$
    $5x + 6y - 5z = 3$

7. $x + 2y - z = -2$
    $2x + 2y + 2z = 3$
    $6x - 4y - 2z = 2$

8. $3x + y - z = 8$
    $2x - y + 2z = 3$
    $x + 2y - 3z = 5$

Answers to Exercise Set 4.2

1. $\left(3, -1, \dfrac{1}{2}\right)$

2. $(1, -2, 1)$

3. $(2, 1, 2)$

4. $(2, 1, -1)$

5. $(2, -2, 3)$

6. No solution

7. $\left(\dfrac{1}{2}, -\dfrac{1}{2}, \dfrac{3}{2}\right)$

8. Infinite number of solutions

4.3 Systems of Linear Equations: Applications and Problem Solving

Summary

Many of the applications solved in earlier chapters using only one variable can now be solved using two variables.

Example 1
Two angles are supplementary if the sum of their measures is 180°. Find two supplementary angles if one angle is 20° more than three times the other.

Solution
Let x = first angle
Let y = second angle
$x + y = 180$
    $y = 3x + 20$
Solve using the substitution method.
$x + 3x + 20 = 180$
    $4x + 20 = 180$
        $4x = 160$
          $x = 40$
$y = 3(40) + 20 = 140$
Thus, the two angles have measures of 40° and 140°.

Example 2
A boat can go upstream (against the current) a distance of 36 miles in 4 hours. It can return downstream (with the current) a distance of 45 miles in 3 hours. Determine the rate of the boat in still water and the rate of the current.

Solution
Let s = rate of boat in still water
Let c = rate of current
Use distance = rate $\cdot$ time

	Rate	Time	Distance
Upstream	$s - c$	4	36
Downstream	$s + c$	3	45

$4(s - c) = 36 \quad \rightarrow \quad 4s - 4c = 36$
$3(s + c) = 45 \quad \rightarrow \quad 3x + 3y = 45$

Solve using the addition method.
$3(4s - 4c) = 36(3) \quad \rightarrow \quad 12s - 12c = 108$
$4(3s + 3c) = 45(4) \quad \rightarrow \quad 12s + 12c = 180$
$$12s = 288$$
$$s = 12$$
Substituting $s = 12$ into the first equation,
$4(12 - c) = 36$
$48 - 4c = 36$
$-4c = -12$
$c = 3$
Thus, the rate of the boat in still water is 12 mph and the rate of the current is 3 mph.

Example 3
How many ounces of pure water and how many ounces of 16% butterfat solution should be mixed to obtain 32 ounces of a 10% butterfat solution?

Solution
Let x = number of ounces of pure water
Let y = number of ounces of 16% solution

Solution	Strength	# of ounces	Amt of butterfat
0%	0	x	$x(0)$
16%	0.16	y	$0.16y$
10%	0.10	32	$0.10(32)$

$x + y = 32$
$0(x) + 0.16y = 0.10(32) \rightarrow 0.16y = 3.2 \rightarrow 16y = 320$
Solve using the substitution method.

$16y = 320$
$\quad y = 20$
Substituting $y = 20$ into the first equation,
$x + 20 = 32$
$\quad x = 12$
Thus, 12 ounces on pure water and 20 ounces of 16% butterfat are needed.
This same approach can be applied to using a system with three equations and three unknowns.

Example 4
A box contains nickels, dimes, and quarters. It has 8 more dimes than nickels, and there are three less quarters than there are dimes and nickels together. The total value of the coins is $8.55. How many of each kind of coins is in the collection?

Solution
Let x = number of nickels
Let y = number of dimes
Let z = number of quarters

$y = x + 8$ (1)
$z = x + y - 3$ (2)
$5x + 10y + 25z = 855$ (3)

Substituting (1) and (2) into (3), we have $5x + 10(x + 8) + 25(x + y - 3) = 855$.
Now, substitute $y = x + 8$ for y into the above equation.
$5x + 10(x + 8) + 25(x + x + 8 - 3) = 855$
$\qquad 5x + 10x + 80 + 25(2x + 5) = 855$
$\qquad 5x + 10x + 80 + 50x + 125 = 855$
$\qquad\qquad\qquad\qquad 65x + 205 = 855$
$\qquad\qquad\qquad\qquad\quad 65x = 650$
$\qquad\qquad\qquad\qquad\qquad x = 10$
Substitute $x = 10$ in equation (1) to get $y = 10 + 8 = 18$.
Substitute $x = 10$ and $y = 18$ in equation (2), $z = 10 + 18 - 3 = 25$.
Thus, the box contains 10 nickels, 18 dimes, and 25 quarters.

Exercise Set 4.3

For the following,

a. express the problem as a system of linear equations, and

b. use the method of your choice to solve the problems.

    1. Two numbers have a sum of 84. If twice the smaller number is three more than the larger number, find the numbers.

    2. How many ounces of 5% hydrochloric acid and 20% hydrochloric acid must be added together to get 10 ounces of solution that is 12.5% hydrochloric acid?

3. A person has $10,000 to invest from which he wishes to earn an annual income of $650 interest per year? He decided to bank part of the money at 5% interest and invest the remainder in bonds at $7\frac{1}{2}$% interest. How much should be invested at each rate?

4. A boat travels upstream (against the current) a distance of 18 miles in 1 hour. It returns downstream (with the current) in $\frac{3}{4}$ hour. Find the speed of the current and the speed of the boat in still water.

5. Two cars start out together and travel in opposite directions. At the end of three hours, they are 345 miles apart. If one car travels 15 mph faster than the other, what are their speeds?

6. A box has some fives, tens and twenties. It contains 30 bills worth $370. There are two more fives than tens. Find the number of each type of bill.

Answers to Exercise Set 4.3

1. **a.** $x + y = 84$
   $2x = 3 + y$
   b. The smaller number is 29. The larger number is 55.

2. **a.** $x + y = 10$
   $0.05x + 0.20y = 1.25$
   b. Five ounces each of the 5% and 20% solutions.

3. **a.** $x + y = 10,000$
   $0.05x + 0.075y = 650$
   b. $4000 at 5%; $6000 at 7.5%

4. **a.** $\frac{3}{4}(s + c) = 18$
   $1(s - c) = 18$
   b. Boat rate is 21 mph; current rate is 3 mph

5. **a.** $y = x + 15$
   $3y + 3x = 345$
   b. One rate is 50 mph; the other rate is 65 mph

6. **a.** $x + y + z = 30$
   $5x + 10y + 20z = 370$
   $x = y + 2$
   b. 10 fives, 8 tens, 12 twenties

4.4 Solving Systems of Equations Using Matrices

Summary

A **matrix** is a rectangular array of numbers within brackets. The numbers inside the brackets are referred to as **elements** of the matrix.

Summary

For the system of equations $a_1 x + b_1 y = c_1$
$$a_2 x + b_2 y = c_2$$
the **augmented** matrix is written
$$\begin{bmatrix} a_1 & b_1 & c_1 \\ a_2 & b_2 & c_2 \end{bmatrix}$$

Summary

Procedures for Row Transformations

1. Any two rows of a matrix may be interchanged. (This is the same as interchanging any two equations in the system of equations.)

2. All the numbers in a row may be multiplied (or divided) by any nonzero real number. (This is the same as multiplying both sides of an equation by a nonzero real number.)

3. All the number in a row may be multiplied by any, nonzero real number. These products may then be added to the corresponding numbers in any other row. (This is equivalent to eliminating a variable from a system of equations using the addition method.)

Summary

To Write a 2 × 2 Augmented Matrix in The Form
$$\begin{bmatrix} 1 & a & p \\ 0 & 1 & q \end{bmatrix}$$

1. First, use row transformations to change the element in the first column, first row to 1.

2. Then use row transformations to change the element in the first column, second row to 0.

3. Next, use row transformations to change the element in the second column, second row to 1.

Example 2
Solve the following system of equations using matrices.
$$2x + 3y = -1$$
$$3x + 2y = 1$$

Solution
First write the augmented matrix.
$$\left[\begin{array}{cc|c} 2 & 3 & -1 \\ 3 & 2 & 1 \end{array}\right]$$

Multiply the first row by $\dfrac{1}{2}$ to obtain

$$\left[\begin{array}{cc|c} 2\left(\frac{1}{2}\right) & 3\left(\frac{1}{2}\right) & -1\left(\frac{1}{2}\right) \\ 3 & 2 & 1 \end{array}\right] \Rightarrow \left[\begin{array}{cc|c} 1 & \frac{3}{2} & -\frac{1}{2} \\ 3 & 2 & 1 \end{array}\right]$$

Next, multiply the first row by –3 and add that product to the second row. Replace the second row by the resulting sum. This results in the matrix,

$$\left[\begin{array}{cc|c} 1 & -\frac{3}{2} & -\frac{1}{2} \\ 3+1(-3) & 2+\left(-\frac{3}{2}\right)(-3) & 1+\left(-\frac{1}{2}\right)(-3) \end{array}\right] \Rightarrow \left[\begin{array}{cc|c} 1 & \frac{3}{2} & -\frac{1}{2} \\ 0 & -\frac{5}{2} & \frac{5}{2} \end{array}\right]$$

Finally, multiply the second row by $-\dfrac{2}{5}$ to obtain

$$\left[\begin{array}{cc|c} 1 & \frac{3}{2} & -\frac{1}{2} \\ 0\left(-\frac{2}{5}\right) & -\frac{5}{2}\left(-\frac{2}{5}\right) & \frac{5}{2}\left(-\frac{2}{5}\right) \end{array}\right] \Rightarrow \left[\begin{array}{cc|c} 1 & \frac{3}{2} & -\frac{1}{2} \\ 0 & 1 & -1 \end{array}\right]$$

We can now write the equivalent triangular system of equations,
$$x + \frac{3}{2}y = -\frac{1}{2}$$
$$y = -1$$
Solve by substitution. Let $y = -1$ in the top equation.
$$x + \frac{3}{2}(-1) = -\frac{1}{2}$$
$$x - \frac{3}{2} = -\frac{1}{2}$$
$$x = 1$$
Thus, the solution to the system is (1, –1).

Summary

For a system of three linear equations we use a row transformation to write the augmented matrix in the form

$$\left[\begin{array}{ccc|c} 1 & a & b & p \\ 0 & 1 & c & q \\ 0 & 0 & 1 & r \end{array}\right]$$

Example 3
Use matrices to solve the following system of equations.

$2x - y - z = 5$
$x + 2y + 3z = -2$
$3x - 2y + z = 2$

Solution
Write the augmented matrix.

$$\left[\begin{array}{ccc|c} 2 & -1 & -1 & 5 \\ 1 & 2 & 3 & -2 \\ 3 & -2 & 1 & 2 \end{array}\right]$$

Exchange rows 1 and 2 to obtain

$$\left[\begin{array}{ccc|c} 1 & 2 & 3 & -2 \\ 2 & -1 & -1 & 5 \\ 3 & -2 & 1 & 2 \end{array}\right]$$

Now, multiply row 1 by –2 and add to row 2. Replace row 2 by the resulting sum.

$$\left[\begin{array}{ccc|c} 1 & 2 & 3 & -2 \\ 0 & -5 & -7 & 9 \\ 3 & -2 & 1 & 2 \end{array}\right]$$

Next, multiply row 1 by –3 and add to row 3. Replace row 3 by the resulting sum.

$$\left[\begin{array}{ccc|c} 1 & 2 & 3 & -2 \\ 0 & -5 & -7 & 9 \\ 0 & -8 & -8 & 8 \end{array}\right]$$

Exchange rows 2 and 3 to obtain

$$\left[\begin{array}{ccc|c} 1 & 2 & 3 & -2 \\ 0 & -8 & -8 & 8 \\ 0 & -5 & -7 & 9 \end{array}\right]$$

Multiply row 2 by $-\dfrac{1}{8}$ to obtain

$$\left[\begin{array}{ccc|c} 1 & 2 & 3 & -2 \\ 0 & 1 & 1 & -1 \\ 0 & -5 & -7 & 9 \end{array}\right]$$

Multiply row 2 by 5 and add to row 3. Replace row 3 by the resulting sum.

$$\left[\begin{array}{ccc|c} 1 & 2 & 3 & -2 \\ 0 & 1 & 1 & -1 \\ 0 & 0 & -2 & 4 \end{array}\right]$$

Multiply row 3 by $-\dfrac{1}{2}$ to obtain

$$\left[\begin{array}{ccc|c} 1 & 2 & 3 & -2 \\ 0 & 1 & 1 & -1 \\ 0 & 0 & 1 & -2 \end{array}\right]$$

Now write the equivalent triangular system of equations and solve by substitution.

$$x + 2y + 3z = -2$$
$$y + z = -1$$
$$z = -2$$

Let $z = -2$ in the second equation.

$$y + (-2) = -1$$
$$y = 1$$

Let $y = 1$ and $z = -2$ in first equation.

$$x + 2(1) + 3(-2) = -2$$
$$x - 4 = -2$$
$$x = 2$$

Finally, the solution is $(2, 1, -2)$.

Note: If row transformations yield a row of the form $\begin{bmatrix} 0 & 0 & | & K \end{bmatrix}$ or $\begin{bmatrix} 0 & 0 & 0 & | & K \end{bmatrix}$, $K \neq 0$, then the system has no solution. If row transformations yield a row of the form $\begin{bmatrix} 0 & 0 & | & 0 \end{bmatrix}$ or $\begin{bmatrix} 0 & 0 & 0 & | & 0 \end{bmatrix}$, then the system is dependent and has an infinite number of solutions.

Exercise Set 4.4

Solve the following systems using matrices.

1. $x + 3y = 7$
    $-2x + y = 0$

2. $2x + 5y = 8$
    $x + 2y = 3$

3. $2x + 4y = 2$
    $3x + 7y = 1$

4. $2x + 5y = 4$
    $3x - 6y = 33$

5. $x + 2y + 2z = 3$
    $2x + 3y + 6z = 2$
    $-x + y + z = 0$

6. $2x + 5y + 2z = 9$
    $x + 3y + z = 4$
    $2x + 3y - 3z = 1$

7. $x + 3y - 2z = 1$
    $2x + 5y - 2z = 6$
    $-2x - 4y + 3z = -1$

8. $5x - 9y - 9z = 7$
    $3x - 4y + z = 7$
    $x - 2y - z = 1$

Answers to Exercise Set 4.4

1. $(1, 2)$

2. $(-1, 2)$

3. $(5, -2)$

4. $(7, -2)$

5. $(1, 2, -1)$

6. $(5, -1, 2)$

7. $(1, 2, 3)$

8. $(5, 2, 0)$

4.5 Solving Systems of Equations Using Determinants and Cramer's Rule

Summary

> ### Value of a Second-order Determinant
>
> The determinant is evaluated as $\begin{vmatrix} a_1 & b_1 \\ a_2 & b_2 \end{vmatrix} = a_1 b_2 - a_2 b_1$.

Example 1

Evaluate $\begin{vmatrix} 2 & 4 \\ -3 & 7 \end{vmatrix}$

Solution

$\begin{vmatrix} 2 & 4 \\ -3 & 7 \end{vmatrix} = 2(7) - (-3)(4) = 14 + 12 = 26$

Summary

> ### Cramer's Rule for Systems of Linear Equations
>
> For a system of linear equations of the form
>
> $$a_1 x + b_1 y = c_1$$
> $$a_2 x + b_2 y = c_2$$
>
> $$x = \frac{\begin{vmatrix} c_1 & b_1 \\ c_2 & b_2 \end{vmatrix}}{\begin{vmatrix} a_1 & b_1 \\ a_2 & b_2 \end{vmatrix}} = \frac{D_x}{D} \text{ and } y = \frac{\begin{vmatrix} a_1 & c_1 \\ a_2 & c_2 \end{vmatrix}}{\begin{vmatrix} a_1 & b_1 \\ a_2 & b_2 \end{vmatrix}} = \frac{D_y}{D}, \ D \neq 0$$

Example 2
Use determinants to solve the following system.
$5x + 7y = -1$
$6x + 8y = 1$

Solution
Let $a_1 = 5, \ b_1 = 7, \ c_1 = -1$
$\quad a_2 = 6, \ b_2 = 8, \ c_2 = 1$

$D = \begin{vmatrix} a_1 & b_1 \\ a_2 & b_2 \end{vmatrix} = \begin{vmatrix} 5 & 7 \\ 6 & 8 \end{vmatrix} = 5(8) - 6(7) = -2$

$D_x = \begin{vmatrix} c_1 & b_1 \\ c_2 & b_2 \end{vmatrix} = \begin{vmatrix} -1 & 7 \\ 1 & 8 \end{vmatrix} = (-1)(8) - (1)(7) = -15$

$$D_y = \begin{vmatrix} a_1 & c_1 \\ a_2 & c_2 \end{vmatrix} = \begin{vmatrix} 5 & -1 \\ 6 & 1 \end{vmatrix} = (5)(1) - (6)(-1) = 11$$

$$x = \frac{D_x}{D} = \frac{15}{2} \qquad\qquad y = \frac{D_y}{D} = -\frac{11}{2}$$

Therefore, the solution to the system is the ordered pair $\left(\dfrac{15}{2}, -\dfrac{11}{2}\right)$.

Summary

Expansion of the Determinant by the Minors of the First Column

$$\begin{vmatrix} a_1 & b_1 & c_1 \\ a_2 & b_2 & c_2 \\ a_3 & b_3 & c_3 \end{vmatrix} = a_1 \begin{vmatrix} b_2 & c_2 \\ b_3 & c_3 \end{vmatrix} - a_2 \begin{vmatrix} b_1 & c_1 \\ b_3 & c_3 \end{vmatrix} + a_3 \begin{vmatrix} b_1 & c_1 \\ b_2 & c_2 \end{vmatrix}$$

Example 3

Evaluate $\begin{vmatrix} 2 & -1 & 3 \\ 4 & 0 & 7 \\ -2 & 3 & -2 \end{vmatrix}$ using expansion by the minors of the first column.

Solution

Let $a_1 = 2 \qquad b_1 = -1 \qquad c_1 = 3$
$\quad\;\; a_2 = 4 \qquad b_2 = 0 \qquad c_2 = 7$
$\quad\;\; a_3 = -2 \quad\; b_3 = 3 \qquad c_3 = -2$

$$\begin{vmatrix} 2 & -1 & 3 \\ 4 & 0 & 7 \\ -2 & 3 & -2 \end{vmatrix} = 2\begin{vmatrix} 0 & 7 \\ 3 & -2 \end{vmatrix} - 4\begin{vmatrix} -1 & 3 \\ 3 & -2 \end{vmatrix} + (-2)\begin{vmatrix} -1 & 3 \\ 0 & 7 \end{vmatrix}$$

$$= 2[(0)(-2) - (3)(7)] - 4[(-1)(-2) - (3)(3)] + (-2)[(-1)(7) - (0)(3)]$$
$$= 2[-21] - 4[-7] + (-2)[-7]$$
$$= -42 + 28 + 14$$
$$= 0$$

The determinant has a value of 0.

Summary

Cramer's Rule for a System of Equations in Three Variables

To evaluate the system
$$a_1x + b_1y + c_1z = d_1$$
$$a_2x + b_2y + c_2z = d_2$$
$$a_3x + b_3y + c_3z = d_3$$

with $D = \begin{vmatrix} a_1 & b_1 & c_1 \\ a_2 & b_2 & c_2 \\ a_3 & b_3 & c_3 \end{vmatrix}$, $D_x = \begin{vmatrix} d_1 & b_1 & c_1 \\ d_2 & b_2 & c_2 \\ d_3 & b_3 & c_3 \end{vmatrix}$, $D_y = \begin{vmatrix} a_1 & d_1 & c_1 \\ a_2 & d_2 & c_2 \\ a_3 & d_3 & c_3 \end{vmatrix}$, $D_z = \begin{vmatrix} a_1 & b_1 & d_1 \\ a_2 & b_2 & d_2 \\ a_3 & b_3 & d_3 \end{vmatrix}$

$$x = \frac{D_x}{D} \qquad y = \frac{D_y}{D} \qquad z = \frac{D_z}{D}, D \neq 0$$

Example 4
Solve the following system of equations using detemrinants.
$$x + y - z = -2$$
$$2x - y + z = -5$$
$$x - 2y + 3z = 4$$

Solution
Let $a_1 = 1 \quad b_1 = 1 \quad c_1 = -1 \quad d_1 = -2$
$ a_2 = 2 \quad b_2 = -1 \quad c_2 = 1 \quad d_2 = -5$
$ a_3 = 1 \quad b_3 = -2 \quad c_3 = 3 \quad d_3 = 4$

$$D = \begin{vmatrix} 1 & 1 & -1 \\ 2 & -1 & 1 \\ 1 & -2 & 3 \end{vmatrix}$$

$$= 1\begin{vmatrix} -1 & 1 \\ -2 & 3 \end{vmatrix} - 2\begin{vmatrix} 1 & -1 \\ -2 & 3 \end{vmatrix} - 1\begin{vmatrix} 1 & -1 \\ -1 & 1 \end{vmatrix}$$

$$= 1(-1) - 2(1) - 1(0)$$

$$= -3$$

$$D_x = \begin{vmatrix} -2 & 1 & -1 \\ -5 & -1 & 1 \\ 4 & -2 & 3 \end{vmatrix} = -2\begin{vmatrix} -1 & 1 \\ -2 & 3 \end{vmatrix} - (-5)\begin{vmatrix} 1 & -1 \\ -2 & 3 \end{vmatrix} - 4\begin{vmatrix} 1 & -1 \\ -1 & 1 \end{vmatrix} = 7$$

$$D_y = \begin{vmatrix} 1 & -2 & -1 \\ 2 & -5 & 1 \\ 1 & 4 & 3 \end{vmatrix} = -22$$

$$D_z = \begin{vmatrix} 1 & 1 & -2 \\ 2 & -1 & -5 \\ 1 & -2 & 4 \end{vmatrix} = -21$$

$$x = \frac{D_x}{D} = \frac{7}{-3}, \ y = \frac{D_y}{D} = \frac{-22}{-3} = \frac{22}{3}, \ z = \frac{D_z}{D} = \frac{-21}{-3} = 7$$

The solution to the system is the ordered triple $\left(-\frac{7}{3}, \frac{22}{3}, 7\right)$.

Note: If the value of D is zero, then the system is either dependent or inconsistent. It is probably better to use another method to solve the system.

Exercise Set 4.5

Evaluate the following determinants.

1. $\begin{vmatrix} 3 & -1 \\ 2 & -6 \end{vmatrix}$

2. $\begin{vmatrix} 1 & 3 & -2 \\ -1 & -2 & -3 \\ 1 & 1 & 2 \end{vmatrix}$

Solve the system of equations using determinants.

3. $8x - 4y = 8$
    $x + 3y = 22$

4. $4x + 3y = 0$
    $3x - 4y = 25$

5. $3x + 8y = 17$
    $2x - 4y = 2$

6. $5x - 4y = 2$
    $-3x + 3y = -3$

7. $2x + 3y + 2z = 10$
    $x - y + 2z = 3$
    $x + 2y - 6z = -15$

8. $x - y + 5z = -6$
    $3x + 3y - z = 10$
    $x + 3y + 2z = 5$

9. $x + y - 3z = 1$
    $2x - y + z = 9$
    $3x + y - 4z = 8$

Answers to Exercise Set 4.5

1. -16

2. -6

3. $(4, 6)$

4. $(3, -4)$

5. $(3, 1)$

6. $(-2, -3)$

7. $(-1, 2, 3)$

8. $(1, 2, -1)$

9. $(4, 0, 1)$

4.6 Solving Systems of Linear Inequalities

Summary

To Solve a System of Linear Inequalities
Graph each inequality on the same axes. The solution is the set of points whose coordinates satisfy all the inequalities in the system.

Example 1
Determine the solution to the system of inequalities.
$x - 3y > 6$
$2x - y \le 0$

Solution
First graph $x - 3y > 6$.
$x - 3y > 6$
$\quad -3y > -x + 6$
$\qquad y < \dfrac{1}{3}x - 2$

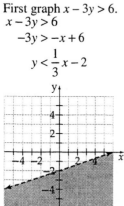

Now graph $2x - y \le 0$ and consider the region of the plane of intersection.
$2x - y \le 0$
$\quad -y \le -2x$
$\qquad y \ge 2x$

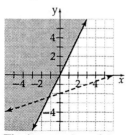

The intersection of the regions is the darkest section.

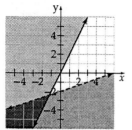

The solution is the triangular shaped region of overlap in the third quadrant.

Example 2
Determine the solution to the following system of inequalities.

$$x \geq 0$$
$$y \geq 0$$
$$x + 2y \leq 6$$
$$2x - y \geq 4$$

Solution
Since we are given the inequalities $x \geq 0$, $y \geq 0$, we restrict our attention to the first quadrant.
Graph.
$$x + 2y \leq 6$$
$$2y \leq -x + 6$$
$$y \leq -\frac{1}{2}x + 3$$

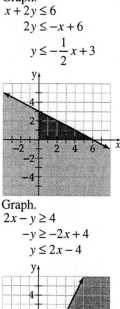

Graph.
$$2x - y \geq 4$$
$$-y \geq -2x + 4$$
$$y \leq 2x - 4$$

Solution is the darkest section:

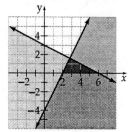

Example 3
Graph the system of inequalities.
$$|y| \leq 2$$
$$|x - 1| \geq 1$$

Solution
Recall:
If $|x| < a$ and $a > 0$, then $-a < x < a$. If $|x| > a$ and $a > 0$, then $x < -a$ or $x > a$.
$|y| \leq 2$ means $-2 \leq y \leq 2$.
$|x - 1| > 1$ means $x - 1 \leq -1$ or $x - 1 \geq 1$
$$\qquad\qquad\qquad x \leq 0 \qquad\qquad x \geq 2$$

Exercise Set 4.6

Determine the solution to each system of inequalities.

1. $x - y \leq 4$
   $x + y \geq 2$

2. $3x - y < 1$
   $x + 2y > 5$

3. $2x + y \geq 3$
   $x - 2y > 4$

4. $2x - 3y \leq 4$
   $2x - y > -2$

5. $|x - 1| \leq 3$

6. $|y + 2| > 1$

7. $|y| \geq 1$
   $|x - 1| < 2$

8. $x \geq 0$
   $y \geq 0$
   $y \leq x + 1$
   $x + 2y \leq 4$

9. $x \geq 0$
   $y \geq 0$
   $2x - 3y \leq 6$
   $x + y \leq 4$

Answers to Exercise Set 4.6

1.

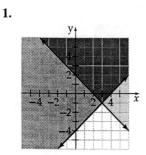

2.

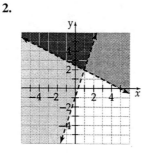

3.

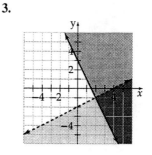

4.   **5.**   **6.**

7.   **8.**   **9.**

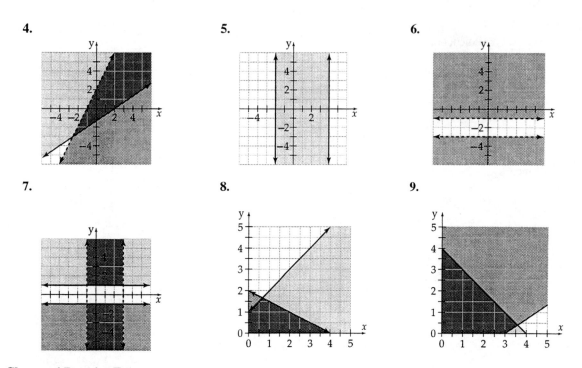

Chapter 4 Practice Test

Determine, without solving the system, whether the system of equations is consistent, inconsistent, or dependent. State whether the system has exactly one solution, no solution, or an infinite number of solutions.

1. $y = \dfrac{3}{2}x + 2$
$3x - 2y = 0$

2. $2x - 5y = 6$
$3x + 2y = 3$

Solve the system of equations by the method indicated.

3. $y = 2x - 5$
$y = x + 1$
(Graphically)

4. $2x + y = 4$
$3x - 2y = -1$
(Substitution)

5. $2x + 3y = 15$
$2x - 7y = 5$
(Addition)

6. $5x + 4y = 12$
$-\dfrac{3}{2}x + 2y = -2$
(Addition)

7. $5x + 6y = -3$
$-4x + 9y = 7$
(Determinants)

8. $2x - 3y = 7$
$x - 2y = 4$
(Matrices)

9. $x - y - z = -3$
$x - y + z = -1$
$x + y + z = -1$
(Addition)

10. $x - 2y + z = 2$
$x + y + z = 8$
$x - y - z = 2$
(Any method)

11. **a.** Express the problem as a system of linear equations and

b. use the method of your choice to find the solution to the problem.

A boat travels downstream (with the current) a distance of 40 miles in 5 hours. It takes 8 hours to make the return trip against the current. Find the rate of the boat in still water and the rate of the current.

Graph the system of inequalities and indicate its solution.

12. $2x + y \le 6$
$3x - y \ge 3$

13. $|x| \le 1$
$|y| < 2$

Answers to Chapter 4 Practice Test

1. Inconsistent, no solution

2. Consistent, one solution

3. $(6, 7)$

4. $(1, 2)$

5. $(6, 1)$

6. $\left(2, \dfrac{1}{2}\right)$

7. $\left(-1, \dfrac{1}{3}\right)$

8. $(2, -1)$

9. $(-2, 0, 1)$

10. $(5, 2, 1)$

11. **a.** $(x + y)(5) = 40$
$(x - y)(8) = 40$

b. Boat rate is $= 6\dfrac{1}{2}$ mph; current rate is $1\dfrac{1}{2}$ mph

12.

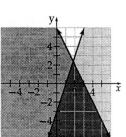

13.

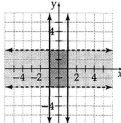

CHAPTER 4 SUMMARY

IMPORTANT FACTS

Solutions for Systems of Equations

Exactly 1 Solution (intersecting lines)	**No Solution** (parallel lines)	**Infinite Number of Solutions** (same line)
Consistent	**Inconsistent**	**Dependent**

Augmented Matrices

- The matrix $\begin{bmatrix} 1 & a & | & p \\ 0 & 1 & | & q \end{bmatrix}$ represents the system
$$\begin{aligned} x + a &= p \\ y &= q \end{aligned}$$

- The matrix $\begin{bmatrix} 1 & a & b & | & p \\ 0 & 1 & c & | & q \\ 0 & 0 & 1 & | & r \end{bmatrix}$ represents the system
$$\begin{aligned} x + ay + bz &= p \\ y + cz &= q \\ z &= r \end{aligned}$$

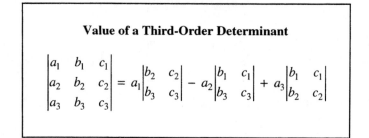

Value of a Second-Order Determinant	**Value of a Third-Order Determinant**
$\begin{vmatrix} a_1 & b_1 \\ a_2 & b_2 \end{vmatrix} = a_1 b_2 - a_2 b_1$	$\begin{vmatrix} a_1 & b_1 & c_1 \\ a_2 & b_2 & c_2 \\ a_3 & b_3 & c_3 \end{vmatrix} = a_1 \begin{vmatrix} b_2 & c_2 \\ b_3 & c_3 \end{vmatrix} - a_2 \begin{vmatrix} b_1 & c_1 \\ b_3 & c_3 \end{vmatrix} + a_3 \begin{vmatrix} b_1 & c_1 \\ b_2 & c_2 \end{vmatrix}$

Cramer's Rule

- For a system of equations of the form
$$a_1x + b_1y = c_1$$
$$a_2x + b_2y = c_2$$

$$x = \frac{\begin{vmatrix} c_1 & b_1 \\ c_2 & b_2 \end{vmatrix}}{\begin{vmatrix} a_1 & b_1 \\ a_2 & b_2 \end{vmatrix}} = \frac{D_x}{D} \quad \text{and} \quad y = \frac{\begin{vmatrix} a_1 & c_1 \\ a_2 & c_2 \end{vmatrix}}{\begin{vmatrix} a_1 & b_1 \\ a_2 & b_2 \end{vmatrix}} = \frac{D_y}{D}, \quad D \neq 0$$

- For a system of equations of the form
$$a_1x + b_1y + c_1z = d_1$$
$$a_2x + b_2y + c_2z = d_2$$
$$a_3x + b_3y + c_3z = d_3$$

$$x = \frac{\begin{vmatrix} d_1 & b_1 & c_1 \\ d_2 & b_2 & c_2 \\ d_3 & b_3 & c_3 \end{vmatrix}}{\begin{vmatrix} a_1 & b_1 & c_1 \\ a_2 & b_2 & c_2 \\ a_3 & b_3 & c_3 \end{vmatrix}} = \frac{D_x}{D}, \quad y = \frac{\begin{vmatrix} a_1 & d_1 & c_1 \\ a_2 & d_2 & c_2 \\ a_3 & d_3 & c_3 \end{vmatrix}}{\begin{vmatrix} a_1 & b_1 & c_1 \\ a_2 & b_2 & c_2 \\ a_3 & b_3 & c_3 \end{vmatrix}} = \frac{D_y}{D}, \quad z = \frac{\begin{vmatrix} a_1 & b_1 & d_1 \\ a_2 & b_2 & d_2 \\ a_3 & b_3 & d_3 \end{vmatrix}}{\begin{vmatrix} a_1 & b_1 & c_1 \\ a_2 & b_2 & c_2 \\ a_3 & b_3 & c_3 \end{vmatrix}} = \frac{D_z}{D}, \quad D \neq 0$$

HELPFUL HINTS

- The solution of a system requires a numerical solution for each variable in the form of (x, y) or (x, y, z).

- If an equation in a system contains fractions, eliminate the fractions by multiplying each term in the equation by the least common denominator, and then solve the system. For example, if one equation in the system is $x + \frac{3}{4}y + \frac{5}{6}z = \frac{1}{2}$, multiply both side of the equation by 12 to obtain the equivalent equation $12x + 9y + 10z = 6$.

- When using matrices, be careful to keep all the numbers lined up neatly in rows and columns. One slight mistake in copying numbers from one matrix to another will lead to an incorrect solution of the system.

- The elements in determinant D are the coefficients of the x and y terms in the equations, listed in the same order as listed in the equations. To obtain the determinant D_x from determinant D, replace the coefficients of the x-terms (first column) with the constants of the equations. To obtain the determinant D_y from determinant D, replace the coefficients of the y-terms (second column) with the constants of the equations.

- When evaluting determinants, if any two rows or columns are identical, or identical except for opposite signs, the determinant has a value of 0. For example, $\begin{vmatrix} 6 & -3 \\ 6 & -3 \end{vmatrix} = 0$ and $\begin{vmatrix} 6 & -3 \\ -6 & 3 \end{vmatrix} = 0$.

Chapter 5

5.1 Addition and Subtraction of Polynomials

Summary

Polynomials
1. A **polynomial** is a finite sum of terms in which all variables have whole number exponents and no variable appears in the denominator.
2. The **degree of a term** is the sum of the exponents on the variables in the term.
3. The **degree of a polynomial** is the same as that of its highest-degree term.

Example 1

Find the degree of the term $2x^3y^2z^5$.

Solution

The sum of the exponents on the variables is $3 + 2 + 5 = 10$. Thus, $2x^3y^2z^5$ is of degree 10.

Example 2

Write the polynomials in descending order of the variable x. Give the degree of each polynomial.

   a. $x^3 + 5 - 6x^2 + 9x$

   b. $9x^5 + 11x - 4x^8$

   c. $6x^3 + 7x^2 - 9x + 12$

   d. $7x^2y - 9x^3y^2 + 10xy^2$

Solution

   a. $x^3 + 5 - 6x^2 + 9x = x^3 - 6x^2 + 9x + 5$ and is a third degree polynomial. (x^3 is the highest-degree term.)

   b. $9x^5 + 11x - 4x^8 = -4x^8 + 9x^5 + 11x$ and is an eighth-degree polynomial since $-4x^8$ is the highest-degree term.

   c. $6x^3 + 7x^2 - 9x + 12$ is already in descending order of the variable x and is a third degree polynomial.

d. $7x^2y - 9x^3y^2 + 10xy^2 = -9x^3y^2 + 7x^2y + 10xy^2$ in descending order of the variable x; the degree of $-9x^3y^2$ is 5. The degree of $7x^2y$ is 3 and the degree of $10xy^2$ is also 3. Thus, the polynomial is of the fifth degree.

Summary

Polynomial Function of degree n

A polynomial function of degree n is a function which can be expressed in the following form:
$$f(x) = a_n x^n + a_{n-1} x^{n-1} + a_{n-2} x^{n-2} + \cdots + a_1 x + a_0$$
where all exponents are whole numbers and all coefficients of the variables are all real numbers with a_n not equal to zero.

Example 3
Determine if the following are polynomial functions. If a function is not a polynomial, explain why. If it is a polynomial function, give its degree.

a. $f(x) = x^6 - 7x^5 + 8x^2 - 9$ **b.** $f(x) = x^{1/3} + 2x^2$

c. $f(x) = \sqrt{3}x^4 + \frac{1}{2}x^2 + 5$ **d.** $f(x) = 2x^{-4} + 3x^{-2} + 5$

Solution

a. This is a polynomial function of degree 6.

b. This is not a polynomial function because fractional exponents are not allowed.

c. This is a polynomial function of degree 4.

d. This is not a polynomial function because negative exponents are not allowed.

Example 4
Graph $y = x^2 - 2x - 1$ and show where it is increasing and decreasing.

Solution
Construct a table of values and draw the graph.

x	y
–2	7
–1	2
0	–1
1	–2
2	–1
3	2
4	7

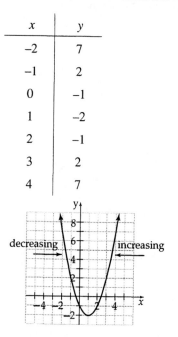

Example 5
Let $P(x) = 2x^3 - 3x^2 + 5x - 7$. Find $P(-1)$ and $P(2)$.

Solution
$$P(-1) = 2(-1)^3 - 3(-1)^2 + 5(-1) - 7$$
$$= -2 - 3 - 5 - 7$$
$$= -17$$
and
$$P(2) = 2(2)^3 - 3(2)^2 + 5(2) - 7$$
$$= 16 - 12 + 10 - 7$$
$$= 7$$

Summary

┌───┐

Adding and Subtracting Polynomials

1. To add polynomials, combine the like terms of the polynomials.

2. To subtract polynomials,

    a. Remove the parentheses from the polynomial being subtracted and change the sign of every term of the polynomial being subtracted.

    b. Combine like terms.

└───┘

Example 6
Simplify the following.

    a. $(6x^2 - 5x + 9) + (4x^2 - 3x - 7)$

    b. $(2x^2 y - 3xy + y) + (4x^2 y + 2xy - 3y + 3)$

    c. $(-3x^2 - 4x - 6) - (5x^2 + 4y - 7)$

    d. $(x^2 y - 3xy + 5) - (-2x^2 y - 4xy^2 - 7)$

Solution

    a. $(6x^2 - 5x + 9) + (4x^2 - 3x - 7) = 6x^2 - 5x + 9 + 4x^2 - 3x - 7$ (remove parentheses)

$$= 6x^2 + 4x^2 - 5x - 3x + 9 - 7 \text{ (rearrange terms)}$$

$$= 10x^2 - 8x + 2 \text{ (combine like terms)}$$

    b. $(2x^2 y - 3xy + y) + (4x^2 y + 2xy - 3y + 3) = 2x^2 y - 3xy + y + 4x^2 y + 2xy - 3y + 3$ (remove parentheses)

$$= 2x^2 y + 4x^2 y - 3xy + 2xy + y - 3y + 3 \text{ (rearrange terms)}$$

$$= 6x^2 y - xy - 2y + 3 \text{ (combine like terms)}$$

    c. $(-3x^2 - 4x - 6) - (5x^2 + 4y - 7) = -3x^2 - 4x - 6 - 5x^2 - 4y + 7$ (remove parentheses;

change sign of every term of
polynomial being subtracted)

$$= -3x^2 - 5x^2 - 4x - 4y - 6 + 7 \text{ (rearrange terms)}$$

$$= -8x^2 - 4x - 4y + 1 \text{ (combine like terms)}$$

d. $(x^2y - 3xy + 5) - (-2x^2y - 4xy^2 - 7) = x^2y - 3xy + 5 + 2x^2y + 4xy^2 + 7$ (remove parentheses;
change signs of every term of
second polynomial)

$$= x^2y + 2x^2y - 3xy + 4xy^2 + 5 + 7 \text{ (rearrange terms)}$$

$$= 3x^2y - 3xy + 4xy^2 + 12 \text{ (combine like terms)}$$

Exercise Set 5.1

State whether the given algebraic expression is a polynomial. Classify all polynomials as a monomial, binomial or trinomial.

1. $3x^2 - 2x + 1$

2. $\dfrac{3}{5}x^2 + x$

3. $\dfrac{1}{x} + 2x$

4. $2x^{-3} + x^3$

Write each polynomial in descending order of the variable x. Give the degree of each polynomial.

5. $2 + x^2 - 5x$

6. $5xy^2 + 3x^2y - 6 - 2x^3$

Simplify.

7. $(7x^2 - 6x + 2) + (-4x^2 + 7x - 8)$

8. $(7x^2 - 6x + 2) - (-4x^2 + 7x - 8)$

9. $(3x^2 + 2) - (3x^2 - 2x + 2)$

10. Subtract $(6x^2y + 3xy)$ from $(2x^2y + 12xy)$

11. Let $P(x) = 5x^2 - 7x + 11$. Find $P(-2)$, $P(0)$, $P(3)$, and $P(10)$.

12. Graph $y = x^2 + 2x - 3$.

13. Graph $y = -x^2 + 4x$.

Answers to Exercise Set 5.1

1. Yes; trinomial

2. Yes; binomial

3. No

4. No

5. $x^2 - 5x + 2$; second degree

6. $-2x^3 + 3x^2y + 5xy^2 - 6$; third

7. $3x^2 + x - 6$

8. $11x^2 - 13x + 10$

9. $2x$

10. $-4x^2y + 9xy$

11. $P(-2) = 45$, $P(0) = 11$, $P(3) = 35$, $P(10) = 441$

12.   **13.**

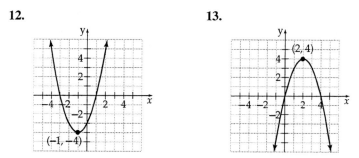

5.2 Multiplication of Polynomials

Summary

Multiplying Polynomials

1. To multiply polynomials, each term of the first polynomial is multiplied by each term of the second polynomial. Then, like terms are combined.

2. To multiply a monomial by another polynomial which is **not** a monomial, use the expanded form of the distributive property:

$$a(b + c + d + \cdots + n) = ab + ac + ad + \cdots + an.$$

Example 1
Multiply the following.

     a. $(4x^2 y)(-3x^7 y^5)$ **b.** $(-2x^4 y^7)(-4x^5 y^3 z^2)$ **c.** $2x^2\left(\dfrac{1}{6}x + 3xy + 9y^2\right)$

Solution

     a. $(4x^2 y)(-3x^7 y^5) = 4(-3)x^2 \cdot x^7 \cdot y \cdot y^5$ (rearrange factors)
                             $= -12x^9 y^6$ (product rule of exponents)

     b. $(-2x^4 y^7)(-4x^5 y^3 z^2) = (-2)(-4)(x^4 \cdot x^5)(y^7 \cdot y^3)z^2$ (rearrange factors)
                                   $= 8x^9 y^{10} z^2$ (product rule of exponents)

     c. $2x^2\left(\dfrac{1}{6}x + 3xy + 9y^2\right) = 2x^2\left(\dfrac{1}{6}x\right) + 2x^2(3xy) + 2x^2(9y^2)$ (expanded distributive property)

                                       $= \dfrac{1}{3}x^3 + 6x^3 y + 18x^2 y^2$

Summary

Multiplying Binomials

Two methods:

1. Multiply each term of the first binomial by each term of the second binomial and combine all like terms.

2. Use FOIL method. FOIL indicates that you multiply **F**irst terms, **O**uter terms, **I**nner terms and **L**ast terms of the two binomials.

Example 2
Multiply $(2x + 3)(-3x + 4)$.

Solution
Binomials can be multiplied vertically as well as horizontally. Write the binomials beneath each other. Next, multiply each term of the top binomial by each term of the bottom binomial and then combine like terms.

$$
\begin{array}{r}
2x + 3 \\
\times\ -3x + 4 \\
\hline
\end{array}
$$

$4(2x+3) \rightarrow 8x + 12$

$-3x(2x+3) \rightarrow \underline{-6x^2 - 9x}$

$ -6x^2 - x + 12$

Example 3
Multiply $(2x + 3)(-3x + 4)$ using the **FOIL** method.

Solution

$$
\begin{array}{ccccc}
& \text{F} & \text{O} & \text{I} & \text{L} \\
(2x + 3)(-3x + 4) = & 2x(-3x) & + 2x(4) & + 3(-3x) & + 3(4)
\end{array}
$$

$$
\begin{array}{rcccccc}
= -6x^2 & + & 8x & - & 9x & + & 12 \\
= -6x^2 & - & x & & & + & 12
\end{array}
$$

Example 4

Multiply $3x^2 - 2x + 5$ by $5x - 3$.

Solution

We will use a procedure similar to multiplying a three digit number by a two digit number. The longer polynomial is placed on top. Then multiply each term of the top polynomial by each term of the binomial. Like terms are aligned so that terms can easily be combined.

$$3x^2 - 2x + 5$$

$-3(3x^2 - 2x + 5) \rightarrow$ $\underline{\times \qquad 5x - 3}$

$5x(3x^2 - 2x + 5) \rightarrow$ $-9x^2 \quad + 6x - 15$

$\underline{15x^3 - 10x^2 + 25x \qquad}$

$15x^3 - 19x^2 + 31x - 15$

Summary

Special Formulas
1. Square of a binomial
$(a+b)^2 = a^2 + 2ab + b^2$
$(a-b)^2 = a^2 - 2ab + b^2$
2. Product of the sum and difference of the same two terms.
$(a+b)(a-b) = a^2 - b^2$

Example 5

Multiply $(3x + 2y)^2$.

Solution

Use $(a+b)^2 = a^2 + 2ab + b^2$.

Let $a = 3x$ and $b = 2y$: $(3x + 2y)^2 = (3x)^2 + 2(3x)(2y) + (2y)^2$

$$= 9x^2 + 12xy + 4y^2$$

Example 6

Multiply $(3x^2 - 2y)^2$.

Solution

Use the formula $(a-b)^2 = a^2 - 2ab + b^2$.

Let $a = 3x^2$ and $b = 2y$: $(3x^2 - 2y)^2 = (3x^2)^2 - 2(3x^2)(2y) + (2y)^2$

$$= 9x^4 - 12x^2y + 4y^2$$

Example 7
Expand $[y + (2x - 1)]^2$.

Solution
Use $(a + b)^2 = a^2 + 2ab + b^2$.
Let $a = y$ and $b = (2x - 1)$: $[y + (2x - 1)]^2 = y^2 + 2y(2x - 1) + (2x - 1)^2$
Now, use the formula $(a - b)^2 = a^2 - 2ab + b^2$ to expand $(2x - 1)^2$.
Let $a = 2x$ and $b = 1$:
$[y + (2x - 1)]^2 = y^2 + 2y(2x - 1) + (2x)^2 - 2(2x)(1) + 1^2$
$[y + (2x - 1)]^2 = y^2 + 4xy - 2y + 4x^2 - 4x + 1$
Since all terms are unlike terms, this will be the final answer.

Example 8
Multiply $\left(2x + \dfrac{3}{4} \right)\left(2x - \dfrac{3}{4} \right)$.

Solution
Observe that this problem is of the general form $(a + b)(a - b)$, where $a = 2x$ and $b = \dfrac{3}{4}$. Since

$(a + b)(a - b) = a^2 - b^2$, then $\left(2x + \dfrac{3}{4} \right)\left(2x - \dfrac{3}{4} \right) = (2x)^2 - \left(\dfrac{3}{4} \right)^2 = 4x^2 - \dfrac{9}{16}$.

Thus, $\left(2x + \dfrac{3}{4} \right)\left(2x - \dfrac{3}{4} \right) = 4x^2 - \dfrac{9}{16}$.

Exercise Set 5.2

Multiply. Use the formula for the square of a binomial or for the product of the sum and the difference of the same two terms when appropriate.

1. $\left(\dfrac{3}{2}x \right)\left(\dfrac{3}{2}x^3 \right)$ 2. $-4y(-3y^2 + 2y - 2)$ 3. $(3x + 2)(4x + 3)$

4. $(a + 2b)(a - 3b)$ 5. $(x^2 - 2x + 3)(x - 1)$ 6. $(x^2 - 2xy + y^2)(x - y)$

7. $(x + 10)^2$ 8. $(2x - 7)^2$ 9. $(3w^2 + 4)(3w^2 - 4)$

10. $[3 + (x - y)][3 - (x - y)]$

Answers to Exercise Set 5.2

1. $\dfrac{9}{4}x^4$ 2. $12y^3 - 8y^2 + 8y$ 3. $12x^2 + 17x + 6$

4. $a^2 - ab - 6b^2$ 5. $x^3 - 3x^2 + 5x - 3$ 6. $x^3 - 3x^2y + 3xy^2 - y^3$

7. $x^2 + 20x + 100$　　　　**8.** $4x^2 - 28x + 49$　　　　**9.** $9w^4 - 16$

10. $-x^2 + 2xy - y^2 + 9$

5.3　Division of Polynomials and Synthetic Division

Summary

> **To divide a polynomial by a monomial,** divide each term of the polynomial by the monomial.

Example 1

Divide $\dfrac{3x^2 - 6x + 4}{9x}$.

Solution

$$\frac{3x^2 - 6x + 4}{9x} = \frac{3x^2}{9x} - \frac{6x}{9x} + \frac{4}{9x} = \frac{1}{3}x - \frac{2}{3} + \frac{4}{9x}$$

Summary

> **Division of Polynomials**
>
> Division of a polynomial by a polynomial of two or more terms is similar to long division in arithmetic. In particular, the process used to divide a trinomial by a binomial is similar to dividing a three-digit numeral by a two-digit numeral. When dividing a polynomial by a binomial, the polynomial and binomial should be written in descending order. If a term of any degree is missing, it is often helpful to include that term with a numerical coefficient of zero.

Example 2

Divide $x^2 + 5x + 8$ by $x + 3$.

Solution

1. $x + 3 \overline{\smash{\big)}\, x^2 + 5x + 8}$

Notice that both polynomials are written in descending order.

2. Divide x into x^2: $\dfrac{x^2}{x} = x$

$$x+3\overline{)x^2+5x+8} \quad \overset{x}{}$$

3. Multiply the partial quotient by the divisor and subtract.

$$\begin{array}{r} x \\ x+3\overline{)x^2+5x+8} \\ \underline{x^2+3x} \\ 2x+8 \end{array}$$

4. Use the remainder as the new dividend and repeat the procedure above until the remainder is of lower degree than the divisor.

$$\begin{array}{r} x+2 \\ x+3\overline{)x^2+5x+8} \\ \underline{x^2+3x} \\ 2x+8 \\ \underline{2x+6} \\ 2 \end{array}$$

5. Since the remainder of 2 is of lesser degree than the divisor, we can stop dividing. The remainder of 2 is placed over the divisor and our final result is:

$$\frac{x^2+5x+8}{x+3} = x+2+\frac{2}{x+3}$$

Example 3
Divide x^3+8 by $x+2$.

Solution
Since x^3+8 is a third degree polynomial with missing x^2 and x terms, we will include $0x^2$ and $0x$ terms in the dividend and then divide using our normal procedure.

$$\begin{array}{r} x^2 \\ x+2\overline{)x^3+0x^2+0x+8} \\ \underline{x^3+2x^2} \end{array}$$

(Divide x into $x^3 = x^2$ and multiply the x^2 term by the divisor, $x+2$.)

$$\begin{array}{r}
x^2 - 2x + 4 \\
x + 2\overline{\smash{\big)}\,x^3 + 0x^2 + 0x + 8} \\
\underline{x^3 + 2x^2} \\
-2x^2 + 0x \\
\underline{-2x^2 - 4x} \\
4x + 8 \\
\underline{4x + 8} \\
0
\end{array}$$

(Subtract; bring down next term and repeat process.)

Thus, $\dfrac{x^3 + 8}{x + 2} = x^2 - 2x + 4.$

Summary

+---+
| **Synthetic Division** |
| |
| 1. When a polynomial is divided by a binomial of |
| the form $x - a$, the division process can be greatly |
| shortened using a procedure called **synthetic |
| division**. |
| |
| 2. When using synthetic division, the variables are |
| not written since they do not play a role in |
| determining the numerical coefficients of the |
| quotient. |
+---+

Example 4

Use synthetic division to divide $(4x^3 - 6x^2 + 8x + 2)$ by $(x - 2)$.

Solution

1. Write the dividend in descending powers of x. Then list the numerical coefficients of each term in the dividend. If a term of any degree is missing, place a 0 in the appropriate position to serve as a placeholder.
   4　–6　8　2

2. When dividing by $x - a$, place the "a" to the left of the row of coefficients of the dividend. Our divisor is of the form $x - 2$, so $a = 2$ in this case.
   2⌋　4　–6　8　2

3. Bring down the 4. Multiply 4 by 2 (the value of a) and place the product 8 underneath the –6.

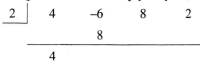

4. Find the sum of –6 and 8 to obtain 2. Multiply 2 by 2 (value of a) to obtain 4. Place the 4 under the 8.

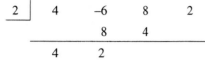

```
2 |  4    −6    8    2
            8    4
   _____
      4     2
```

5. Find the sum of 8 and 4 and obtain 12. Multiply 12 by 2 (value of a) to get 24. Place the 24 underneath the 2. Add 24 and 2 to obtain 26.

```
2 |  4    −6    8    2
            8    4    24
   _____
      4     2    12   26
```

6. The first three numbers in the last row, 4, 2, and 12 are the coefficients of the quotient. The last number, 26, is the remainder. The degree of the quotient is **always** one less than the degree of the dividend. Since the dividend is a third-degree polynomial, this means that our quotient is a second-degree polynomial. We can interpret the division problem as follows:

$$(4x^2 - 6x^2 + 8x + 2) \div (x - 2) = (4x^2 + 2x + 12) + \frac{26}{x - 2}$$

Example 2

Find the quotient using synthetic division: $(3x^4 - 25x^2 - 20) \div (x - 3)$

Solution

We can use synthetic division since our divisor is of the form $x - a$. ($a = 3$)

1. Write the coefficients of the dividend in descending powers of x and observe that there is a missing x^3 term and a missing x term so zeroes will be used for the coefficients of these terms. Place the 3 in front of this row of coefficients.

```
3 |  3   0   −25   0   −20
```

2. Bring down the 3 and multiply 3 by 3 (value of a) to obtain 9. Place the 9 underneath 0 and add 0 to 9 to obtain 9.

```
3 |  3     0    −25    0    −20
            9
   _____
      3     9
```

3. Repeat the above process to obtain the following result.

```
3 |  3     0    −25    0    −20
            9    27     6    18
   _____
      3     9     2     6    −2
```

4. Interpret the results. The degree of the dividend is 4. So the degree of the quotient will be 3. The remainder is –2. The remainder will **always be** the last number in the third row.

Thus, $(3x^4 - 25x^2 - 20) \div (x - 3) = 3x^3 + 9x^2 + 2x + 6 + \dfrac{-2}{x-3}$.

Summary

> ### Remainder Theorem
>
> If the polynomial $P(x)$ is divided by $(x - a)$, the remainder is equal to $P(a)$.

Example 6

Use the Remainder Theorem to find the remainder when $8x^3 - 6x^2 - 5x + 3$ is divided by $x + \dfrac{3}{4}$.

Solution

First write the divisor $\left(x + \dfrac{3}{4}\right)$ in the form $x - a$. Since $\left(x + \dfrac{3}{4}\right) = \left(x - \dfrac{-3}{4}\right)$, we will evaluate $P\left(\dfrac{-3}{4}\right)$.

First let $P(x) = 8x^3 - 6x^2 - 5x + 3$.

$$P\left(\frac{-3}{4}\right) = 8\left(\frac{-3}{4}\right)^3 - 6\left(\frac{-3}{4}\right)^2 - 5\left(\frac{-3}{4}\right) + 3$$

$$P\left(\frac{-3}{4}\right) = 8\left(\frac{-27}{64}\right) - 6\left(\frac{9}{16}\right) + \frac{15}{4} + 3$$

$$P\left(\frac{-3}{4}\right) = \frac{-27}{8} - \frac{54}{16} + \frac{15}{4} + \frac{3}{1}$$

$$P\left(\frac{-3}{4}\right) = \frac{-54}{16} + \frac{-54}{16} + \frac{60}{16} + \frac{48}{16} = 0$$

Thus, when $8x^3 - 6x^2 - 5x + 3$ is divided by $\left(x + \dfrac{3}{4}\right)$, the remainder is 0. Since the remainder is 0, this implies that $\left(x + \dfrac{3}{4}\right)$ is a factor of $8x^3 - 6x^2 - 5x + 3$. In general, whenever a polynomial $P(x)$ is divided by $(x - a)$ and the remainder is 0, then $(x - a)$ will be a factor of $P(x)$. To determine the remaining factor, divide $P(x)$ by $x - a$ using synthetic division. The quotient will be the remaining factor.

Example 7

Find the remaining factor of $8x^3 - 6x^2 - 5x + 3$ given that $\left(x + \dfrac{3}{4}\right)$ is a factor of $8x^3 - 6x^2 - 5x + 3$.

Solution

Divide $8x^3 - 6x^2 - 5x + 3$ by $\left(x + \dfrac{3}{4}\right)$ using synthetic division. Recall, $\left(x + \dfrac{3}{4}\right) = \left(x - \dfrac{-3}{4}\right)$. So $a = \dfrac{-3}{4}$.

$$
\begin{array}{r|rrrr}
-\frac{3}{4} & 8 & -6 & -5 & 3 \\
 & & -6 & 9 & -3 \\
\hline
 & 8 & -12 & 4 & 0
\end{array}
$$

Since the dividend was a third-degree polynomial, the quotient in a second-degree polynomial, $8x^2 - 12x + 4$, and is the remaining factor.

Exercise Set 5.3

Find each quotient.

1. $\dfrac{12n^3 - 4n^2 + n}{2n^2}$

2. $\dfrac{24xy - 18x^2y^2}{-6xy^2}$

3. $\dfrac{a^3 + 3a^2b + 3ab^2 + b^3}{a^2b^2}$

4. $(3x^2 + 2x + 1) \div (x - 1)$

5. Divide $3y^2 - 13y + 12$ by $y - 3$

6. $\dfrac{4x^2 - 4x - 17}{2x - 5}$

7. $\dfrac{n^3 - 1}{n + 1}$

8. $\dfrac{4x^2 + 9}{2x + 3}$

9. $(9x^4 + 5x^2 + x + 3) \div (3x - 1)$

10. $\dfrac{2x^5 + 2x^4 - 3x^3 - 15x^2 + 18}{2x^2 - 3}$

11. $\dfrac{3y^4 + 4y^3 - 32y^2 - 5y - 20}{3y^3 - 8y^2 - 5}$

Divide using synthetic division.

12. $(x^2 + 15x + 56) \div (x - 7)$

13. $(15x^3 - 2x + 7) \div (x + 5)$

14. $(x^3 - 8) \div (x - 2)$

15. $(x^2 - 4x - 32) \div (x + 4)$

16. $(9x^3 + 9x^2 - x + 2) \div \left(x + \dfrac{2}{3}\right)$

Determine the remainder for the following division problems using the Remainder Theorem. If the divisor is a factor of the dividend, so state.

17. $(x^3 - 6x + 4) \div (x - 1)$

18. $(x^4 - 5x^3 - 6x + 30) \div (x - 5)$

Answers to Exercise Set 5.3

1. $6n - 2 + \dfrac{1}{2n}$

2. $\dfrac{-4}{y} + 3x$

3. $\dfrac{a}{b^2} + \dfrac{3}{b} + \dfrac{3}{a} + \dfrac{b}{a^2}$

4. $3x + 5 + \dfrac{6}{x-1}$

5. $3y - 4$

6. $2x + 3 - \dfrac{2}{2x-5}$

7. $n^2 - n + 1 - \dfrac{2}{n+1}$

8. $2x - 3 + \dfrac{18}{2x+3}$

9. $3x^3 + x^2 + 2x + 1 + \dfrac{4}{3x-1}$

10. $x^3 + x^2 - 6$

11. $y + 4$

12. $x + 22 + \dfrac{210}{x-7}$

13. $15x^2 - 75x + 373 - \dfrac{1858}{x+5}$

14. $x^2 + 2x + 4$

15. $x - 8$

16. $9x^2 + 3x - 3 + \dfrac{4}{x+\frac{2}{3}}$

17. -1

18. 0; factor

5.4 Factoring a Monomial From a Polynomial and Factoring by Grouping

Summary

The **greatest common factor** (GCF) of two or more expressions is the greatest factor that divides (without remainder) each expression.

Example 1
Find the GCF of the following terms:

a. b^3, b^7, b^2, b^8

b. $c^2 d^4, c^3 d^4, c^5 d^3, c^2 d^6$

c. $12x^2 y, 16x^4 y^2, 8x^5 y^4$

d. $3(x+3)^4, 2(x+3)^7, 5(x+3)^3$

Solution

a. The GCF is b^2 since b^2 is the lowest power of b that appears in all terms.

b. The lowest power of c that appears in all terms is c^2. The lowest power of d that appears in all terms is d^3. Thus, the GCF is $c^2 d^3$.

c. The coefficients have a common factor of 4. The lowest power of x that appears in all terms is x^2. The lowest power of y that appears in all terms is y. Thus, the GCF is $4x^2 y$.

   d. The coefficients have a common factor of 1. The lowest power of $(x + 3)$ that appears in all terms is $(x+3)^3$. Thus, the GCF is $1(x+3)^3$ or just $(x+3)^3$.

Summary

> ### To Factor a Monomial From a Polynomial
>
> **1.** Determine the greatest common factor of all terms in the polynomial.
>
> **2.** Write each term as the product of the GCF and its other factors.
>
> **3.** Use the distributive property of factor out the GCF.

Example 2
Factor.

   a. $8x^3 + 16x^5 - 24x^2$ **b.** $5x^2y^4 + 25x^3y^7 - 15x^4y^2$ **c.** $6a^4(2c+5) - 12a^3(2c+5)$

Solution

   a. The GCF is $8x^2$.
$$3x^3 + 16x^5 - 24x^2 = (8x^2 \cdot x) + (8x^2 \cdot 2x^3) + (8x^2 \cdot (-3))$$
$$= 8x^2(x + 2x^3 - 3)$$

   b. The GCF is $5x^2y^2$.
$$5x^2y^4 + 25x^3y^7 - 15x^4y^2 = (5x^2y^2 \cdot y^2) + (5x^2y^2 \cdot 5xy^5) + (5x^2y^2 \cdot (-3x^2))$$
$$= 5x^2y^2(y^2 + 5xy^5 - 3x^2)$$

   c. The GCF is $6a^3(2c+5)$.
$$6a^4(2c+5) - 12a^3(2c+5) = 6a^3(2c+5) \cdot a + 6a^3(2c+5)(-2)$$
$$= 6a^3(2c+5)(a-2)$$

Summary

```
┌─────────────────────────────────────────────┐
│        To Factor Four Terms by Grouping      │
│                                              │
│  1. Arrange the four terms into two groups   │
│     of two terms each. Each group of two     │
│     terms must have a GCF.                    │
│                                              │
│  2. Factor the GCF from each group of two    │
│     terms.                                    │
│                                              │
│  3. If the two terms formed in step two      │
│     have a GCF, factor it out.                │
└─────────────────────────────────────────────┘
```

Example 3
Factor by grouping.

   a. $2x^2 - 8x + 3x - 12$ **b.** $rm - rn - sm + sn$

Solution

   a. $2x^2 - 8x + 3x - 12$ (Step 1)
   $= 2x(x - 4) + 3(x - 4)$ (Step 2)
   $= (x - 4)(2x + 3)$ (Step 3)

   b. $rm - rn - sm + sn$ (Step 1)
   $= r(m - n) - s(m - n)$ (Step 2)
   $= (m - n)(r - s)$ (Step 3)
   Note: Need to factor $-s$ from second pair to obtain GCF.

Exercise Set 5.4

Factor out the greatest common factor.

   1. $x^2y - xy^2$ **2.** $21a^2b - 14ab^2 + 7ab$ **3.** $15 - 5a$

   4. $-18x^5 - 27x^4$ **5.** $5(a + 2) + b(a + 2)$ **6.** $a(z + 2)^3 - b(z + 2)^2$

Factor by grouping.

   7. $2x^2 + 5x + 6x + 15$ **8.** $5x^2 - 10x + 7x - 14$ **9.** $7x + 7y + ax + ay$

   10. $5r + s^2 - 5s - rs$

Factor completely.

   11. $b^4z - b^4 - b^2 + b^2z$ **12.** $uz - vz + uz^2 - vz^2$

Answers to Exercise Set 5.4

1. $xy(x-y)$

2. $7ab(3a-2b+1)$

3. $5(3-a)$

4. $-9x^4(2x+3)$

5. $(a+2)(b+5)$

6. $(z+2)^2(az+2a-b)$

7. $(2x+5)(x+3)$

8. $(x-2)(5x+7)$

9. $(x+y)(a+7)$

10. $(r-s)(5-s)$

11. $b^2(z-1)(b^2+1)$

12. $z(u-v)(z+1)$

5.5 Factoring Trinomials

Summary

To Factor Trinomials of the Form
$$x^2 + bx + c \ \ \text{(note } a = 1)$$

1. Find two numbers (or factors) whose product is c and whose sum is b.

2. The factors of the trinomial will be of the form

 $(x + \_)$ $(x + \_)$
 One factor   One factor
 determined in   determined in
 step one   step one

Example 1
Factor

a. $x^2 - x - 20$

b. $16y^3 - 32y^2 - 48y$

Solution

a. We need two numbers whose product is –20 and whose sum is –1.

Factors of –20	Sum of Factors
(1)(–20)	–19
(2)(–10)	–8
(4)(–5)	–1
(5)(–4)	1
(10)(–2)	8
(20)(–1)	19

We note that the two numbers are 4 and –5. Therefore, $x^2 - x - 20 = (x-5)(x+4)$.

b. First factor out $16y$ from each term.

$16y(y^2 - 2y - 3)$

Now, find two numbers whose product is –3 and whose sum is –2. The numbers are –3 and 1. Therefore, $16y^3 - 32y^2 - 48y = 16y(y-3)(y+1)$.

Summary

To Factor Trinomials of the Form $ax^2 + bx + c$, $a \neq 1$, Using Trial and Error

1. Write all pairs of factors of the coefficient of the squared term, a.

2. Write all pairs of factors of the constant, c.

3. Try various combinations of these factors until the correct middle term, bx, is found.

Example 2

Factor $3y^2 + 14y + 8$.

Solution

The only factors of 3 are 3 and 1. So, we write $(3y \quad)(y \quad)$.
Now, try different factors of 8 to determine which pair yields the term $14y$.

Factors	Middle Term	
$(3y + 1)(y + 8)$	$25y$	
$(3y + 8)(y + 1)$	$11y$	
$(3y + 4)(y + 2)$	$10y$	
$(3y + 2)(y + 4)$	$14y$	← Correct middle term

Therefore, $3y^2 + 14y + 8 = (3y + 2)(y + 4)$.

Example 3

Factor $10x^2 - 11x + 3$.

Solution

The factors of 10 are 1 and 10 or 5 and 2. Let's try using 5 and 2 and start with $(5x \quad)(2x \quad)$.
Now try the factors of 3 to determine which pair yields the term $-11x$.

Factors	Middle Term	
$(5x - 1)(2x - 3)$	$-17x$	
$(5x - 3)(2x - 1)$	$-11x$	← Correct middle term

Therefore, $10x^2 - 11x + 3 = (5x - 3)(2x - 1)$.

Summary

To Factor Trinomials of the Form $ax^2 + bx + c,\ a \neq 1,$
Using Grouping

1. Find two number whose product is $a \cdot c$ and whose sum is b.

2. Rewrite the bx term using the numbers found in step one.

3. Factor by grouping.

Example 4
Factor $8x^2 - 13x - 6$.

Solution
$a = 8,\ b = -13,\ c = -6$
We must find two numbers whose product is $a \cdot c$ or $(8)(-6) = -48$ and whose sum is -13.
$-48 = (-16)(3)$ and $-16 + 3 = -13$
Rewrite $-13x$ as $-16x + 3x$. So, $8x^2 - 13x - 6 = 8x^2 - 16x + 3x - 6$. Now, factor by grouping.
$8x(x - 2) + 3(x - 2) = (8x + 3)(x - 2)$

Example 5
Factor $u^4 - 3u^2 - 10$.

Solution
Sometimes a more complicated trinomial can be factored by substituting one variable for another. This is called factoring using substitution.
For $u^4 - 2u^2 - 10$, we note that $(u^2)^2 = u^4$.
So, let $x = u^2$ and rewrite the problem:
$u^4 - 3u^2 - 10 = (u^2)^2 - 3u^2 - 10$
$$= x^2 - 3x - 10$$
$x^2 - 3x - 10 = (x - 5)(x + 2)$
Finally, substitute u^2 in place of x to obtain $(u^2 - 5)(u^2 + 2)$.
Thus, $u^4 - 3u^2 - 10 = (u^2 - 5)(u^2 + 2)$.

Exercise Set 5.5

Factor each trinomial completely.

1. $x^2 - 8x + 12$ 2. $y^2 + 3y - 28$ 3. $p^2 + 6p + 8$

4. $4q^2 + 8q - 12$ 5. $m^3 - m^2 - 30m$ 6. $5y^2 + y - 6$

7. $2r^2 - r - 3$ **8.** $12x^2 + 26x + 12$ **9.** $k^4 + k^2 - 12$

10. $2z^4 - 14z^2 - 60$

Answers to Exercise Set 5.5

1. $(x - 6)(x - 2)$ **2.** $(y + 7)(y - 4)$ **3.** $(p + 2)(p + 4)$

4. $4(q + 3)(q - 1)$ **5.** $m(m - 6)(m + 5)$ **6.** $(5y + 6)(y - 1)$

7. $(2r - 3)(r + 1)$ **8.** $2(2x + 3)(3x + 2)$ **9.** $(k^2 + 4)(k^2 - 3)$

10. $2(z^2 - 10)(z^2 + 3)$

5.6 Special Factoring Formulas

Summary

Difference of Two Squares

$$a^2 - b^2 = (a + b)(a - b)$$

Example 1

Factor each of the following differences of squares using the difference of two squares formula.

a. $x^2 - 25$ **b.** $9x^4 - 4y^6$ **c.** $t^4 - s^4$

Solution

a. $x^2 - 25 = (x)^2 - (5)^2$
$\qquad\quad = (x + 5)(x - 5)$

b. $9x^4 - 4y^6 = (3x^2)^2 - (2y^3)^2$
$\qquad\qquad\; = (3x^2 + 2y^3)(3x^2 - 2y^3)$

c. $t^4 - s^4 = (t^2)^2 - (s^2)^2$
$\qquad\quad\; = (t^2 + s^2)(t^2 - s^2)$
$\qquad\quad\; = (t^2 + s^2)(t + s)(t - s)$

Summary

$$
\boxed{
\begin{array}{l}
\textbf{Perfect Square Trinomials} \\[6pt]
a^2 + 2ab + b^2 = (a+b)^2 \\[6pt]
a^2 - 2ab + b^2 = (a-b)^2
\end{array}
}
$$

Example 2
Factor.

    a. $c^2 - 6c + 9$ **b.** $9x^4 + 24x^2 + 16$ **c.** $x^2 + 4xy + 4y^2 - 9$

Solution

    a. $c^2 - 6c + 9$
Since the first and last terms c^2, 3^2 are squares, this trinomial might be a perfect square trinomial. To determine if it is, take twice the product of 3 and c to see if we obtain $6c$.
$2(3)(c) = 6c$
It is a perfect square trinomial and the sign of the middle term is negative, so we have
$c^2 - 6c + 9 = (c - 3)^2$.

    b. $9x^4 + 24x^2 + 16$
The first term is a square $(3x^2)^2$, and the last term is a square, 4^2. Checking the product of twice the $3x^2$ and 4 we obtain $2(3x^2)(4) = 24x^2$. Therefore, $9x^4 + 24x^2 + 16 = (3x^2 + 4)^2$.

    c. $x^2 + 4xy + 4y^2 - 9$
Note that the first three terms, $x^2 + 4xy + 4y^2$ is a perfect square.
So, $x^2 + 4xy + 4y^2 - 9 = (x + 2y)^2 - 9$.
Now, we have the difference of two squares.
$$
\begin{aligned}
(x + 2y)^2 - 9 &= (x + 2y)^2 - (3)^2 \\
&= (x + 2y + 3)(x + 2y - 3)
\end{aligned}
$$

Summary

$$
\boxed{
\begin{array}{c}
\textbf{Sum of Two Cubes} \\[4pt]
a^3 + b^3 = (a + b)(a^2 - ab + b^2) \\[10pt]
\textbf{Difference of Two Cubes} \\[4pt]
a^3 - b^3 = (a - b)(a^2 + ab + b^2)
\end{array}
}
$$

Example 3
Factor.

a. $y^3 + 64$ **b.** $27c^6 - d^9$ **c.** $3x^3 + 24y^6$

Solution

a. Write $y^3 + 64$ as $(y)^3 + (4)^3$.
Use $a^3 + b^3 = (a+b)(a^2 - ab + b^2)$, to obtain
$$y^3 + 4^3 = (y+4)(y^2 - y(4) + 4^2)$$
$$= (y+4)(y^2 - 4y + 16)$$

b. Write $27c^6 - d^9$ as $(3c^2)^3 - (d^3)^3$.
Use $a^3 - b^3 = (a-b)(a^2 + ab + b^2)$, to obtain
$$(3c^2)^3 - (d^3)^3 = (3c^2 - d^3)((3c^2)^2 + (3c^2)(d^3) + (d^3)^2)$$
$$= (3c^2 - d^3)(9c^4 + 3c^2 d^3 + d^6)$$

c. $3x^3 + 24y^6 = 3(x^3 + 8y^6)$
Now, write $x^3 + 8y^6$ as $x^3 + (2y^2)^3$.
Use $a^3 + b^3 = (a+b)(a^2 - ab + b^2)$, to obtain.
$$x^3 + (2y^2)^3 = (x + 2y^2)(x^2 - x(2y^2) + (2y^2)^2)$$
$$= (x + 2y^2)(x^2 - 2xy^2 + 4y^4)$$
Thus, $3x^3 + 24y^6 = 3(x + 2y^2)(x^2 - 2xy^2 + 4y^4)$.

Exercise Set 5.6

Factor using a special factoring form.

1. $9 - p^2$ **2.** $4x^2 - 49$ **3.** $9m^2 - 100r^4$

4. $3x^4 - 12x^2$ **5.** $y^2 + 6y + 9$ **6.** $a^2 - 10a + 25$

7. $x^2 + 6x + 9 - y^2$ **8.** $a^6 - 8a^3 + 16$ **9.** $8a^3 + 1$

10. $125a^6 - 1$ **11.** $64x^3 + 125y^9$ **12.** $4x^6 + 32$

Answers to Exercise Set 5.6

1. $(3 + p)(3 - p)$ **2.** $(2x + 7)(2x - 7)$ **3.** $(3m + 10r^2)(3m - 10r^2)$

4. $3x^2(x + 2)(x - 2)$ **5.** $(y + 3)^2$ **6.** $(a - 5)^2$

7. $(x + 3 + y)(x + 3 - y)$ **8.** $(a^3 - 4)^2$ **9.** $(2a + 1)(4a^2 - 2a + 1)$

10. $(5a^2 - 1)(25a^4 + 5a^2 + 1)$ **11.** $(4x + 5y^3)(16x^2 - 20xy^3 + 25y^6)$

12. $4(x^2 + 2)(x^4 - 2x^2 + 4)$

5.7 A General Review of Factoring

Summary

To Factor a Polynomial

1. Determine whether all the terms in the polynomial have a greatest common factor other than 1. If so, factor out the GCF.

2. If the polynomial has two terms, determine whether it is a difference of two squares or a sum or difference of two cubes. If so, factor using the appropriate formula.

3. If the polynomial has three terms, determine whether it is a perfect square trinomial. If so, factor accordingly. If it is not, then factor the trinomial using the methods presented in 5.5.

4. If the polynomial has more than three terms, try factoring by grouping. If that does not work, see if three of the terms are the square of a binomial.

5. As a final step, examine your factored polynomial to see if any factors listed have a common factor and can be factored further. If you find a common factor, factor it out at this point.

Example 1
Factor $50x - 2x^3$.

Solution
First factor the GCF, $2x$, from each term $2x(25 - x^2)$.
Since $25 - x^2$ is a difference of two squares, use the appropriate formula to obtain $25 - x^2 = (5 - x)(5 + x)$.
Thus, $50x - 2x^3 = 2x(5 - x)(5 + x)$.

Example 2
Factor $2a^2 t^4 - 20t^4 a + 50t^4$.

Solution
First factor the GCF, $2t^4$, from each term.
$2t^4(a^2 - 10a + 25)$
We have a trinomial that is a perfect square, so that $a^2 - 10a + 25 = (a - 5)^2$.
Thus, $2a^2 t^4 - 20t^4 a + 50t^4 = 2t^4(a - 5)^2$.

Example 3
Factor $4x^3 - 16x^2 - 48x$.

Solution
First factor the GCF, $4x$, from each term.
$4x(x^2 - 4x - 12)$
The resulting trinomial must be factored by trial and error. The final factored form is $4x(x - 6)(x + 2)$.

Example 4
Factor $6r^2 t - 2rt^2 + 3rst - st^2$.

Solution
First factor the GCF, t, from each term.
$t(6r^2 - 2rt + 3rs - st)$
Now, since there are four terms in the second expression, factor by grouping.
$6r^2 - 2rt + 3rs - st = 2r(3r - t) + s(3r - t)$
$\qquad\qquad\qquad\qquad = (3r - t)(2r + s)$
Thus, the final factored form is $t(3r - t)(2r + s)$.

Example 5
Factor $x^2 - 4x + 4 - 9y^2$.

Solution
Though the polynomial has four terms, we cannot factor by grouping. Since the first three terms are a perfect square trinomial, we factor as follows:
$x^2 - 4x + 4 - 9y^2 = (x - 2)^2 - 9y^2$
Now, apply the difference of two squares formula.
$(x - 2)^2 - 9y^2 = (x - 2 + 3y)(x - 2 - 3y)$
Thus, $x^2 - 4x + 4 - 9y^2 = (x - 2 + 3y)(x - 2 - 3y)$.

Exercise Set 5.7

Factor each of the following completely.

1. $16x^2 - 16$ 2. $w^3 + 125x^3$ 3. $225a^5 b^2 c - 90a^2 b^2 c$

4. $x^9 - y^6$

5. $12x^2 - 38x - 14$

6. $x^4 - 15x^2 - 16$

7. $2ax + 4x + 2a + 4$

8. $3y^3 - 11y^2 + 8y$

9. $16x^2a^2 + 8xa^2 + a^2$

10. $27a^3 - 3a$

11. $x^2 + 4x + 4 - z^2$

12. $x^2 + z^2 - 2xz - y^2$

Answers to Exercise Set 5.7

1. $16(x+1)(x-1)$

2. $(w+5x)(w^2 - 5wx + 25x^2)$

3. $45a^2b^2c(5a^3 - 2)$

4. $(x^3 - y^2)(x^6 + x^3y^2 + y^4)$

5. $2(3x+1)(2x-7)$

6. $(x-4)(x+4)(x^2+1)$

7. $2(a+2)(x+1)$

8. $y(3y-8)(y-1)$

9. $a^2(4x+1)^2$

10. $3a(3a+1)(3a-1)$

11. $(x+2+z)(x+2-z)$

12. $(x-z+y)(x-z-y)$

5.8 Polynomial Equations

Summary

Standard Form of a Quadratic Equation

$ax^2 + bx + c = 0$, $a \neq 0$, where a, b, and c are real numbers.

Summary

Zero-Factor Property

For all real numbers a and b, if $a \cdot b = 0$, then either $a = 0$ or $b = 0$, or both a and $b = 0$.

Example 1
Solve the equation.
$(x+4)(2x-1) = 0$

Solution
Since the product of the factor equals zero, use the zero-factor property and set each factor equal to zero and solve each equation.

$$x + 4 = 0 \quad \text{or} \quad 2x - 1 = 0$$
$$x = -4 \qquad\qquad 2x = 1$$
$$x = \frac{1}{2}$$

Thus, either -4 or $\dfrac{1}{2}$ is a solution.

Check:

$x = 4$

$$(x+4)(2x-1) = 0$$
$$(-4+4)[2(-4)-1] = 0$$
$$(0)(-9) = 0$$
$$0 = 0 \text{ True}$$

$x = \dfrac{1}{2}$

$$(x+4)(2x-1) = 0$$
$$\left(\frac{1}{2}+4\right)\left[2\left(\frac{1}{2}\right)-1\right] = 0$$
$$\left(\frac{9}{2}\right)(0) = 0$$
$$0 = 0 \text{ True}$$

Summary

> ### To Solve and Equation by Factoring
>
> 1. Use the addition property to remove all terms from one side of the equation. This will result in one side of the equation being equal to 0.
>
> 2. Combine like terms in the equation and then factor.
>
> 3. Set each factor containing a variable equal to zero, solve the equation, and find the solutions.
>
> 4. Check the solutions in the original equation.

Example 2
Solve the equation $4x^2 = 24x$.

Solution
$4x^2 - 24x = 0$ (Step 1)
$\quad 4x(x-6) = 0$ (Step 2)
$4x = 0$ or $x - 6 = 0$ (Step 3)
$\quad x = 0 \qquad\quad x = 6$
A check shows that 0 and 6 are solutions to the equation. (Step 4)

Example 3
Solve the equation $(r-5)(r-3) = 3r(r-3)$.

Solution
$(r-5)(r-3) - 3r(r-3) = 0$ (Step 1)
$\quad r^2 - 8r + 15 - 3r^2 + 9r = 0$ (Step 2)
$\qquad\qquad -2r^2 + r + 15 = 0$
$\qquad\qquad\quad 0 = 2r^2 - r - 15$
$\qquad$ Note: It is usually easier to have the coefficient of the squared term positive.

$$0 = (2r+5)(r-3)$$
$$2r+5=0 \quad \text{or} \quad r-3=0 \text{ (Step 3)}$$
$$2r=-5 \qquad\qquad r=3$$
$$r=-\frac{5}{2}$$

Example 4
The area of a rectangle is 65 square units. If the length is three more than twice the width, find the length and width of the rectangle.

Solution
Let: $x =$ width
Area = (length)(width)
$$65 = (2x+3)(x)$$
Now, solve the equation $(2x + 3)(x) = 65$.
$$(2x+3)(x)-65=0$$
$$2x^2+3x-65=0$$
$$(2x+13)(x-5)=0$$
$$2x+13=0 \qquad \text{or} \quad x-5=0$$
$$2x=-13 \qquad\qquad x=5$$
$$x=-\frac{13}{2}$$
Only $x = 5$ is possible. So width is 5 units and length is 2(5) + 3 = 13 units.

Example 5
Use factoring to find the x-intercepts of the graph of $y = 2x^2 + 3x - 5$.

Solution
At the x-intercepts the value of y is 0. Therefore, set $y = 0$ and solve.
$$2x^2+3x-5=0$$
$$(2x+5)(x-1)=0$$
$$2x+5=0 \quad \text{or} \quad x-1=0$$
$$2x=-5 \qquad\qquad x=1$$
$$x=-\frac{5}{2}$$
Thus, the x-intercepts are at $-\dfrac{5}{2}$ and 1.

Exercise Set 5.8

Solve each equation.

1. $(x+7)(x+3)=0$ 2. $x^2-6x=0$ 3. $6x^2=16x$

4. $x^2-x-2=0$ 5. $4v^2+5v+1=0$ 6. $4t^3+6t^2+2t=0$

7. $3x^2+x=10$ 8. $x^2+10x=-24$ 9. $(x+4)^2=9$

10. $(x - 5)(x - 4) = 12$

Write the problem as an equation. Solve the equation and answer the equation.

11. The product of two consecutive even negative integers is 48. Find the two integers.

12. The product of a triangle is 10 square units. If the height is one more than the base, find the base and height of the triangle.

Use factoring to find the *x*-intercepts of the graph of the equation.

13. $y = x^2 - 3x - 4$ **14.** $y = 9x^2 + 3x - 2$

Answers to Exercise Set 5.8

1. -7 or -3 **2.** 0 or 6 **3.** 0 or $\dfrac{8}{3}$

4. -1 or 2 **5.** -1 or $-\dfrac{1}{4}$ **6.** 0 or $-\dfrac{1}{2}$ or -1

7. -2 or $\dfrac{5}{3}$ **8.** -6 or -4 **9.** -7 or -1

10. 1 or 8 **11.** $x(x + 2) = 48$ **12.** $\dfrac{1}{2}x(x + 1) = 10$

                                   The integers are -6 and -8.   height $= 5$, base $= 4$

13. $x = 4, x = -1$ **14.** $x = \dfrac{1}{3}, x = -\dfrac{2}{3}$

Chapter 5 Practice Test

Multiply

1. $(7x^2 y^5)(-3xy^4)$ **2.** $3x^2(5x^5 - 3xy + 7y^2)$

Let $P(x) = 7x^2 - 8x + 15$. Find

3. $P(-1)$ **4.** $P(2)$

Express each number in scientific notation.

5. 0.0000123 **6.** $270,000,000$

Simplify using scientific notation. Express the answer in scientific notation.

7. $\dfrac{51,000,000}{0.000017}$

Indicate if the expression is a polynomial. If so, state its degree. If not, tell why.

8. $8x^4 - 7x^2 + 3x - 4$

9. $\sqrt{2}x^{-1} + 3x^2 - 9x$

Perform the indicated operations and simplify.

10. $(5x^2 - 3x + 7) - (7x^2 + 4x - 7)$

11. $3x(2x^2 - 9x + 6)$

12. $(2xy + 1)(3x + 2y)$

13. $(2x - 3y^2)^2$

Determine the remainder of the division problem using the remainder theorem.

14. $(2x^3 - 6x^2 + 2x) \div (x + 4)$

Use synthetic division to determine the quotient.

15. $(2x^3 + 3x^2 - 5x + 12) \div (x + 3)$

Factor completely.

16. $8a^3 - 27$

17. $4x^2 + 18x - 10$

18. $ax - bx + 2a - 2b$

19. $x(p - q) - y(q - p)$

20. $a^4 - 2a^2 - 8$

21. $x^2 + 14x + 49$

22. $x^2 + 2xy + y^2 - 9$

23. $4y^2 - 25$

24. $27a^2b^3 - 36a^3b^2 + 45a^4b^4$

25. $2x^6 - 16$

26. $100d^2 - 9b^6$

27. $6x^2 + 7x - 5$

28. $x^4 - x^2 - 6$

29. $x^3 - 9x$

Solve the equation.

30. $(2x + 5)(x - 6) = 0$

31. $x^2 + 3x = -2$

32. $(3x + 5)(2x + 1) = -1$

33. Use factoring to find the *x*-intercepts of the graph of $y = 4x^2 + 5x - 6$.

34. The product of two consecutive integers is 156. Find the two numbers.

35. The area of a rectangle is 60 square units. If the length of the rectangle is two less than twice the width, find the length and width of the rectangle.

Answers to Chapter 5 Practice Test

1. $-21x^3y^9$

2. $15x^7 - 9x^3y + 21x^2y^2$

3. 30

4. 27

5. 1.23×10^{-5}

6. 2.7×10^8

7. 3.0×10^{12}

8. Polynomial; degree 4

9. Not a polynomial; negative exponent not allowed

10. $-2x^2 - 7x + 14$

11. $6x^3 - 27x^2 + 18x$

12. $6x^2 y + 3x + 4xy^2 + 2y$

13. $4x^2 - 12xy^2 + 9y^4$

14. -232

15. $2x^2 - 3x + 4$

16. $(2a - 3)(4a^2 + 6a + 9)$

17. $2(2x - 1)(x + 5)$

18. $(a - b)(x + 2)$

19. $(p - q)(x + y)$

20. $(a - 2)(a + 2)(a^2 + 2)$

21. $(x + 7)^2$

22. $(x + y + 3)(x + y - 3)$

23. $(2y + 5)(2y - 5)$

24. $9a^2 b^2 (3b - 4a + 5a^2 b^2)$

25. $2(x^2 - 2)(x^4 + 2x^2 + 4)$

26. $(10d + 3b^3)(10d - 3b^3)$

27. $(2x - 1)(3x + 5)$

28. $(x^2 - 3)(x^2 + 2)$

29. $x(x - 3)(x + 3)$

30. $-\dfrac{5}{2}, 6$

31. $-2, -1$

32. $-\dfrac{2}{3}, -\dfrac{3}{2}$

33. $-2, \dfrac{3}{4}$

34. $12, 13$

35. Length is 10 units, width is 6 units.

CHAPTER 5 SUMMARY

IMPORTANT FACTS

FOIL Method to Multiply Binomials

   F — Multiply First terms

   O — Multiply Outer terms

   I — Multiply Inner terms

   L — Multiply Last terms

$$(a + b)(c + d) = ac + ad + bc + bd$$

$$\textbf{F} \quad \textbf{O} \quad \textbf{I} \quad \textbf{L}$$

Special Product Formulas

- Square of a binomial: $\begin{cases} (a+b)^2 = a^2 + 2ab + b^2 \\ (a-b)^2 = a^2 - 2ab + b^2 \end{cases}$

- Product of sum and difference of same two terms: $(a+b)(a-b) = a^2 - b^2$

Dividing a Polynomial by a Binomial

- The polynomial and binomial should both be written in descending order.

- Replace a missing term of any degree with a numerical coefficient of 0.

Remainder Theorem

If the polynomial $P(x)$ is divided by $x - a$, the remainder is equal to $P(a)$.

Special Factoring Formulas

- Difference of two squares: $a^2 - b^2 = (a+b)(a-b)$

- Perfect square trinomials: $\begin{cases} a^2 + 2ab + b^2 = (a+b)^2 \\ a^2 - 2ab + b^2 = (a-b)^2 \end{cases}$

- Sum of two cubes: $a^3 + b^3 = (a+b)(a^2 - ab + b^2)$

- Difference of two cubes: $a^3 - b^3 = (a-b)(a^2 + ab + b^2)$

    NOTE: The sum of two squares, $a^2 + b^2$, cannot be facotred over the set of real numbers.

Standard Form of a Quadratic Equation

$$ax^2 + bx + c = 0, \ a \neq 0$$

Zero–Factor Property

If $a \cdot b = 0$, then either $a = 0$ or $b = 0$, or both a and $b = 0$.

Pythagorean Theorem

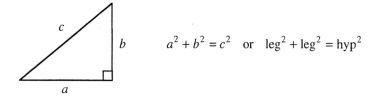

$$a^2 + b^2 = c^2 \quad \text{or} \quad \text{leg}^2 + \text{leg}^2 = \text{hyp}^2$$

HELPFUL HINTS

- Remember that $-$ x means $-1 \cdot$ x. Therefore, $-\left(6x^2 + 5x - 3\right)$ means the same as $-1\left(6x^2 + 5x - 3\right)$, and the distributive property applies. Thus when you subtract one polynomial from another, **the signs of every term** of the polynomial being subtracted must change.

- The rules for exponents were covered in Section 1.5. Some of these rules were presented again for use in this chapter. If you feel you need more examples of the use of these rules, review Section 1.5.

- Use the following guidelines when factoring four terms by grouping:

  - When the *first* and *third* terms are positive—factor a **positive** expression from both the first two and the last two terms to get a factor common to the remaining two terms.

  - When the *first* term is positive and the *third* term is negative—factor a **positive** expression from the first two terms and a **negative** expression from the last two terms to get a factor common to the remaining two terms.

- When factoring trinomials, pay close attention to the factors and their sums. This will help you to find the factors and their correct signs. For example, the factors -5 and 3 have a sum of -2, while the factors 5 and -3 have a sum of 2.

- You can easily check if your factors are correct by multiplying them back together. If the product comes out to be the same trinomial that you factored, then you will know that your factoring is correct.

- When you factor a trinomial in the form of $ax^2 + bx + c$ $(a > 0)$, the sign of the third term (c) is very helpful in finding the answer:

  - When the third term is positive and the numerical coefficient of the x term is positive, both of the numerical factors will be **positive**.

  - When the third term is positive and the coefficient of the x term is negative, both numerical factors will be **negative**.

  - When the third term is negative, one of the numerical factors will be **positive** and the other will be **negative**.

- When you square a binomial, there will be a **2** as part of the middle term of the trinomial. When you factor the sum or difference of two cubes, the trinomial factor is similar to that of a binomial squared, but there will not be a **2** as part of the middle term of this trinomial factor.

The square of a binomial	**The sum or difference of two cubes**
$(a+b)^2 = a^2 + 2ab + b^2$	$a^3 + b^3 = (a+b)(a^2 - ab + b^2)$
$(a-b)^2 = a^2 - 2ab + b^2$	$a^3 - b^3 = (a-b)(a^2 + ab + b^2)$

- All the factoring techniques have been reviewed in Section 5.7. However, if you are still have difficulty with factoring, you should go back to Sections 5.4 through 5.6 to study and practice your factoring skills.

AVOIDING COMMON ERRORS

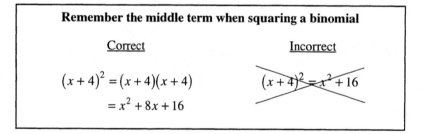

Remember the middle term when squaring a binomial	
<u>Correct</u>	<u>Incorrect</u>
$(x+4)^2 = (x+4)(x+4)$	$(x+4)^2 = x^2 + 16$
$\quad = x^2 + 8x + 16$	

Chapter 6

6.1 The Domains of Rational Functions and Multiplication and Division of Rational Expressions

Summary

Rational Functions

Whenever we write a rational expression containing a variable in the denominator, we always assume that the value or values of the variable that make the denominator equal to zero are excluded.

Example 1

Find the values of the variable that must be excluded in the rational expression $\dfrac{3x-2}{5x-3}$.

Solution
Find the number(s) that make the denominator equal to zero:

$5x - 3 = 0$

$$x = \frac{3}{5}$$

Thus, the rational expression is defined for all real numbers **except** $\dfrac{3}{5}$. The excluded value is $x = \dfrac{3}{5}$.

Example 2

Find the values of the variable that must be excluded in the rational expression $\dfrac{2}{3x^2 - x - 2}$.

Solution
Solve $3x^2 - x - 2 = 0$. We can factor $3x^2 - x - 2$ as $(3x + 2)(x - 1)$. Solve the equation $(3x + 2)(x - 1) = 0$. This implies that $(3x + 2) = 0$ or $(x - 1) = 0$. Thus, $x = -\dfrac{2}{3}$ or $x = 1$, and they are excluded values.

Summary

Domain of a Rational Function

A **rational function** is a quotient of two polynomials. The **domain** of a rational function is the set of values that can be used to replace the variable of the rational function.

Example 3
Find the domain of the rational functions.

a. $y = \dfrac{3}{2x-5}$
        b. $f(x) = \dfrac{2x^2}{x^2-81}$

Solution

a. Find the value that makes the denominator of the rational function equal to zero. Solve $2x - 5 = 0$ which implies that $x = \dfrac{5}{2}$. Thus, the domain $= \left\{ x \middle| x \text{ is a real number and } x \neq \dfrac{5}{2} \right\}$.

b. Solve $x^2 - 81 = 0$. Since $x^2 - 81 = (x+9)(x-9)$, then $(x+9)(x-9) = 0$, then $x = 9$ or $x = -9$. These are the numbers which are **excluded** from the domain. Thus, the domain is $\left\{ x \middle| x \text{ is a real number and } x \neq 9 \text{ and } x \neq -9 \right\}$.

Summary

> **To Simplify Rational Expression**
>
> 1. Factor both numerator and denominator as completely as possible.
>
> 2. Divide both the numerator and the denominator by any common factors.

Example 4
Simplify $\dfrac{x+4}{x^2-5x-36}$ to lowest terms.

Solution
Factor the denominator and divide out any common factors.
$$\frac{x+4}{x^2-5x-36} = \frac{x+4}{(x-9)(x+4)} = \frac{1}{x-9}$$

Example 5
Simplify $\dfrac{-3x^2-11x+20}{3x-4}$.

Solution
Negative 1 is factored out.
$$\frac{-3x^2-11x+20}{3x-4} = \frac{-(3x^2+11x-20)}{3x-4} = \frac{-(3x-4)(x+5)}{3x-4} = -(x+5)$$

Example 6

Write the rational expression $\dfrac{x^2 + 2x - 3}{x^3 + 27}$ in simplified form.

Solution

$$\frac{x^2 + 2x - 3}{x^3 + 27} = \frac{x^2 + 2x - 3}{x^3 + 3^3} = \frac{(x+3)(x-1)}{(x+3)(x^2 - 3x + 9)} = \frac{x-1}{x^2 - 3x + 9}$$

The formula $a^3 + b^3 = (a+b)(a^2 - ab + b^2)$ was used to factor $x^3 + 3^3$.

Example 7

Write the rational expression $\dfrac{5x}{x+3}$ with the denominator of $x^2 - 3x - 18$.

Solution

Factor $x^2 - 3x - 18$ to determine the factor which will be multiplied by the numerator and denominator of the expression $\dfrac{5x}{x+3}$ to produce a denominator of $x^2 - 3x - 18$.

$$\frac{x^2 - 3x - 18}{x+3} = \frac{(x-6)(x+3)}{x+3} = x - 6$$

Therefore, $\dfrac{5x}{x+3} = \dfrac{(5x)(x-6)}{(x+3)(x-6)} = \dfrac{5x^2 - 30x}{x^2 - 3x - 18}$. This is the new rational expression.

Summary

To Multiply Rational Expressions

1. Factor all numerators and denominators as far as possible.

2. Divide out any common factors.

3. Multiply the numerators and multiply the denominators.

4. Simplify the answer when possible.

Example 8

Multiply $\dfrac{x^2 + 3x - 10}{2x} \cdot \dfrac{x^2 - 3x}{x^2 - 5x + 6}$.

Solution

Factor all numerators and denominators: $\dfrac{x^2 + 3x - 10}{2x} \cdot \dfrac{x^2 - 3x}{x^2 - 5x + 6} = \dfrac{(x+5)(x-2)}{2x} \cdot \dfrac{x(x-3)}{(x-2)(x-3)} = \dfrac{x+5}{2}$

Example 9

Multiply and express answer in lowest terms: $\dfrac{x^2-9}{x+3}\cdot\dfrac{x+2}{6+x-x^2}$

Solution

$$\dfrac{x^2-9}{x+3}\cdot\dfrac{x+2}{6+x-x^2}=\dfrac{(x+3)(x-3)}{(x+3)}\cdot\dfrac{(x+2)}{(-1)(x^2-x-6)}=\dfrac{(x+3)(x-3)}{(x+3)}\cdot\dfrac{(x+2)}{(-1)(x-3)(x+2)}=-1$$

(after all common factors have been divided out)

Summary

To Divide Rational Expressions

Invert the divisor (the second fraction or the bottom fraction) and then multiply the resulting rational expressions.

Example 10

Divide and express answer in lowest terms.

$$\dfrac{x-5}{10x}\div\dfrac{25-x^2}{6x^2}$$

Solution

$$\dfrac{x-5}{10x}\div\dfrac{25-x^2}{6x^2}=\dfrac{x-5}{10x}\cdot\dfrac{6x^2}{25-x^2}=\dfrac{x-5}{10x}\cdot\dfrac{6x^2}{(5-x)(5+x)}=\dfrac{x-5}{5}\cdot\dfrac{3x}{(-1)(x-5)(x+5)}=\dfrac{-3x}{5(5+x)}$$

Exercise Set 6.1

Determine the values that are excluded in the following rational expressions.

1. $\dfrac{2}{4x-5}$

2. $\dfrac{2x}{x^2-1}$

3. $\dfrac{y+3}{y^2+9}$

Determine the domain of each function.

4. $y=\dfrac{3}{x^2+7x+6}$

5. $f(x)=\dfrac{4-2x}{x^3-9x}$

Write each rational expression in simplified form.

6. $\dfrac{w^2+3w+2}{w^2+5w+6}$

7. $\dfrac{5s+15}{6s+18}$

8. $\dfrac{2b^3-4b^2}{b^3-8}$

9. $\dfrac{x-5}{5-x}$

Write each rational expression with the denominator indicated.

10. $\dfrac{x+2}{x+3}$, $x^2 - 9$

11. $\dfrac{y+1}{2y}$, $10y^3$

Multiply or divide as indicated and write all answers in lowest terms.

12. $\dfrac{2x+6}{x^2} \cdot \dfrac{x}{x^2 - 9}$

13. $\dfrac{t^2 + 4t - 5}{t^2 - 2t - 3} \cdot \dfrac{t^2 - 4t + 3}{t^2 + 6t + 5}$

14. $\dfrac{(y-2)^2}{5y} \div \dfrac{y^2 - 4}{15y}$

15. $\dfrac{3-x}{y^2 - y} \div \dfrac{x^2 - 9}{y^2 - 2y + 1}$

Answers to Exercise Set 6.1

1. $x = \dfrac{5}{4}$

2. $x = 1; x = -1$

3. No value is excluded.

4. $\{x | x \text{ is a real number and } x \neq -1 \text{ and } x \neq -6\}$

5. $\{x | x \text{ is a real number and } x \neq 0 \text{ and } x \neq 3 \text{ and } x \neq -3\}$

6. $\dfrac{w+1}{w+3}$

7. $\dfrac{5}{6}$

8. $\dfrac{2b^2}{b^2 + 2b + 4}$

9. -1

10. $\dfrac{(x^2 - x - 6)}{x^2 - 9}$

11. $\dfrac{5y^3 + 5y^2}{10y^3}$

12. $\dfrac{2}{x(x-3)}$

13. $\dfrac{(t-1)^2}{(t+1)^2}$

14. $\dfrac{3(y-2)}{y+2}$

15. $\dfrac{-y+1}{y(x+3)}$

6.2 Addition and Subtraction of Rational Expressions

Summary

To Add or Subtract Rational Expressions with a Common Denominator

1. Add or subtract the numerators.

2. Place the sum or difference of the numerators found in step one over the common denominator.

3. Simplify the expression, if possible.

Example 1

Add $\dfrac{x^2 + 2x}{x^2 + 1} + \dfrac{3x^2 - 4x}{x^2 + 1}$.

Solution

$$\frac{x^2 + 2x}{x^2 + 1} + \frac{3x^2 - 4x}{x^2 + 1} = \frac{x^2 + 2x + 3x^2 - 4x}{x^2 + 1} = \frac{4x^2 - 2x}{x^2 + 1}$$

Example 2

Subtract $\dfrac{2x + 1}{3x - 5} - \dfrac{x + 4}{3x - 5}$.

Solution

$$\frac{2x + 1}{3x - 5} - \frac{x + 4}{3x - 5} = \frac{(2x + 1) - (x + 4)}{3x - 5} = \frac{2x + 1 - x - 4}{3x - 5} = \frac{x - 3}{3x - 5}$$

Summary

Finding the Least Common Denominator

1. Write each non-prime coefficient that appears in a denominator as a product of prime numbers.

2. Factor each denominator completely. Express factors which occur more than once as powers.

3. The LCD is the product of all the different factors, with each factor appearing the most number of times it appears in any one factorization.

Example 3

Add, after finding the LCD: $\dfrac{7}{12}+\dfrac{3}{100}$

Solution

Find the LCD by expressing 12 and 100 as products of primes.

$12 = 2\cdot2\cdot3 = 2^2\cdot3,\ 100 = 2^2\cdot5^2$

The LCD is the product of all the different factors with each factor appearing the most number of times in any one factorization.

The LCD is $2^2\cdot3\cdot5^2 = 300$.

Rename fractions: $\dfrac{7}{12}=\dfrac{7\cdot25}{12\cdot25}=\dfrac{175}{300},\ \dfrac{3}{100}=\dfrac{3\cdot3}{100\cdot3}=\dfrac{9}{300}$

Add: $\dfrac{7}{12}+\dfrac{3}{100}=\dfrac{175}{300}+\dfrac{9}{300}=\dfrac{184}{300}=\dfrac{46}{75}$

Summary

To Add or Subtract Rational Expressions with Unlike Denominators

1. Completely factor each denominator and find the LCD.

2. Rewrite each fraction as an equivalent fraction with the LCD. This is done by multiplying both the numerator and denominator of each fraction by any factors needed to obtain the LCD.

3. Leave the denominator in factored form, but multiply out the numerator.

4. Add or subtract numerators while maintaining the LCD.

5. When possible, factor the numerator and reduce fractions.

Example 4

Find the sum or difference.

a. $\dfrac{5}{12x^2y}+\dfrac{4}{9xy^3}$

b. $\dfrac{x}{x-2}-\dfrac{3x+2}{x^2-4}$

Solution

a. $\dfrac{5}{12x^2y} + \dfrac{4}{9xy^3}$

The LCD is $36x^2y^3$.

Rename the fractions: $\dfrac{5}{12x^2y} \cdot \dfrac{3y^2}{3y^2} = \dfrac{15y^2}{36x^2y^3}$

$\dfrac{4}{9xy^3} \cdot \dfrac{4x}{4x} = \dfrac{16x}{36x^2y^3}$

Thus, $\dfrac{15y^2}{36x^2y^3} + \dfrac{16x}{36x^2y^3} = \dfrac{15y^2 + 16x}{36x^2y^3}$.

b. $\dfrac{x}{x-2} - \dfrac{3x+2}{x^2-4} = \dfrac{x}{x-2} + \dfrac{-(3x+2)}{(x-2)(x+2)}$

The LCD is $(x-2)(x+2)$.

Rename $\dfrac{x}{x-2} = \dfrac{x(x+2)}{(x-2)(x+2)}$. The remaining rational expression already has the LCD in its

denominator.

Thus, $\dfrac{x(x+2)}{(x-2)(x+2)} + \dfrac{-(3x+2)}{(x-2)(x+2)} = \dfrac{x^2+2x-3x-2}{(x-2)(x+2)}$

$= \dfrac{x^2-x-2}{(x-2)(x+2)}$

$= \dfrac{(x-2)(x+1)}{(x-2)(x+2)}$

$= \dfrac{x+1}{x+2}$

Example 5

Add $\dfrac{2x-4}{3x-1} + \dfrac{x-5}{1-3x}$.

Solution

Notice that the denominators are opposite. Multiply numerator and denominator of **either** fraction by -1 to obtain the LCD. We will select the second fraction.

$\dfrac{2x-4}{3x-1} + \dfrac{x-5}{1-3x} = \dfrac{2x-4}{3x-1} + \dfrac{(x-5)\cdot(-1)}{(1-3x)\cdot(-1)}$

$= \dfrac{2x-4}{3x-1} + \dfrac{5-x}{3x-1}$

$= \dfrac{2x-4+5-x}{3x-1}$

$= \dfrac{x+1}{3x-1}$

Example 6

Add $\dfrac{3}{x^2-13x+36}+\dfrac{4}{2x^2-7x-4}$.

Solution

$$\frac{3}{x^2-13x+36}+\frac{4}{2x^2-7x-4}=\frac{3}{(x-4)(x-9)}+\frac{4}{(2x+1)(x-4)}$$

The LCD is $(x-4)(x-9)(2x+1)$.

Rename $\dfrac{3}{(x-4)(x-9)}=\dfrac{3(2x+1)}{(x-4)(x-9)(2x+1)}$

$$=\frac{6x+3}{(x-4)(x-9)(2x+1)}$$

Rename $\dfrac{4}{(2x+1)(x-4)}=\dfrac{4(x-9)}{(2x+1)(x-4)(x-9)}$

$$=\frac{4x-36}{(2x+1)(x-4)(x-9)}$$

Add: $\dfrac{6x+3}{\text{LCD}}+\dfrac{4x-36}{\text{LCD}}=\dfrac{10x-33}{\text{LCD}}=\dfrac{10x-33}{(2x+1)(x-4)(x-9)}$

Summary

An Application of Rational Expressions:
Finding the Profit

1. Substitute the revenue function, $R(x)$ and the cost function, $C(x)$, into the profit function, $P(x)=R(x)-C(x)$.

2. Subtract the cost function from the revenue function.

3. Simplify the result, if possible.

Example 7

Find the profit function, $P(x)$, when $R(x)=\dfrac{6x-5}{x+3}$ and $C(x)=\dfrac{3x-2}{x+2}$

Solution

Substitute $R(x)$ and $C(x)$ into the profit function $P(x)$.

$$P(x)=\frac{6x-5}{x+3}-\frac{3x-2}{x+2}=\frac{6x-5}{x+3}+\frac{-(3x-2)}{x+2}$$

The LCD is $(x+3)(x+2)$.

Rename $\dfrac{6x-5}{x+3}=\dfrac{(6x-5)(x+2)}{(x+3)(x+2)}$

$$=\frac{6x^2+7x-10}{(x+3)(x+2)}$$

Rename $\dfrac{-(3x-2)}{x+2} = \dfrac{-(3x-2)(x+3)}{(x+2)(x+3)}$ Multiply the binomials first, then distribute the -1.

$$= \dfrac{-3x^2 - 7x + 6}{(x+2)(x+3)}$$

Add: $\dfrac{6x^2 + 7x - 10}{(x+3)(x+2)} + \dfrac{-3x^2 - 7x + 6}{(x+3)(x+2)} = \dfrac{3x^2 - 4}{(x+3)(x+2)}$

Exercise Set 6.2

Add or subtract and express answer in lowest terms.

1. $\dfrac{x-7}{2x-3} + \dfrac{x+4}{2x-3}$

2. $\dfrac{2}{x} - \dfrac{3}{-x}$

3. $\dfrac{x^3 - 10x^2 + 35x}{x(x-6)} - \dfrac{x^2 + 5x}{x(x-6)}$

4. $\dfrac{5}{4x} + \dfrac{3}{8y}$

5. $\dfrac{4x}{x-4} + \dfrac{x+4}{x+1}$

6. $\dfrac{x}{x+3} + \dfrac{5x-3}{x^2-9}$

7. $\dfrac{x+1}{x^2+5x+6} - \dfrac{x+3}{x^2+3x+2}$

8. $\dfrac{-4}{8x^2y^2} + \dfrac{7}{5x^4y^5}$

9. $\dfrac{x+2y}{3x^2-8xy+4y^2} - \dfrac{3x+2y}{x^2-4xy+4y^2}$

10. Find the profit function, $P(x)$, when $R(x) = \dfrac{4x-1}{x+1}$ and $C(x) = \dfrac{2x-3}{x+3}$

Answers to Exercise Set 6.2

1. 1

2. $\dfrac{5}{x}$

3. $x-5$

4. $\dfrac{10y+3x}{8xy}$

5. $\dfrac{5x^2+4x-16}{(x-4)(x+1)}$

6. $\dfrac{x-1}{x-3}$

7. $\dfrac{-4}{(x+1)(x+3)}$

8. $\dfrac{-20x^2y^3+56}{40x^4y^5}$

9. $\dfrac{-8x^2}{(x-2y)^2(3x-2y)}$

10. $\dfrac{2x^2+12x}{(x+3)(x+2)}$

6.3 Complex Fractions

Summary

Complex Fractions

A **complex fraction** is one that has a fractional expression in its numerator or its denominator or both its numerator and denominator.

To Simplify a Complex Fraction by Multiplying by a Common Denominator

1. Find the LCD of all fractions appearing within the complex fraction. This is the LCD of the complex fraction.

2. Multiply both the numerator and denominator of the complex fraction by this LCD.

3. Simplify when possible.

Example 1

Simplify $\dfrac{\frac{3}{4}+\frac{1}{3}}{\frac{2}{3}-\frac{1}{2}}$.

Solution
The LCD of all the fractions that appear in the numerator or denominator is 12. Multiply the numerator and denominator by 12.

$$\frac{12\left(\frac{3}{4}+\frac{1}{3}\right)}{12\left(\frac{2}{3}-\frac{1}{2}\right)} = \frac{12\left(\frac{3}{4}\right)+12\left(\frac{1}{3}\right)}{12\left(\frac{2}{3}\right)-12\left(\frac{1}{2}\right)} = \frac{\frac{36}{4}+\frac{12}{3}}{\frac{24}{3}-\frac{12}{2}} = \frac{9+4}{8-6} = \frac{13}{2}$$

Example 2

Simplify $\dfrac{n+\frac{1}{m}}{n-\frac{1}{m}}$.

Solution
Multiply numerator and denominator of the complex fraction by the LCD of m:

$$\frac{m\left(n+\frac{1}{m}\right)}{m\left(n-\frac{1}{m}\right)} = \frac{mn+\frac{m}{m}}{mn-\frac{m}{m}} = \frac{mn+1}{mn-1}$$

Summary

> **To Simplify a Complex Fraction by Simplifying Numerator and Denominator**
>
> 1. Add or subtract as necessary to get one rational expression in the numerator.
>
> 2. Add or subtract as necessary to get one rational expression in the denominator.
>
> 3. Invert and multiply the denominator of the complex fraction by the numerator of the complex fraction.
>
> 4. Simplify when possible.

Example 3

Simplify $\dfrac{x^{-1}+1}{1-x^{-2}}$.

Solution

$$\frac{x^{-1}+1}{1-x^{-2}} = \frac{\frac{1}{x}+1}{1-\frac{1}{x^2}} = \frac{\frac{1}{x}+\frac{x}{x}}{\frac{x^2}{x^2}-\frac{1}{x^2}} = \frac{\frac{1+x}{x}}{\frac{x^2-1}{x^2}} = \frac{1+x}{x} \cdot \frac{x^2}{x^2-1} = \frac{1+x}{x} \cdot \frac{x^2}{(x-1)(x+1)} = \frac{x}{x-1}$$

Exercise Set 6.3

Simplify each complex fraction.

1. $\dfrac{2+\frac{5}{8}}{\frac{1}{3}-\frac{1}{4}}$

2. $\dfrac{\frac{1}{x}}{\frac{2}{x}-\frac{3}{y}}$

3. $\dfrac{\frac{a-b}{a+b}}{\frac{1}{b}-\frac{1}{a}}$

4. $\dfrac{\frac{x^2-y^2}{x}}{\frac{x+y}{x^3}}$

5. $\dfrac{1-\frac{1}{a}-\frac{1}{b}}{b+\frac{1}{a}+1}$

6. $\dfrac{x^{-2}-2}{x^{-4}-4}$

7. $\dfrac{x^{-2}+\frac{1}{x}}{x^{-1}+x^{-2}}$

Answers to Exercise Set 6.3

1. $\dfrac{63}{2}$

2. $\dfrac{y}{2y-3x}$

3. $\dfrac{ab}{a+b}$

4. $x^2(x-y)$

5. $\dfrac{ab-b-a}{ab^2+b+ab}$

6. $\dfrac{x^2}{1+2x^2}$

7. 1

6.4 Solving Rational Equations

Summary

To Solve Rational Equations

1. Determine the LCD of all rational expressions in the equation.

2. Multiply both sides of the equation by the LCD. This will result in every term in the equation being multiplied by the LCD.

3. Remove any parentheses and combine like terms.

4. Solve the resulting equation.

5. Check the solution.

Example 1

Solve the equation $5-\dfrac{x}{2}=x$.

Solution
Multiply both sides of the equation by the LCD of 2:

$$2\left(5-\frac{x}{2}\right)=2(x)$$

$$2(5)-2\left(\frac{x}{2}\right)=2(x)$$

$$10-x=2x$$

Solve for x: $10-x=2x$

$$10=3x$$

$$\frac{10}{3}=x$$

If you substitute $\dfrac{10}{3}$ for x in the original equation, the resulting equation is true.

Example 2

Solve $\dfrac{1}{x} - \dfrac{2}{x} = \dfrac{3}{x}$.

Solution

Multiply each side of the equation by the LCD of x:

$$x\left(\dfrac{1}{x} - \dfrac{2}{x}\right) = x\left(\dfrac{3}{x}\right)$$

$$\dfrac{x}{x} - \dfrac{2x}{x} = \dfrac{3x}{x}$$

$$1 - 2 = 3$$

$$-1 = 3 \text{ is false.}$$

There is no solution to this equation.

Example 3

Solve $3 = \dfrac{2x}{x^2 - 9} + \dfrac{x+9}{x+3}$.

Solution

1. Find the LCD of $x^2 - 9$ and $x + 3$. Since $x^2 - 9 = (x+3)(x-3)$, the LCD is $(x+3)(x-3)$.

2. Multiply each side of the equation by the LCD.

$$3(x+3)(x-3) = \left(\dfrac{2x}{x^2-9} + \dfrac{x+9}{x+3}\right)(x+3)(x-3)$$

$$3(x^2-9) = \dfrac{2x(x+3)(x-3)}{x^2-9} + \dfrac{(x+9)(x+3)(x-3)}{x+3}$$

$$3(x^2-9) = 2x + (x+9)(x-3)$$

$$3x^2 - 27 = x^2 + 8x - 27$$

$$2x^2 - 8x = 0$$

$$2x^2 - 8x = 0$$

$$2x(x-4) = 0$$

$$x = 0, x = 4$$

Both values check in the original equation.

Example 4

Solve $\dfrac{x-4}{x-5} = \dfrac{4}{x-5}$.

Solution

This rational equation is a proportion. Any rational equation of the form $\dfrac{a}{b} = \dfrac{c}{d}$ can be solved using cross

multiplication: If $\dfrac{a}{b} = \dfrac{c}{d}$, then $ad = bc$.

Thus, since $\dfrac{x-4}{x-5} = \dfrac{4}{x-5}$, then $(x-4)(x-5) = 4(x-5)$.

$$x^2 - 9x + 20 = 4x - 20$$
$$x^2 - 13x + 40 = 0$$
$$(x - 5)(x - 8) = 0$$

This means that $x = 5$ or $x = 8$. If the number 5 is substituted into the original equation, we have $\dfrac{5-1}{5-5} = \dfrac{4}{5-5}$ or $\dfrac{4}{0} = \dfrac{4}{0}$. This equation is false since you cannot divide by zero. As a result, $x = 5$ does not check. The value $x = 8$ docs check.

Example 5

Solve the formula $\dfrac{1}{a} = \dfrac{1}{b} - \dfrac{1}{c}$ for c.

Solution
Multiply each side of this equation by the LCD of abc.

$$abc\left(\frac{1}{a}\right) = abc\left(\frac{1}{b} - \frac{1}{c}\right)$$
$$bc = ac - ab$$
$$bc - ac = -ab$$
$$c(b - a) = -ab$$

Now, divide by $(b - a)$ to obtain $c = \dfrac{-ab}{b-a} = \dfrac{ab}{a-b}$.

Exercise Set 6.4

Solve each equation and check the solution.

1. $\dfrac{2y}{3} - \dfrac{3y}{4} = 1$ 2. $\dfrac{x}{5} = \dfrac{x-3}{2}$ 3. $\dfrac{x}{3} - \dfrac{3x}{4} = -\dfrac{5x}{12}$

4. $\dfrac{3}{x} - \dfrac{4}{x} = \dfrac{2}{x}$ 5. $\dfrac{6}{x+1} - \dfrac{4}{x-1} = \dfrac{10}{x^2 - 1}$ 6. $\dfrac{2}{3x+1} + \dfrac{4}{3x-1} = \dfrac{6x+8}{9x^2 - 1}$

7. $\dfrac{1}{3x-1} - \dfrac{2}{x-2} = \dfrac{5x}{3x^2 - 7x + 2}$ 8. $\dfrac{6}{5x} + \dfrac{4}{5} - 2x = 0$

Solve the given equation for the specified variable.

9. $p = \dfrac{1}{1+w}$ for w 10. $d = \dfrac{fl}{f+w}$ for f

Solutions for Exercise Set 6.4

1. -12 2. 5 3. All real numbers

4. No solution   **5.** 10   **6.** $\dfrac{1}{2}$

7. 0   **8.** $-\dfrac{3}{5}, 1$ **9.** $w = \dfrac{1-p}{p}$

10. $f = \dfrac{dw}{l-d}$

6.5 Rational Equations: Applications and Problem Solving

Summary

Work Problems

Work problems often involve rational equations. The goal in such problems is to find the time needed to complete a job when two or more people or machines work together.

If a job requires x units of time to complete, then $\dfrac{1}{x}$ of the job is completed in **one time unit.**

Example 1
Nick can paint a certain room in 4 hours while Diane can paint the same room in 3 hours. How long would it take both Nick and Diane to paint this room working together?

Solution

Nick can complete the job in 4 hours. So in **1 hour**, he completes $\dfrac{1}{4}$ of the job. Diane can complete the job in 3 hours, so she can do $\dfrac{1}{3}$ of the job in 1 hour. Together, assume they can complete the entire job in x hours. Then in 1 hour, both should be able to complete $\dfrac{1}{x}$ of the job. Set up the equation:

(Portion of job done + (Portion of job done   =   (Portion done by both in one hour)
by Nick in one hour)   by Diane in one hour)

$$\dfrac{1}{4} \quad + \quad \dfrac{1}{3} \quad = \quad \dfrac{1}{x}$$

The LCD is $12x$. Multiply both sides of this equation by the LCD.

$$12x\left(\frac{1}{4}+\frac{1}{3}\right)=12x\left(\frac{1}{x}\right)$$
$$3x+4x=12$$
$$7x=12$$
$$x=\frac{12}{7}=1\frac{5}{7}\text{ hours,}$$

the time for both to do the job.

Example 2

One machine can complete a job in 2 hours. At what rate would a second machine need to operate so that together they could complete the job in $\frac{1}{2}$ hour?

Solution

Let x be the number of minutes the second machine needs to complete the job. Minutes are used as the unit of time since we are given that $\frac{1}{2}$ hour is needed to complete the job working together. Then, in one minute, the first machine can complete $\frac{1}{120}$ of the job, since 2 hours = 120 minutes. The second machine can do $\frac{1}{x}$ of the job in x minutes while both machines can do $\frac{1}{30}$ of the job in 1 minute, since $\frac{1}{2}$ hour is 30 minutes.

(portion of job 1st machine + (portion of job 2nd machine = (portion of job both can do working together)
can do in 1 minute)   can do in 1 minute)

$$\frac{1}{120} \qquad + \qquad \frac{1}{x} \qquad = \qquad \frac{1}{30}$$

The LCD is $120x$.

$$120x\left(\frac{1}{120}+\frac{1}{x}\right)=120x\left(\frac{1}{30}\right)$$
$$x+120=4x$$
$$120=3x$$
$$40=x$$

Thus, the second machine would need to complete the job in 40 minutes if both machines working together are to complete the entire job in one half hour.

Example 3

What number multiplied by the numerator and added to the denominator of the fraction $\frac{2}{3}$ makes the resulting number equal to 1?

Solution

Let x = the unknown number.

Equation

$$\frac{2x}{3+x}=1$$

Since this is a proportion, we can cross multiply as follows.

$$\frac{2x}{3+x} = \frac{1}{1}$$
$$(2x)(1) = 1(3+x)$$
$$2x = 3+x$$
$$x = 3$$
Check: $\dfrac{2(3)}{3+3} = \dfrac{6}{6} = 1$

Summary

Motion Problems

Motion problems involve forms of the distance-rate-time formula: Recall, **distance = rate · time** or

$$\textbf{time} = \frac{\textbf{distance}}{\textbf{rate}}.$$

Example 4

A boat can travel 12 km downstream in the same time it can travel 8 km upstream. If the current of the river is 1 km/hour, what is the boat's rate in still water?

Solution

Organize the information in a table and use the formula **distance = rate · time**. Let x = boat's speed in still water. When the boat is traveling downstream, the speed of the boat will increase by 1 km/hour to $(x + 1)$. When the boat is going upstream, its speed will decrease by 1 km/hour to $(x - 1)$.

Boat	Distance	Rate	Time
downstream	12	$x + 1$	$\dfrac{12}{x+1}$
upstream	8	$x - 1$	$\dfrac{8}{x-1}$

Since $t = \dfrac{d}{r}$, we obtain the expressions for time in the table. We are told that the time going downstream is equal to the time going upstream, so we can write the equation: $\dfrac{12}{x+1} = \dfrac{8}{x-1}$.

Cross-multiplying, we have
$$12(x-1) = 8(x+1)$$
$$12x - 12 = 8x + 8$$
$$12x - 8x = 12 + 8$$
$$4x = 20$$
$$x = 5$$
Thus, 5 km/hour is the rate of the boat in still water.

Example 5
A bicyclist pedaled 2 miles against a 5 mile/hour wind. With the same wind at her back, she pedaled 2 miles in 20 **minutes** less time. At what speed would the bicyclist have been pedaling if there was no wind?

Solution
Let x = speed of the bicycle with no wind. When the cyclist goes against the wind, the speed will be reduced by 5 miles per hour to $(x-5)$ and when the cyclist goes with the wind, the speed will be $(x+5)$. Again, we can organize the information in a chart:

Bicyclist	Distance	Rate	Time
Against wind	2	$x-5$	$\dfrac{2}{x-5}$
With wind	2	$x+5$	$\dfrac{2}{x+5}$

In this case, the times are not equal. They differ by 20 minutes or $\dfrac{1}{3}$ hour. The equation becomes:

$$\frac{2}{x-5} - \frac{2}{x+5} = \frac{1}{3}$$

Since the LCD is $3(x-5)(x+5)$, we can clear fractions in the equation by multiplying both sides of the equation by the LCD.

$$(3)(x-5)(x+5)\left(\frac{2}{x-5} - \frac{2}{x+5}\right) = (3)(x-5)(x+5)\left(\frac{1}{3}\right)$$

$$(3)(x+5)(2) - 2(3)(x-5) = (x-5)(x+5)$$

$$6x + 30 - 6x + 30 = x^2 - 25$$

$$60 = x^2 - 25$$

$$85 = x^2$$

$$\sqrt{85} = x$$

Thus, $x = \sqrt{85} \approx 9.2$ miles/hour.

Exercise Set 6.5

1. Coin sorter X can process a sack of coins in 20 minutes; sorter Y can process the sack in one-half hour. How long would it take the two machines working together to process the sack of coins?

2. One electrician can wire a house in 20 hours, while another can wire the same house in 16 hours. If they work together, will they both be able to complete the job in less than 10 hours? Explain.

3. Ezra can paint a bedroom in 6 hours. Ruth can paint the same bedroom in 4 hours. How long should it take them to paint the bedroom if they work together?

4. What number multiplied by the numerator and added to the denominator of $\dfrac{1}{5}$ makes the resulting fraction $\dfrac{1}{2}$?

5. The speed of an airplane with no wind is 250 miles per hour. If the plane travels 150 miles with a tailwind (pushing the plane) in the same amount of time that it travels 130 miles against the headwind, find the speed of the wind.

6. Two runners run along the same course. One runner runs at 5 miles per hour, while the other travels at 4 miles per hour. If it takes the slower runner $\frac{1}{2}$ hour longer than the faster runner to complete the course, how long is the course?

7. When a husband and a wife work together, they can rake a certain lawn in 3.2 hours. When the wife rakes the lawn alone, it takes her 5.7 hours. How long would it take the husband to rake the lawn alone?

8. When only the cold water valve is opened, a washtub will fill in 8 minutes. When only the hot water valve is opened, the washtub will fill in 12 minutes. When the drain of the washtub is open, it will drain completely in 7 minutes. If both the hot and cold water valves are open and the drain is open, how long will it take for the washtub to fill?

9. What number added to the numerator and multiplied by the denominator of the fraction $\frac{3}{2}$ makes the resulting fraction $\frac{1}{8}$?

10. The rate of a bicyclist is 8 miles per hour faster than that of a jogger. If the bicyclist travels 10 miles in the same amount of time that the jogger travels 5 miles, find the rate of the jogger.

Answers to Exercise Set 6.5

1. 12 minutes
2. Yes, in about 8 hours and 54 minutes.
3. 2.4 hours
4. 5
5. $17\frac{6}{7}$ miles per hour
6. 10 miles
7. 7.3 hours
8. About 15.27 minutes
9. –4
10. 8 miles per hour

6.6 Variation

Summary

Direct Variation

If a variable y varies directly as x, then $y = kx$, where k is the **constant of proportionality**. The two related variables will both **increase** together or both **decrease** together.

Example 1
The property tax, T, varies directly as the assessed value, v, of the home. Write a variation equation for this statement.

Solution
Since T = property tax and v = assessed value, the equation is $T = kv$, where k is the constant of proportionality.

Example 2
Suppose y varies directly as x and $y = 5$ when $x = 4$.

Solution
If y varies directly as x, then $y = kx$, where k is the constant of proportionality. If $y = 5$ when $x = 4$, then $5 = k(4)$. Thus, $k = \dfrac{5}{4}$. We now have $y = \dfrac{5}{4}x$. If $x = 20$, then $y = \dfrac{5}{4}(20) = 25$.

Summary

Inverse Variation

If a variable y varies inversely with a variable x, then $y = \dfrac{k}{x}$ (or $xy = k$), where k is the constant of proportionality. This means that as one quantity **increases** the other quantity **decreases** or vice versa.

Example 3
The time to do a job, T, varies inversely as the number of workers, n. If it takes 7 hours for 3 workers to do a certain job, how long should it take 4 workers to do the same job?

Solution
We have $T = \dfrac{k}{n}$, since T varies inversely as n. Substitute the given values into the equation: $7 = \dfrac{k}{3}$, or $k = 21$.

Our new equation is $T = \dfrac{21}{n}$. If $n = 4$, then $T = \dfrac{21}{4} = 5.25$. It should take 4 workers 5.25 hours to do the same job.

Summary

Joint Variation

The general form a **joint variation** where y varies directly as x and z is

$y = kxz$, where k is the constant of proportionality.

The following examples illustrate combined variations.

Example 4
V varies jointly as l, w and h and inversely as n; $V = 5$ when $l = 2$, $w = 3$, $h = 4$, and $n = 6$. Find V when $l = 4$, $w = 3$, $h = 1$, and $n = 5$.

Solution
$$V = \frac{klwh}{n}$$

Substitute the values to get $5 = \frac{k(2)(3)(4)}{6}$ or $5 = 4k$. Thus, $\frac{5}{4} = k$.

Now use this value of k and the new values of the four variables to find V: $V = \frac{\frac{5}{4}(4)(3)(1)}{5}$ or $V = 3$.

Example 5
The electrical resistance of a wire, R, varies directly as its length, L, and inversely as its cross-sectional area, A. If the resistance of a wire is 0.2 ohm when the length is 200 feet and its cross-sectional area is 0.05 square inches, find the resistance of a wire whose length is 5000 feet with a cross-sectional area of 0.01 square inches.

Solution
Use the equation $R = \frac{kL}{A}$. Now, substitute the first set of values into this equation: $0.2 = \frac{k(200)}{0.05}$.

Now solve for k to get $0.2 = 4000k$ or $k = \frac{0.2}{4000} = 5 \times 10^{-5}$. Now, substitute the second set of values into the

equation: $R = \frac{(5 \times 10^{-5})(5000)}{0.01} = 25$ ohms.

Exercise Set 6.6

Write the variation equation and find the quantities indicated.

1. x varies directly as y. Find x when $y = 12$ and $k = 6$.

2. T varies directly as the square of D and inversely as F. Find T when $D = 8$, $F = 15$ and $k = 12$ (the constant of proportionality).

3. y varies inversely as x, and $y = 2$ when $x = 7$. Find y when $x = 5$.

4. y varies directly as x and inversely as z^2; $y = 0.5$ when $x = 8$ and $z = 2$. Find y when $x = 4$ and $z = -1$.

5. F varies directly as q_1 and q_2 and inversely as the square of d. If $F = 8$ when $q_1 = 2$, $q_2 = 8$ and $d = 4$, find F when $q_1 = 28$, $q_2 = 12$ and $d = 2$.

6. The wattage rating, W, of an appliance varies jointly as the square of the current I and the resistance R. If the wattage is 1 watt when the current is 0.1 amperes and the resistance is 100 ohms, find the wattage when the current is 0.5 amperes and the resistance is 500 ohms.

7. The volume, V, of a cylinder varies jointly as the square of the radius r of the cylinder and the height h of the cylinder. If the volume of a cylinder is $\dfrac{400\pi}{3}$ cubic inches when the radius is 5 inches and the height is 4 inches, find the volume of the cylinder with radius 10 inches and height 4 inches.

8. W varies jointly as A and h and inversely as d^2; $w = 1$ when $A = 9$, $h = 2$, and $d = 6$. Find w when $A = 9$, $h = 2$ and $d = 2$.

9. The weight (w) of a solid cube varies directly as the cube of an edge (e). If a cube with edge 8 inches weighs 10 pounds, what will a cube with edge 7 inches made of the same material weigh? Round to the nearest tenth of a pound.

10. Write the relationship algebraically: w varies jointly as s and t and inversely as the square of r.

Answers to Exercise Set 6.6

1. 72

2. 51.2 or $\dfrac{256}{5}$

3. 2.8 or $\dfrac{14}{5}$

4. 1

5. 672

6. 25 watts

7. $\dfrac{800\pi}{3}$ cu in.

8. 9

9. 6.7 pounds

10. $w = \dfrac{kst}{r^2}$

Chapter 6 Practice Set

1. Write the rational expression in lowest terms.
$$\frac{2x^2 - 6x + 5x - 15}{2x^2 + 7x + 5}$$

2. Multiply $\dfrac{1}{x-2} \cdot \dfrac{2-x}{2}$.

3. Subtract $\dfrac{5x}{3xy} - \dfrac{4}{x^2}$.

4. Multiply $\dfrac{1}{a-3} \cdot \dfrac{a^2 - 2a - 3}{a^2 + 3a + 2}$.

5. Add or subtract as indicated.
$$\frac{1}{x+3} - \frac{2}{x-3} + \frac{6}{x^2 - 9}$$

6. Simplify the complex fraction.

$$\frac{4 - \frac{9}{16}}{1 + \frac{5}{8}}$$

7. Simplify the complex fraction.

$$\frac{x^{-2} + \frac{1}{x}}{\frac{1}{x^2} - \frac{1}{x}}$$

8. Solve the equation.

$$\frac{x+3}{5} = \frac{9}{5}$$

9. Solve the equation.

$$\frac{3x+4}{5} = \frac{2x-8}{3}$$

10. It takes Bob 3 hours to mow Mr. Gonzales' lawn. It takes Jan 4 hours to mow the same lawn. How long will it take them together to mow Mr. Gonzales' lawn?

11. Susan's boat can travel 15 miles per hour in still water. Traveling with the current of a river, the boat can travel 20 miles in the same time it takes to go 10 miles against the current. Find the rate of the current.

12. P varies directly as Q and inversely as R. If $P = 8$ when $Q = 4$ and $R = 10$, find P when $Q = 10$ and $R = 20$.

Answers to Chapter 6 Practice Test

1. $\dfrac{x-3}{x-1}$

2. $-\dfrac{1}{2}$

3. $\dfrac{5x^2 - 12y}{3x^2 y}$

4. $\dfrac{1}{a+2}$

5. $-\dfrac{1}{x-3}$

6. $\dfrac{55}{26}$

7. $\dfrac{x+1}{1-x}$

8. 6

9. 52

10. $\dfrac{12}{7}$ or 1.71 hours

11. 5 miles per hour

12. 10

CHAPTER 6 SUMMARY

IMPORTANT FACTS

Summary of Operations on Rational Expressions.

Operation	Use this Rule
To Multiply	$\dfrac{a}{b} \cdot \dfrac{c}{d} = \dfrac{a \cdot c}{b \cdot d}, \quad b \neq 0, d \neq 0$
To Divide	$\dfrac{a}{b} \div \dfrac{c}{d} = \dfrac{a}{b} \cdot \dfrac{d}{c} = \dfrac{a \cdot d}{b \cdot c}, \quad b \neq 0, c \neq 0$
To Add	$\dfrac{a}{c} + \dfrac{b}{c} = \dfrac{a+b}{c}, \quad c \neq 0$
To Subtract	$\dfrac{a}{c} - \dfrac{b}{c} = \dfrac{a-b}{c}, \quad c \neq 0$

Summary of Variation

▫ Direct: $y = kx$

▫ Inverse: $y = \dfrac{k}{x}$

▫ Joint: $y = kxz$

HELPFUL HINTS

- You must be proficient with your factoring to be successful in working with rational expressions and equations. Therefore, if you are still having any difficulty factoring, review Sections 5.4 – 5.7.

- Use the following guidelines when working with rational expressions.

    ▫ To add or subtract, find the LCD. Write an equivalent fraction with the LCD. Add or subtract the numerators and write this result over the LCD.

    ▫ To multiply, factor each expression in the numerator and denominator. Divide out common factors.

    ▫ To divide, multiply the first (or top) fraction by the reciprocal of the second (or bottom) fraction. Then follow the guideline for multiplication.

- When simplifying a complex fraction that consists of a single fraction over a single fraction, you may prefer to invert the denominator and multiply it by the numerator, instead of multiplying the numerator and the denominator by the LCD.

- Whenever there is a variable in the denominator of an equation, you must check the apparent solution in the original equation to make sure it is not an extraneous solution. A solution is extraneous if the apparent solution makes any denominator zero. Therefore it is not a true solution to the equation and you should write "No Solution" as your answer.

AVOIDING COMMON ERRORS

- When simplifying rational expressions, you must first factor the numerator and denominator because you can only divide out common factors, *not terms*. When an expression is written as multiplication, they are factors. If there is a plus or minus sign, they are terms. For example:

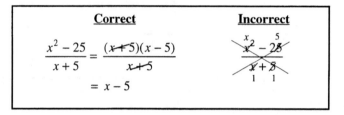

- Be careful not to confuse the role of the LCD in adding or subtracting rational expressions with the role of the LCD in solving rational equations.

  - When you are adding or subtracting rational expressions, you would write the fractions *with* the LCD and the common denominator must be a part of the answer.

  - When solving an equation, you would multiply both sides of the equation by the LCD to *remove* the common denominator.

Adding or Subtracting Rational Expressions	Solving an Equation
$\dfrac{x}{x-2} + \dfrac{5}{x-2} = \dfrac{x+5}{x-2}$	$\dfrac{x}{x-2} + \dfrac{5}{x-2} = (x-2)\left(\dfrac{x}{x-2} + \dfrac{5}{x-2}\right)$ $= x+5$

Chapter 7

7.1 Roots and Radicals

Summary

Principal Square Roots

The **principal** or **positive square root** of a positive real number a, written $\sqrt{a}$, is that positive number whose square is a. That is, $\sqrt{a} = b$ if $a = b^2$.

Example 1
Find

   a. $\sqrt{49}$ **b.** $\sqrt{\dfrac{25}{36}}$

Solution

   a. $\sqrt{49} = 7$ since $7^2 = 49$.

   b. $\sqrt{\dfrac{25}{36}} = \dfrac{5}{6}$ since $\left(\dfrac{5}{6}\right)^2 = \dfrac{25}{36}$.

Summary

Nth Root of a

The nth root of a, $\sqrt[n]{a}$, where n is an **even index** and a is a positive real number, is the positive real number b such that $b^n = a$.

The nth root of a, $\sqrt[n]{a}$, where n is an **odd index** and a is any real number, is the real number b such that $b^n = a$.

Note: the nth root of a, $\sqrt[n]{a}$, is not defined if n is even and a is less than 0. For all other cases, the nth root of a is defined.

Example 2
Indicate whether or not the radical expression is a real number. If it is a real number, find its value.

　　a. $\sqrt[3]{27}$　　　　　　　　**b.** $\sqrt[3]{-27}$　　　　　　　　**c.** $\sqrt[4]{16}$

　　d. $\sqrt[4]{-16}$　　　　　　　**e.** $-\sqrt[4]{81}$

Solution

　　a. $\sqrt[3]{27}$ is real and equals 3.

　　b. $\sqrt[3]{-27}$ is real and equals –3.

　　c. $\sqrt[4]{16}$ is real and equals 2.

　　d. $\sqrt[4]{-16}$ is not a real number since the index is even but the radicand is a negative number.

　　e. $-\sqrt[4]{81}$ is real and equals –3.

Summary

> **For any real number** a, $\sqrt{a^2} = |a|$.

Example 3
Use absolute values to evaluate the following.

　　a. $\sqrt{15^2}$　　　　　　　　**b.** $\sqrt{(-15)^2}$　　　　　　　　**c.** $\sqrt{(-21)^2}$

　　d. $\sqrt{(x+7)^2}$　　　　　　　**e.** $\sqrt{(5-a)^2}$

Solution

　　a. $\sqrt{15^2} = |15| = 15$　　　　**b.** $\sqrt{(-15)^2} = |-15| = 15$　　　　**c.** $\sqrt{(-21)^2} = |-21| = 21$

　　d. $\sqrt{(x+7)^2} = |x+7|$　　　　**e.** $\sqrt{(5-a)^2} = |5-a|$

Example 3
Simplify $\sqrt{49x^2}$ assuming x is a positive value.

Solution
$$\sqrt{49x^2} = \sqrt{(7x)^2} = 7x$$

Exercise Set 7.1

Evaluate the radical expression if it is a real number. If it is not a real number, so state.

1. $\sqrt{81}$

2. $\sqrt[3]{-125}$

3. $-\sqrt[4]{16}$

4. $\sqrt[8]{-1}$

Use absolute value to evaluate the following.

5. $\sqrt{11^2}$

6. $\sqrt{(-18)^2}$

7. $\sqrt{\left(-\dfrac{1}{2}\right)^2}$

8. $-\sqrt{(-4)^2}$

Write as an absolute value.

9. $\sqrt{(x+8)^2}$

10. $\sqrt{(10-2x)^2}$

11. $\sqrt{(x^2-1)^2}$

12. $\sqrt{(x^4+x-1)^2}$

13. Simplify $\sqrt{100y^6}$ assuming y is a positive value.

Answers to Exercise Set 7.1

1. 9

2. –5

3. –2

4. Not a real number

5. 11

6. 18

7. $\dfrac{1}{2}$

8. –4

9. $|x+8|$

10. $|10-2x|$

11. $\left|x^2-1\right|$

12. $\left|x^4+x-1\right|$

13. $10y^3$

7.2 Rational Exponents

Summary

> When a is nonnegative, n can be any index. When a is
> negative, n must be odd.
>
> $$\sqrt[n]{a} = a^{1/n}$$
>
> For any nonnegative number a, and integers m and n,
> $n \geq 2$,
>
> $$\sqrt[n]{a^m} = \left(\sqrt[n]{a}\right)^m = a^{m/n}$$

Example 1
Write the following in exponential form and simplify if possible.

    a. $\sqrt{y^3}$
              b. $\sqrt[5]{y^{10}}$
              c. $\sqrt[9]{x^3}$

Solution

    a. $\sqrt{y^3} = y^{3/2}$
        b. $\sqrt[5]{y^{10}} = y^{10/5} = y^2$
        c. $\sqrt[9]{x^3} = x^{3/9} = x^{1/3}$

Note: The rules of exponents introduced in section 1.5 are applicable with exponents that are rational
        numbers.

Example 2
Evaluate $\left(\dfrac{1}{27}\right)^{-1/3}$.

Solution
First, use the negative exponent rule to write $\left(\dfrac{1}{27}\right)^{-1/3} = \dfrac{1}{\left(\frac{1}{27}\right)^{1/3}}$. Now, rewrite the expression in radical

form.
$$\frac{1}{\left(\frac{1}{27}\right)^{1/3}} = \frac{1}{\sqrt[3]{\frac{1}{27}}} = \frac{1}{\frac{1}{3}} = 3$$

An alternate method: The rule $\left(\dfrac{a}{b}\right)^{-n} = \left(\dfrac{b}{a}\right)^{n}$ can be used here.
$$\left(\frac{1}{27}\right)^{-1/3} = \left(\frac{27}{1}\right)^{1/3} = \sqrt[3]{27} = 3$$

Example 3
Use the rules of exponents to simplify the following.

    a. $a^{2/3} \cdot a^{4/3}$ **b.** $\dfrac{c^{1/4}}{c^{-1/2}}$ **c.** $(x^{1/2} \cdot y^{1/4})^{-3/4}$

Solution

    a. $a^{2/3} \cdot a^{4/3} = a^{\frac{2}{3}+\frac{4}{3}} = a^{6/3} = a^2$

    b. $\dfrac{c^{1/4}}{x^{-1/2}} = c^{\frac{1}{4}-\left(-\frac{1}{2}\right)} = c^{\frac{1}{4}+\frac{2}{4}} = c^{3/4}$

    c. $(x^{1/2} \cdot y^{1/4})^{-3/4} = x^{-3/8} \cdot y^{-3/16} = \dfrac{1}{x^{3/8} \cdot y^{3/16}}$

Note: We can factor expressions involving negative and rational exponents by factoring out the variable with the lesser exponent.

Example 4
Factor.

    a. $t^{4/3} - t^{1/3}$ **b.** $s^{-2} + s^{-6}$

Solution

    a. Since the lesser exponent is $\dfrac{1}{3}$, factor out $t^{1/3}$.

       $t^{4/3} - t^{1/3} = (t^1 \cdot t^{1/3}) - t^{1/3} = t^{1/3}(t-1)$ using the fact that $\dfrac{4}{3} = \dfrac{3}{3} + \dfrac{1}{3} = 1 + \dfrac{1}{3}$.

    b. $s^{-2} + s^{-6}$

       Since the lesser exponent is –6, factor out s^{-6}.
       $s^{-2} - s^{-6} = (s^4 \cdot s^{-6}) - s^{-6} = s^{-6}(s^4 - 1)$ using the fact that $4 + (-6) = -2$.

Note: We can factor three-termed expressions containing rational exponents using the substitution procedure introduced in section 5.5.

Example 5

Factor $x^{2/3} - x^{1/3} - 6$.

Solution

Since $x^{2/3}$ is the square of $x^{1/3}$, substitute y for $x^{1/3}$ and write

$$x^{2/3} - x^{1/3} - 6 = (x^{1/3})^2 - x^{1/3} - 6$$
$$= y^2 - y - 6$$
$$= (y-3)(y+2)$$

Now, substitute $x^{1/3}$ back for each y: $(y-3)(y+2) = (x^{1/3} - 3)(x^{1/3} + 2)$.

Thus, $x^{2/3} - x^{1/3} - 6 = (x^{1/3} - 3)(x^{1/3} + 2)$.

Exercise Set 7.2

Write in exponential form and simplify if possible.

1. $\sqrt{2^3}$

2. $\sqrt[3]{b^5}$

3. $\sqrt{9c^4}$

4. $\sqrt[6]{x^2 y^3}$

Evaluate each of the following if possible. If the expression is not a real number, state so.

5. $9^{1/2}$

6. $27^{-2/3}$

7. $(-16)^{1/4}$

8. $16^{-5/4}$

9. $36^{1/2} + 27^{1/3}$

Simplify each of the following. Write in exponential form.

10. $y^{1/3} \cdot y^{-4/3}$

11. $\dfrac{x^{4/5}}{x^{-1/5}}$

12. $\dfrac{k^{2/3} \cdot k^{-1}}{k^{1/3}}$

13. $(8p^9 q^6)^{2/3}$

14. $\left(\dfrac{z^{10}}{x^{12}}\right)^{1/4}$

15. $\dfrac{(m^2 \cdot h)^{1/2}}{m^{3/4} \cdot h^{-1/4}}$

16. $\left(\dfrac{m^{-1/3}}{a^{-3/4}}\right)^4 (m^{-3/8} \cdot a^{1/4})^{-2}$

Factor the following.

17. $y^{-3/4} + y^{-1/4}$

18. $a^{-2} + a^{-3}$

19. $3x^{2/3} - 6x^{-4/3}$

20. $x^{2/3} + 3x^{1/3} + 2$

21. $t^{2/5} - 3t^{1/5} - 10$

Answers to Exercise Set 7.2

1. $2^{3/2}$

2. $b^{5/3}$

3. $3c^2$

4. $x^{1/3}y^{1/2}$

5. 3

6. $\dfrac{1}{9}$

7. Not a real number

8. $\dfrac{1}{32}$

9. 9

10. y^{-1} or $\dfrac{1}{y}$

11. x

12. $\dfrac{1}{k^{2/3}}$

13. $4p^6q^4$

14. $\dfrac{z^{5/2}}{x^3}$

15. $m^{1/4}h^{3/4}$

16. $\dfrac{a^{5/2}}{m^{7/12}}$

17. $y^{-3/4}(1+y^{1/2})$

18. $a^{-3}(a+1)$

19. $3x^{-4/3}(x^2-2)$

20. $(x^{1/3}+1)(x^{1/3}+2)$

21. $(t^{1/5}-5)(t^{1/5}+2)$

7.3 Simplifying Radicals

Summary

Understanding Perfect Powers

- Rewrite the radicand so that it is written as a base raised to an exponent which matches the index.

- When the exponent matches the index, it is a perfect power. Therefore the base will be the answer.

Example 1
Evaluate the perfect powers.

  a. $\sqrt{25}$

         b. $\sqrt[3]{64}$

         c. $\sqrt[4]{x^{20}}$

Solution

  a. $\sqrt{5^2}=5$

         b. $\sqrt[3]{4^3}=4$

         c. $\sqrt[4]{\left(x^5\right)^4}=x^5$

Summary

Product Rule for Radicals

For nonnegative real numbers a and b,

$$\sqrt[n]{a} \cdot \sqrt[n]{b} = \sqrt[n]{ab}$$

Example 2
Use the product rule to rewrite the following.

    a. $\sqrt{30}$ **b.** $\sqrt[3]{y^6}$

Solution

    a. $\begin{aligned} \sqrt{30} &= \sqrt{1} \cdot \sqrt{30} \\ &= \sqrt{2} \cdot \sqrt{15} \\ &= \sqrt{3} \cdot \sqrt{10} \\ &= \sqrt{5} \cdot \sqrt{6} \end{aligned}$ **b.** $\begin{aligned} \sqrt[3]{y^6} &= \sqrt[3]{y} \cdot \sqrt[3]{y^5} \\ &= \sqrt[3]{y^2} \cdot \sqrt[3]{y^4} \\ &= \sqrt[3]{y^3} \cdot \sqrt[3]{y^3} \end{aligned}$

Summary

To Simplify Radicals Whose Radicands are Natural Numbers

1. Write the radicand as the product of two numbers, one of which is the largest perfect power of the given index.

2. Use the product rule to write the expression as a product of roots.

3. Find the roots of any perfect power numbers.

Note: A number is a **perfect square** if it is the square of a natural number. A number is a **perfect cube** if it is a cube of a natural number.

Example 3
Simplify the following.

    a. $\sqrt{125}$ **b.** $\sqrt[3]{81}$ **c.** $\sqrt[4]{32}$

Solution

    a. $\sqrt{125} = \sqrt{25} \cdot \sqrt{5} = 5\sqrt{5}$ **b.** $\sqrt[3]{81} = \sqrt[3]{27} \cdot \sqrt[3]{3} = 3\sqrt[3]{3}$ **c.** $\sqrt[4]{32} = \sqrt[4]{16} \cdot \sqrt[4]{2} = 2\sqrt[4]{2}$

Summary

+---+
| **To Simplify Radicals Whose Radicands are Variables**

1. Write each variable as the product of two factors, one of which is the largest perfect power of the variable for the index.

2. Use the product rule to write the radical expression as a product of radicals. Place all perfect powers under the same radical.

3. Find the roots of any perfect powers.
+---+

Example 4
Simplify the following.

    a. $\sqrt{b^7}$ **b.** $\sqrt[3]{y^{11}}$ **c.** $\sqrt{x^5 y^6}$

Solution

    a. $\sqrt{b^7} = \sqrt{b^6} \cdot \sqrt{b} = b^3 \sqrt{b}$

    b. $\sqrt[3]{y^{11}} = \sqrt[3]{y^9} \cdot \sqrt[3]{y^2} = y^3 \sqrt[3]{y^2}$

    c. $\sqrt{x^5 y^6} = \sqrt{x^4 y^6} \cdot \sqrt{x} = x^2 y^3 \sqrt{x}$

Summary

+---+
| **To Simplify Radicals**

1. If the radicand contains a numerical factor, write it as a product of two numbers, one of which is the largest perfect power for the index.

2. Write each variable factor as a product of two factors, one of which is the largest perfect power of the variable for the index.

3. Use the product rule to write the radical expression as a product of radicals. Place the perfect powers (numbers and variables) under the same radical.

4. Simplify the radical containing the perfect powers.
+---+

Example 5

Simplify $\sqrt{48c^5d^7}$.

Solution

$$\sqrt{48c^5d^7} = \sqrt{16 \cdot 3 \cdot c^4 \cdot c \cdot d^6 \cdot d}$$
$$= \sqrt{16 \cdot c^4 \cdot d^6 \cdot 3cd}$$
$$= \sqrt{16c^4d^6} \cdot \sqrt{3cd}$$
$$= 4c^2d^3\sqrt{3cd}$$

Summary

Quotient Rule for Radicals

For nonnegative real numbers a and b,

$$\frac{\sqrt[n]{a}}{\sqrt[n]{b}} = \sqrt[n]{\frac{a}{b}}, \ b \neq 0$$

Example 6

Simplify.

a. $\dfrac{\sqrt{50}}{\sqrt{2}}$ b. $\dfrac{\sqrt[3]{24}}{\sqrt[3]{3}}$ c. $\sqrt[3]{\dfrac{125}{8}}$

d. $\sqrt{\dfrac{8x^5}{4x^3}}$

Solution

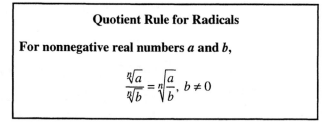

a. $\dfrac{\sqrt{50}}{\sqrt{2}} = \sqrt{\dfrac{50}{2}} = \sqrt{25} = 5$ b. $\dfrac{\sqrt[3]{24}}{\sqrt[3]{3}} = \sqrt[3]{\dfrac{24}{3}} = \sqrt[3]{8} = 2$ c. $\sqrt[3]{\dfrac{125}{8}} = \dfrac{\sqrt[3]{125}}{\sqrt[3]{8}} = \dfrac{5}{2}$

d. $\sqrt{\dfrac{8x^5}{4x^3}} = \sqrt{2x^2} = \sqrt{x^2} \cdot \sqrt{2} = x\sqrt{2}$

Exercise Set 7.3

Simplify.

1. $\sqrt[4]{81}$

2. $\sqrt[3]{y^{18}}$

3. $\sqrt{48}$

4. $\sqrt{300}$

5. $\sqrt[3]{128}$

6. $\sqrt[4]{243}$

7. $\sqrt[3]{250}$

8. $\sqrt[3]{x^5}$

9. $\sqrt[4]{x^5 y^9}$

10. $\sqrt{75y^3}$

11. $\sqrt{800k^{15}n^{10}}$

12. $\sqrt[3]{24z^5 x^9}$

13. $\sqrt[4]{48x^8 y^{11}}$

14. $\dfrac{\sqrt[3]{81}}{\sqrt[3]{3}}$

15. $\sqrt{\dfrac{81a^8 b^{10}}{121c^4}}$

Answers to Exercise Set 7.3

1. 3

2. y^6

3. $4\sqrt{3}$

4. $10\sqrt{3}$

5. $4\sqrt[3]{2}$

6. $3\sqrt[4]{3}$

7. $5\sqrt[3]{2}$

8. $x\sqrt[3]{x^2}$

9. $xy^2 \sqrt[4]{xy}$

10. $5y\sqrt{3y}$

11. $20k^7 n^5 \sqrt{2k}$

12. $2zx^3 \sqrt[3]{3z^2}$

13. $2x^2 y^2 \sqrt[4]{3y^3}$

14. 3

15. $\dfrac{9a^4 b^5}{11c^2}$

7.4 Adding, Subtracting, and Multiplying Radicals

Summary

Like radicals are radicals having the same radicand and index.

Unlike radicals are radicals differing in either the radicand or the index.

Summary

> **To Add or Subtract Radicals**
>
> 1. Simplify each radical expression.
>
> 2. Combine like radicals (if there are any).

Example 1
Simplify.

    a. $\sqrt{3} + \sqrt{48}$ **b.** $\sqrt[3]{16} + \sqrt[3]{54}$ **c.** $9\sqrt{27p^2} - 4p\sqrt{108} - 2\sqrt{48p^2}$

Solution

    a. $\sqrt{3} + \sqrt{48}$
        First, simplify each radical.
        $\sqrt{3} = \sqrt{3}$, $\sqrt{48} = \sqrt{16} \cdot \sqrt{3} = 4\sqrt{3}$
        Now, add like radicals.
        $\sqrt{3} + 4\sqrt{3} = 5\sqrt{3}$

    b. $\sqrt[3]{16} + \sqrt[3]{54}$
        Simplify each radical.
        $\sqrt[3]{16} = \sqrt[3]{8} \cdot \sqrt[3]{2} = 2 \cdot \sqrt[3]{2}$
        $\sqrt[3]{54} = \sqrt[3]{27} \cdot \sqrt[3]{2} = 3 \cdot \sqrt[3]{2}$
        Now add, $2\sqrt[3]{2} + 3\sqrt[3]{2} = 5\sqrt[3]{2}$.

    c. $9\sqrt{27p^2} - 4p\sqrt{108} - 2\sqrt{48p^2}$
        Simplify each radical.
        $9\sqrt{27p^2} = 9\sqrt{9p^2} \cdot \sqrt{3} = 9 \cdot 3p\sqrt{3} = 27p\sqrt{3}$
        $4p\sqrt{108} = 4p\sqrt{36} \cdot \sqrt{3} = 4p \cdot 6\sqrt{3} = 24p\sqrt{3}$
        $2\sqrt{48p^2} = 2\sqrt{16p^2} \cdot \sqrt{3} = 2 \cdot 4p\sqrt{3} = 8p\sqrt{3}$
        Now add, $27p\sqrt{3} - 24p\sqrt{3} - 8p\sqrt{3} = -5p\sqrt{3}$.

Summary

> Multiplying Radicals
>
> 1. Use the distributive property when necessary.
>
> 2. Multiply radicands together to form one radicand.
>
> 3. Simplify the result by using the product rule.

Example 2

Multiply and simplify $\sqrt[3]{4xy^5} \cdot \sqrt[3]{4x^2y}$.

Solution

First, multiply radicals and place product under a single radical. Then, simplify.

$$\sqrt[3]{4xy^5} \cdot \sqrt[3]{4x^2y} = \sqrt[3]{16x^3y^6}$$
$$= \sqrt[3]{8x^3y^6} \cdot \sqrt[3]{2}$$
$$= 2xy^2\sqrt[3]{2}$$

Example 3
Simplify

   a. $\sqrt{5}\left(\sqrt{5} + 3\right)$ **b.** $\left(2\sqrt{3} - 2\right)^2$

Solution

   a. $\sqrt{5}\left(\sqrt{5} + 3\right)$

      First, distribute.

      $\sqrt{5}\left(\sqrt{5}\right) + \sqrt{5}(3)$

      $= \sqrt{25} \;\; + \;\; 3\sqrt{5}$

      Simplify each radical when possible.

      $5 + 3\sqrt{5}$

   b. $\left(2\sqrt{3} - 2\right)^2$

      First, square the binomial.

      $\left(2\sqrt{3} - \sqrt{2}\right)^2 = \left(2\sqrt{3}\right)^2 - 2\left(2\sqrt{3}\right)\left(\sqrt{2}\right) + \left(-\sqrt{2}\right)^2$

      Now, simplify each term.

      $\left(2\sqrt{3}\right)^2 = 4 \cdot 3 = 12$

      $2 \cdot 2\sqrt{3} \cdot \sqrt{2} = 4\sqrt{6}$

      $\left(\sqrt{2}\right)^2 = 2$

      Then add, $12 - 4\sqrt{6} + 2 = 14 - 4\sqrt{6}$.

Exercise Set 7.4

Simplify. Assume all variables represent positive real numbers.

   1. $2\sqrt{48} + 3\sqrt{75}$ **2.** $6\sqrt{18} + \sqrt{32} - 2\sqrt{50}$ **3.** $2\sqrt{5} - 3\sqrt{20} - 4\sqrt{45}$

4. $2\sqrt{40} + 6\sqrt{90} - 3\sqrt{160}$

5. $3\sqrt{72m^2} + 2\sqrt{32m^2} - 3m\sqrt{18}$

6. $\sqrt[3]{54} - 2\sqrt[3]{16}$

7. $2\sqrt[3]{27x} + 2\sqrt[3]{8x}$

8. $\sqrt{48x^2y} \cdot \sqrt{6xy^3}$

9. $\sqrt[3]{27x} \cdot \sqrt[3]{3x^5y^7}$

10. $\sqrt{3}\left(4 + \sqrt{27}\right)$

11. $\left(\sqrt{3} + 1\right)\left(\sqrt{5} - 1\right)$

12. $\left(2\sqrt{3} + \sqrt{5}\right)\left(3\sqrt{3} - 2\sqrt{5}\right)$

Answers to Exercise Set 7.4

1. $23\sqrt{3}$

2. $12\sqrt{2}$

3. $-16\sqrt{5}$

4. $10\sqrt{10}$

5. $17m\sqrt{2}$

6. $-\sqrt[3]{2}$

7. $10\sqrt[3]{x}$

8. $12xy^2\sqrt{2x}$

9. $3x^2y^2\sqrt[3]{3y}$

10. $4\sqrt{3} + 9$

11. $\sqrt{15} - \sqrt{3} + \sqrt{5} - 1$

12. $8 - \sqrt{15}$

7.5 Dividing Radicals

Summary

A Radical Expression is Simplified When the Following are All True
1. No perfect power are factors of the radicand.
2. No radicand contains a fraction.
3. No denominator contains a radical.

Summary

Rationalizing Denominators
To rationalize a denominator, multiply both the numerator and the denominator of the fraction by the denominator, or by a radical that will result in the radicand becoming a perfect power.

Example 1
Simplify

a. $\dfrac{2}{\sqrt{3}}$ **b.** $\sqrt{\dfrac{1}{5}}$ **c.** $\sqrt[3]{\dfrac{3}{4}}$

d. $\sqrt{\dfrac{6x^3y^5}{5z}}$ **e.** $\sqrt[3]{\dfrac{2x}{3y^2}}$ **f.** $\dfrac{1}{\sqrt{5}}+\sqrt{45}$

Solution

a. $\dfrac{2}{\sqrt{3}}\cdot\dfrac{\sqrt{3}}{\sqrt{3}}=\dfrac{2\sqrt{3}}{3}$ **b.** $\sqrt{\dfrac{1}{5}}=\dfrac{\sqrt{1}}{\sqrt{5}}\cdot\dfrac{\sqrt{5}}{\sqrt{5}}=\dfrac{\sqrt{5}}{5}$ **c.** $\sqrt[3]{\dfrac{3}{4}}=\dfrac{\sqrt[3]{3}}{\sqrt[3]{4}}\cdot\dfrac{\sqrt[3]{2}}{\sqrt[3]{2}}=\dfrac{\sqrt[3]{6}}{\sqrt[3]{8}}=\dfrac{\sqrt[3]{6}}{2}$

d. $\sqrt{\dfrac{6x^3y^5}{5z}}=\dfrac{\sqrt{6x^3y^5}}{\sqrt{5z}}$

Now, simplify the numerator: $\sqrt{6x^3y^5}=\sqrt{x^2y^4}\cdot\sqrt{6xy}=xy^2\cdot\sqrt{6xy}$

Thus, we have $\dfrac{xy^2\cdot\sqrt{6xy}}{\sqrt{5z}}$. Now, rationalize the denominator.

$\dfrac{xy^2\cdot\sqrt{6xy}}{\sqrt{5z}}\cdot\dfrac{\sqrt{5z}}{\sqrt{5z}}=\dfrac{xy^2\sqrt{30xyz}}{5z}$

e. $\sqrt[3]{\dfrac{2x}{3y^2}}=\dfrac{\sqrt[3]{2x}}{\sqrt[3]{3y^2}}\cdot\dfrac{\sqrt[3]{9y}}{\sqrt[3]{9y}}=\dfrac{\sqrt[3]{18xy}}{\sqrt[3]{27y^3}}=\dfrac{\sqrt[3]{18xy}}{3y}$

f. $\dfrac{1}{\sqrt{5}}+\sqrt{45}$

Simplify each radical.

$\dfrac{1}{\sqrt{5}}\cdot\dfrac{\sqrt{5}}{\sqrt{5}}=\dfrac{\sqrt{5}}{5}=\dfrac{1}{5}\sqrt{5}$

$\sqrt{45}=\sqrt{9}\cdot\sqrt{5}=3\sqrt{5}$

Now add, $\dfrac{1}{5}\sqrt{5}+3\sqrt{5}=\left(\dfrac{1}{5}+3\right)\sqrt{5}=\dfrac{16}{5}\sqrt{3}.$

Summary

Rationalizing Denominators of Binomials that Contain a Radical

When the denominator of a rational expression is a binomial that contains a radical, we rationalize the denominator. We do this by multiplying both the numerator and the denominator of the fraction by the **conjugate** of the denominator. The **conjugate** of a binomial is a binomial having the same two terms with the sign of the second term changed.

Example 2
Simplify.

a. $\dfrac{4}{3+\sqrt{5}}$
b. $\dfrac{3}{\sqrt{7}-\sqrt{3}}$

Solution

a. $\dfrac{4}{3+\sqrt{5}}$

Multiply numerator and denominator by the conjugate of the denominator, $3-\sqrt{5}$.

$$\frac{4}{3+\sqrt{5}}\cdot\frac{3-\sqrt{5}}{3-\sqrt{5}}=\frac{4\left(3-\sqrt{5}\right)}{9-5}=\frac{4\left(3-\sqrt{5}\right)}{4}=3-\sqrt{5}$$

b. $\dfrac{3}{\sqrt{7}-\sqrt{3}}\cdot\dfrac{\sqrt{7}+\sqrt{3}}{\sqrt{7}+\sqrt{3}}=\dfrac{3\left(\sqrt{7}+\sqrt{3}\right)}{7-3}=\dfrac{3\left(\sqrt{7}+\sqrt{3}\right)}{4}$

Summary

Divide Radical Expressions with Different Indices

1. Write each radical with a rational exponent.

2. Use the rules of exponents to simplify the expression.

3. Rewrite the answer as a radical.

Example 3
Simplify.

a. $\dfrac{\sqrt[6]{4x^8 y^4}}{\sqrt[4]{x^4 y^2}}$ **b.** $\dfrac{\sqrt[6]{(m+4)^5}}{\sqrt[3]{(m+4)^5}}$

Solution

a. $\dfrac{\sqrt[6]{4x^8 y^4}}{\sqrt[4]{x^4 y^2}}$

$= \dfrac{\left(4x^8 y^4\right)^{1/6}}{\left(x^4 y^2\right)^{1/4}}$ Rewrite with rational exponents

$= \dfrac{4^{1/6} x^{3/2} y^{2/3}}{xy^{1/2}}$ Raise the product to a power

$= 4^{1/6} x^{(3/2)-(1)} y^{(2/3)-(1/2)}$ Use the quotient rule for exponents

$= 4^{1/6} x^{1/3} y^{1/6}$

$= 4^{1/6} x^{2/6} y^{1/6}$ Write all fractions with an LCD of 6

$= \left(4x^2 y\right)^{1/6}$ Rewrite using the rules of exponents

$= \sqrt[6]{4x^2 y}$ Rewrite as a radical

b. $\dfrac{\sqrt[6]{(m+4)^5}}{\sqrt[3]{(m+4)^5}}$

$= \dfrac{(m+4)^{5/6}}{(m+4)^{5/3}}$ Rewrite with rational exponents

$= (m+4)^{(5/6)-(5/3)}$ Use the quotient rule for exponents

$= (m+4)^{-5/6}$

$= \dfrac{1}{(m+4)^{5/6}}$ Use the rule for negative exponents

$= \dfrac{1}{\sqrt[6]{(m+4)^5}}$ Rewrite as a radical

Exercise Set 7.5

Simplify. Assume all variables represent positive real numbers.

1. $\sqrt{\dfrac{45}{5}}$

2. $\sqrt[3]{\dfrac{54}{2}}$

3. $\dfrac{\sqrt[3]{24}}{\sqrt[3]{-3}}$

4. $\dfrac{2}{3\sqrt{3}}$

5. $\sqrt{\dfrac{5}{6}}$

6. $\sqrt{\dfrac{11x}{5y}}$

7. $\dfrac{1}{\sqrt[3]{7}}$

8. $\dfrac{x}{\sqrt[3]{9y}}$

9. $\dfrac{3}{2\sqrt{x}}$

10. $\sqrt{\dfrac{8x^5 y}{6z}}$

11. $\dfrac{\sqrt{3}}{2+\sqrt{3}}$

12. $\dfrac{1-\sqrt{5}}{1+\sqrt{5}}$

13. $\dfrac{\sqrt[6]{x^4 y^{11} z^7}}{\sqrt{xy^3 z}}$

14. $\dfrac{\sqrt[5]{(2x+5)^4}}{\sqrt[3]{(2x+5)^2}}$

Answers to Exercise Set 7.5

1. 3

2. 3

3. -2

4. $\dfrac{2\sqrt{3}}{9}$

5. $\dfrac{\sqrt{30}}{6}$

6. $\dfrac{\sqrt{55xy}}{5y}$

7. $\dfrac{\sqrt[3]{49}}{7}$

8. $\dfrac{x\sqrt[3]{3y^2}}{3y}$

9. $\dfrac{3\sqrt{x}}{2x}$

10. $\dfrac{2x^2\sqrt{3xyz}}{3z}$

11. $2\sqrt{3}-3$

12. $\dfrac{\sqrt{5}-3}{2}$

13. $\sqrt[6]{xy^2 z^4}$

14. $\sqrt[15]{(2x+5)^2}$

7.6 Solving Radical Equations

Summary

To Solve Radical Equations

1. Rewrite the equation so that one radical containing a variable is by itself on one side of the equation.

2. Raise each side to a power equal to the index of the radical.

3. Collect and combine like terms.

4. If the equation still contains a term with a variable in a radicand, repeat steps 1 through 3.

5. Solve the resulting equation for the variable.

6. Check all solutions in the original equation for extraneous solutions.

Example 1
Solve the equation $\sqrt{2x+1} = 3$.

Solution
$$\left(\sqrt{2x+1}\right)^2 = 3^2$$
$$2x+1 = 9$$
$$2x = 8$$
$$x = 4$$
Check: $x = 4$
$$\sqrt{2x+1} = 3$$
$$\sqrt{2(4)+1} = 3$$
$$\sqrt{9} = 3$$
$$3 = 3$$
Since $3 = 3$ is true, $x = 4$ is the solution.

Example 2
Solve the equation $\sqrt[3]{x} - 3 = 1$.

Solution
$$\sqrt[3]{x} - 3 = 1$$
$$\sqrt[3]{x} = 4$$
$$\left(\sqrt[3]{x}\right)^3 = 4^3$$
$$x = 64$$

Check: $x = 64$

$\sqrt[3]{x} - 3 = 1$

$\sqrt[3]{64} - 3 = 1$

$4 - 3 = 1$

$1 = 1$

This is a true statement so $x = 64$ is the solution.

Example 3

Solve the equation $x\sqrt{2} = \sqrt{5x - 2}$.

Solution

$$\left(x\sqrt{2}\right)^2 = \left(\sqrt{5x - 2}\right)^2$$

$$2x^2 = 5x - 2$$

$2x^2 - 5x + 2 = 0$

$(2x - 1)(x - 2) = 0$

$2x - 1 = 0 \quad$ or $\quad x - 2 = 0$

$2x = 1 \quad$ or $\quad x = 2$

$x = \dfrac{1}{2} \quad$ or $\quad x = 2$

When these values of x are substituted into the original equation, it is found at **both** values of x make the statement true.

Thus, $x = \dfrac{1}{2}$ and $x = 2$ are solutions.

Example 4

Solve the equation $\sqrt{3x + 1} = \sqrt{x + 1} + 2$.

Solution

$$\left(\sqrt{3x + 1}\right)^2 = \left(\sqrt{x + 1} + 2\right)^2$$

$$3x + 1 = x + 1 + 4\sqrt{x + 1} + 4$$

$$3x + 1 = x + 5 + 4\sqrt{x + 1}$$

$$2x - 4 = 4\sqrt{x + 1}$$

Notice that both sides of the equation have a factor of 2: $2(x - 2) = 2 \cdot 2\sqrt{x + 1}$. We can divide both sides of this equation by 2 and make the equation simpler.

$x - 2 = 2\sqrt{x + 1}$

Now, square both sides to eliminate the radical.

$$(x - 2)^2 = \left(2\sqrt{x + 1}\right)^2$$

$x^2 - 4x + 4 = 4(x + 1)$

$x^2 - 4x + 4 = 4x + 4$

$x^2 - 8x = 0$

$x(x - 8) = 0$; or $x = 0$; $x = 8$

Check $x = 0$.
$$\sqrt{3x+1} = \sqrt{x+1} + 2$$
$$\sqrt{3(0)+1} = \sqrt{0+1} + 2$$
$$1 = 1 + 2$$
$$1 = 3 \text{ is false.}$$
Therefore, $x = 0$ is not a solution.
Check $x = 8$.
$$\sqrt{3x+1} = \sqrt{x+1} + 2$$
$$\sqrt{3(8)+1} = \sqrt{8+1} + 2$$
$$\sqrt{25} = \sqrt{9} + 2$$
$$5 = 3 + 2 \text{ is true.}$$
Thus, $x = 8$ is the only solution.

Summary

Pythagorean Theorem

The square of the hypotenuse of a right triangle is equal to the sum of the squares of the two legs. If a and b represent the legs and c represents the hypotenuse, then

$$a^2 + b^2 = c^2$$

Example 5
A right triangle has a hypotenuse with a length of 13 units and one of the legs has a length of 5 units. Find the length of the other leg.

Solution
Use $a^2 + b^2 = c^2$ with $a = 5$ and $c = 13$.
$$5^2 + b^2 = 13^2$$
$$25 + b^2 = 169$$
$$b^2 = 144$$
$$b = \sqrt{144} = 12$$
The other leg has a length of 12 units.

Example 6
Find the area of a triangle with sides of length 3, 4, and 5 units, respectively.

Solution
Use Heron's formula: $A = \sqrt{s(s-a)(s-b)(s-c)}$, where a, b, and c are the lengths of the sides of the triangle and $s = \dfrac{a+b+c}{2}$ or $\dfrac{3+4+5}{2} = 6$.
Then, $A = \sqrt{6(6-3)(6-4)(6-5)} = \sqrt{6 \cdot 3 \cdot 2 \cdot 1} = \sqrt{36} = 6$
$$A = 6 \text{ square units}$$

Exercise Set 7.6

Solve and check your solution(s).

1. $\sqrt{r-2} = 3$

2. $\sqrt{6k-1} = 1$

3. $\sqrt{3k+1} - 4 = 0$

4. $\sqrt{r+1} = \sqrt{2r-3}$

5. $2\sqrt{x} = \sqrt{3x+4}$

6. $k = \sqrt{k^2 + 4k - 20}$

7. $\sqrt{x^2 + 3x - 3} = x + 1$

8. $\sqrt[3]{2x+5} = \sqrt[3]{6x+1}$

9. $\sqrt[3]{x-8} + 2 = 0$

10. $\sqrt{x^2 + 12} - x = 6$

11. $\sqrt{2x+3} = 2 + \sqrt{x-2}$

12. $-\sqrt{z+5} = -\sqrt{3z+3} + 2$

13. A right triangle has legs of lengths 3 units and 6 units. What is the length of the hypotenuse?

14. A right triangle has a hypotenuse of length 8 units and a leg of length 4 units. Find the length of the other leg,

15. An equilateral triangle has a side of 6 feet. Use Heron's formula to determine its area.

Answers to Exercise Set 7.6

1. 11

2. $\dfrac{1}{3}$

3. 5

4. 4

5. 4

6. 5

7. 4

8. 1

9. 0

10. –2

11. 11, 3

12. 11

13. $3\sqrt{5}$ units

14. $4\sqrt{3}$ units

15. $9\sqrt{3}$ square units

7.7 Complex Numbers

Summary

Imaginary Numbers

$$i = \sqrt{-1}, \; i^2 = -1$$

For any positive real number n, $\sqrt{-n} = i\sqrt{n}$.

Complex Numbers

Every number of the form $a + bi$ where a and b are real numbers, is a complex number.

Example 1
Write each of the following complex numbers in the form $a + bi$.

   a. $\sqrt{-16}$ **b.** $4 - \sqrt{-32}$ **c.** $3 + \sqrt{-9}$

Solution

   a. $\sqrt{-16} = i \cdot \sqrt{16} = 4i$ or $0 + 4i$

   b. $4 - \sqrt{-32} = 4 - i\sqrt{32}$
   $$= 4 - i\left(4\sqrt{2}\right)$$
   $$= 4 - 4\sqrt{2}i$$

   c. $3 + \sqrt{-9} = 3 + i\sqrt{9}$
   $$= 3 + 3i$$

Summary

To Add or Subtract Complex Numbers
1. Change all imaginary numbers to *bi* form.
2. Add (or subtract) the real parts of the complex numbers.
3. Add (or subtract) the imaginary parts of the complex numbers.
4. Write the answer in the form $a + bi$.

Example 2
Add $(5 - 6i) + (-8 + 12i)$.

Solution
$$(5 - 6i) + (-8 + 12i) = 5 - 6i - 8 + 12i$$
$$= 5 - 8 - 6i + 12i$$
$$= -3 + 6i$$

Example 3
Subtract $\left(4 + \sqrt{-27}\right) - \left(3 - \sqrt{-12}\right)$.

Solution
$$\left(4 + \sqrt{-27}\right) - \left(3 - \sqrt{-12}\right) = \left(4 + i\sqrt{27}\right) - \left(3 - i\sqrt{12}\right)$$
$$= 4 + 3\sqrt{3}i - \left(3 - 2\sqrt{3}i\right)$$
$$= 4 + 3\sqrt{3}i - 3 + 2\sqrt{3}i$$
$$= 1 + 5\sqrt{3}i$$

Summary

To Multiply Complex Numbers

1. Change all imaginary numbers to *bi* form.

2. Multiply the complex numbers as you would multiply polynomials.

3. Substitute -1 for i^2.

4. Combine the real parts and the imaginary parts. Write the answer in $a + bi$ form.

Example 4
Multiply

    a. $5i(3 + 4i)$ **b.** $(4 - 2i)(3 + 5i)$ **c.** $\left(2 - \sqrt{-5}\right)\left(3 + \sqrt{-20}\right)$

Solution

    a. $\begin{aligned} 5i(3 + 4i) &= 15i + 20i^2 \\ &= 15i + 20(-1) \\ &= 15i - 20 \\ &= -20 + 15i \end{aligned}$

    b. $\begin{aligned} (4 - 2i)(3 + 5i) &= 12 + 20i - 6i - 10i^2 \\ &= 12 + 20i - 6i - 10(-1) \\ &= 12 + 20i - 6i + 10 \\ &= 22 + 14i \end{aligned}$

    c. $\begin{aligned} \left(2 - \sqrt{-5}\right)\left(3 + \sqrt{-20}\right) &= \left(2 - \sqrt{5}i\right)\left(3 + i\sqrt{20}\right) \\ &= \left(2 - \sqrt{5}i\right)\left(3 + 2\sqrt{5}i\right) \\ &= 6 + 4\sqrt{5}i - 3\sqrt{5}i - \left(\sqrt{5}\right)\left(2\sqrt{5}\right)i^2 \\ &= 6 + 4\sqrt{5}i - 3\sqrt{5}i - \left(\sqrt{5}\right)\left(2\sqrt{5}\right)(-1) \\ &= 6 + 4\sqrt{5}i - 3\sqrt{5}i + 10 \\ &= 16 + \sqrt{5}i \end{aligned}$

Note: The **conjugate** of a complex number $a + bi$ is $a - bi$.

Summary

To Divide Complex Numbers

1. Change all imaginary numbers to *bi* form.

2. Rationalize the denominator by multiplying both the numerator and the denominator by the conjugate of the denominator.

3. Write the answer in $a + bi$ form.

Example 5
Divide.

a. $\dfrac{2-3i}{\sqrt{-4}}$ **b.** $\dfrac{3+2i}{4-i}$

Solution

a.
$$\frac{2-3i}{\sqrt{-4}} = \frac{2-3i}{\sqrt{4}\,i}$$
$$= \frac{2-3i}{2i}$$
$$= \frac{2-3i}{2i} \cdot \frac{-2i}{-2i}$$
$$= \frac{-4i+6i^2}{-4i^2}$$
$$= \frac{-6-4i}{4}$$
$$= \frac{2(-3-2i)}{2\cdot 2}$$
$$= -\frac{3}{2} - i$$

b.
$$\frac{3+2i}{4-i} \cdot \frac{4+i}{4+i} = \frac{12+3i+8i+2i^2}{16-i^2}$$
$$= \frac{12+3i+8i+2(-1)}{16-(-1)}$$
$$= \frac{10+11i}{17}$$
$$= \frac{10}{17} + \frac{11}{17}i$$

215

Exercise Set 7.7

Write each expression as a complex number in the form $a + bi$.

1. $\sqrt{-36}$

2. $4 + \sqrt{-49}$

3. $2 - \sqrt{-72}$

Perform the indicated operations.

4. $(1 - i) + (2 - 3i)$

5. $(5 + 2i) + (3 + 5i)$

6. $\left(3 + \sqrt{-9}\right) - \left(5 + \sqrt{-25}\right)$

7. $i(9i)$

8. $(1 - i)(3 + 2i)$

9. $\left(1 - \sqrt{-9}\right)\left(2 - \sqrt{-9}\right)$

10. $(3 + 4i)^2$

11. $\left(\sqrt{8} + \sqrt{-18}\right)^2$

12. $\dfrac{1}{1+i}$

13. $\dfrac{2}{1 - 3i}$

14. $\dfrac{1 + \sqrt{-4}}{1 + \sqrt{-9}}$

Answers to Exercise Set 7.7

1. $6i$ or $0 + 6i$

2. $4 + 7i$

3. $2 - 6\sqrt{2}i$

4. $3 - 4i$

5. $8 + 7i$

6. $-2 - 2i$

7. -9

8. $5 - i$

9. $-7 - 9i$

10. $-7 + 24i$

11. $-10 + 24i$

12. $\dfrac{1}{2} - \dfrac{1}{2}i$

13. $\dfrac{1}{5} + \dfrac{3}{5}i$

14. $\dfrac{7}{10} - \dfrac{1}{10}i$

Chapter 7 Practice Test

1. Write as an absolute value: $\sqrt{(5x + 2)^2}$.

2. Simplify $\left(\dfrac{c^{2/3} \cdot c^{-2}}{c^{-1/4}}\right)^3$.

3. Factor $3x^{2/3} + 7x^{1/3} - 6$.

Simplify. Assume all variables represent positive real numbers.

4. $\sqrt{48x^5 y^6}$

5. $\sqrt[3]{9x^2 y^4} \cdot \sqrt[3]{6x^3 y^2}$

6. $\sqrt{\dfrac{10x^2 y^5}{8z}}$

7. $\dfrac{1}{5-\sqrt{2}}$ **8.** $\sqrt{128}-\sqrt{32}$ **9.** $\sqrt[3]{-192}-2\sqrt[3]{-375}$

10. $\left(2\sqrt{6}-1\right)\left(\sqrt{2}-\sqrt{3}\right)$ **11.** $\dfrac{\sqrt{x^3y^4z}}{\sqrt[5]{x^7y^6z^2}}$ **12.** $\dfrac{\sqrt[4]{(x-7)}}{\sqrt[6]{(x-7)^5}}$

Solve the equations.

13. $\sqrt{2x-1}-4=0$ **14.** $x=\sqrt{2x+6}-3$ **15.** $\sqrt{2-7t}-3=\sqrt{t+3}$

16. The hypotenuse of a right triangle has a length of 12 feet. One of the legs is 6 feet. Find the length of the other leg.

17. Subtract $\left(2-\sqrt{-16}\right)-\left(3+\sqrt{-25}\right)$.

18. Multiply $\left(1+\sqrt{-4}\right)\left(5-\sqrt{-9}\right)$.

19. Divide $\dfrac{3-\sqrt{-49}}{5+\sqrt{-25}}$.

20. Evaluate x^2-x+2 if $x=-2+i$.

Answers to Chapter 7 Practice Test

1. $|5x+2|$ **2.** $\dfrac{1}{c^{13/4}}$ **3.** $(3x^{1/3}-2)(x^{1/3}+3)$

4. $4x^2y^3\sqrt{3x}$ **5.** $3xy^2\sqrt[3]{2x^2}$ **6.** $\dfrac{xy^2\sqrt{5yz}}{2z}$

7. $\dfrac{5+\sqrt{2}}{23}$ **8.** $4\sqrt{2}$ **9.** $6\sqrt[3]{3}$

10. $5\sqrt{3}-7\sqrt{2}$ **11.** $\sqrt[10]{xy^8z}$ **12.** $\dfrac{1}{\sqrt[12]{(x-7)^7}}$

13. $\dfrac{17}{2}$ **14.** $-3,-1$ **15.** -2

16. $6\sqrt{3}$ feet   **17.** $-1-9i$ **18.** $11+7i$

19. $-\dfrac{2}{5}-i$ **20.** $7-5i$

CHAPTER 7 SUMMARY

IMPORTANT FACTS

If n is Even and $a \geq 0$
$\sqrt[n]{a} = b$ if $b \geq 0$ and $b^n = a$

If n is Odd
$\sqrt[n]{a} = b$ if $b^n = a$

Rules of Radicals

- $\sqrt{a^2} = |a|$

- $\sqrt{a^2} = a, \ a \geq 0$

- $\sqrt[n]{a^n} = a, \ a \geq 0$

- $\sqrt[n]{a} = a^{1/n}, \ a \geq 0$

- $\sqrt[n]{a^m} = \left(\sqrt[n]{a}\right)^m = a^{m/n}, \ a \geq 0$

- $\sqrt[n]{a} \cdot \sqrt[n]{b} = \sqrt[n]{ab}, \ a \geq 0, b \geq 0$

- $\dfrac{\sqrt[n]{a}}{\sqrt[n]{b}} = \sqrt[n]{\dfrac{a}{b}}, \ a \geq 0, b > 0$

A Radical is Simplified When the Following are All True
1. No perfect powers are factors of any radicand, and all exponents in the radicand, are less than the index.
2. No radicand contains a fraction.
3. No denominator contains a radical.

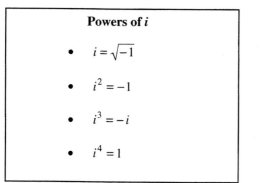

HELPFUL HINTS

- When you raise a real number to an even power, it cannot equal a negative number. Therefore, the square root (or any even root) of a negative number is not a real number. Do not confuse $-\sqrt{25}$ with $\sqrt{-25}$, and do not confuse $-\sqrt[4]{81}$ with $\sqrt[4]{-81}$.

    - $-\sqrt{25} = -5$, but $\sqrt{-25}$ is not a real number.

    - $-\sqrt[4]{81} = -3$, but $\sqrt[4]{-81}$ is not a real number.

- The expressions $-36^{1/2}$ and $(-36)^{1/2}$ are very different and are evaluated in different ways. A good way to distinguish between the two is to remember to what base you are applying the exponent. **An exponent only applies directly to what it is front of it.** Therefore with the expression $-36^{1/2}$, the exponent applies only to the 36 and *not* to the negative sign. Thus the expression $-36^{1/2}$ would be evaluated at $-\sqrt{36}$, which is -6. However, with the expression $(-36)^{1/2}$, the exponent applies to everything in parentheses *including* the negative sign. Thus the expression $(-36)^{1/2}$, would be evaluated as $\sqrt{-36}$, which is not a real number.

- To easily and quickly determine if a radicand, x^n, is a perfect power for an index, determine if the exponent is divisible by the index. For example, consider $\sqrt[4]{x^{24}}$. Since the exponent, 24, is divisible by the index, 4, x^{24} is a perfect fourth power. In the case of $\sqrt[4]{x^{27}}$, the radicand x^{27} would *not* be a perfect fourth power since the exponent, 27, is not divisible by the index, 4.

- When simplifying radicals, it is helpful if you can find the largest perfect square. If you cannot, the final answer will be the same, but it will require more steps to achieve. Here you have $\sqrt{48}$ worked out both ways:

  □ If you are able to find the largest perfect square, your work will appear as:
  $$\sqrt{48} = \sqrt{16 \cdot 3} = \sqrt{16}\sqrt{3} = 4\sqrt{3}.$$

  □ If you are *not* able to find the largest perfect square, your work may appear as:
  $$\sqrt{48} = \sqrt{4 \cdot 12} = \sqrt{4}\sqrt{12} = 2\sqrt{12} = 2\sqrt{4 \cdot 3} = 2\sqrt{4}\sqrt{3} = 2 \cdot 2\sqrt{3} = 4\sqrt{3}.$$

- Radicals with variables can also be simplified by dividing the exponents in the radicand by the index. When you divide the exponent by the index, the quotient becomes the exponent that goes with the variable to the outside of the radical. The remainder becomes the exponent that stays with the variable in the radicand. For example: $\sqrt[4]{x^{14}y^{23}} = x^3y^5\sqrt[4]{x^2y^3}$ because $14 \div 4$ has a quotient of 3 with a remainder of 2, and $23 \div 4$ has a quotient of 5 with a remainder of 3.

- The product rule and quotient rule for radicals are: $\sqrt[n]{a} \cdot \sqrt[n]{b} = \sqrt[n]{ab}$ and $\dfrac{\sqrt[n]{a}}{\sqrt[n]{b}} = \sqrt[n]{\dfrac{a}{b}}$.

  However, these properties do not apply to addition and subtraction. To illustrate this, let n be a square root (index 2), $a = 16$, and $b = 9$.
  $$\sqrt[n]{a} + \sqrt[n]{b} \neq \sqrt[n]{a+b}$$
  $$\sqrt{16} + \sqrt{9} \neq \sqrt{16+9}$$
  $$4 + 3 \neq \sqrt{25}$$
  $$7 \neq 5$$

- With radical equations, always check your solutions in the original equation. When you raise both sides of an equation to a power, you may introduce extraneous solutions. With the equation x = 3, see what happens when you square both side of the equation:
  $$x = 3$$
  $$x^2 = 3^2$$
  $$x^2 = 9$$

  The equation $x^2 = 9$ has two solutions, $+3$ and -3. Since the original equation $x = 3$ has only one solution, 3, you introduced the extraneous solution, -3. An extraneous solution is not part of the answer.

- A quick way of evaluating i^n is to divide the exponent by 4. When you do this, your remainder becomes your new exponent.

  □ When the ramainder is 0, you then have i^0 which equals 1.
  □ When the remainder is 1, you then have i^1 which equals i.
  □ When the remainder is 2, you then have i^2 which equals -1.
  □ When the remainder is 3, you then have i^3 which equals $-i$.

AVOIDING COMMON ERRORS

- When simplifying radicals, both numbers and variables that are not within the radicand can be simplified. But you cannot simplify a number or a variable that is *not* within the radicand with a number or a variable that *is* within the radicand. For example:

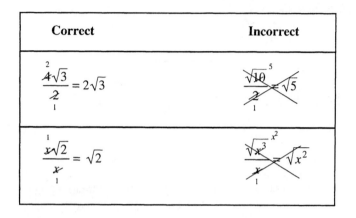

4. Remember that $(a+b)^2 \neq a^2 + b^2$. Therefore when squaring a binomial, you must always multiply the binomial times itself. For example:

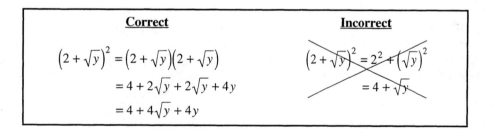

Chapter 8

8.1 Solving Quadratic Equations by Completing the Square

Summary

Square Root Property

If $x^2 = a$, where a is a real number, then $x = \pm\sqrt{a}$.

Example 1
Solve the following by using the square root property:

   a. $x^2 - 17 = 0$ **b.** $x^2 = -4$

Solution

   a. $x^2 - 17 = 0$ should be rewritten as $x^2 = 17$. Now, use the square root property and take the square root of each side of this equation: $x = \pm\sqrt{17}$. This means $x = \sqrt{17}$ and $x = -\sqrt{17}$.

   b. If $x^2 = -4$, then, using the square root property, $x = \pm\sqrt{-4}$. There are no **real solutions** to this equation. However, we can express $\sqrt{-4}$ as $2i$. Thus $2i$ and $-2i$ are our two complex number solutions.

Example 2
Solve $(x+4)^2 - 9 = 0$.

Solution
Rewrite $(x+4)^2 - 9 = 0$ as $(x+4)^2 = 9$ and use the square root property: $\sqrt{(x+4)^2} = x+4$ and $\sqrt{9} = 3$. Thus, we have $(x+4) = \pm 3$; $x = -4 \pm 3$. So one value of x is $-4 + 3$ or -1. The remaining value of x is $-4 - 3$ or -7. The solutions are -1 and -7.

Summary

Pythagorean Theorem

The square of the hypotenuse of a right triangle is equal to the sum of the squares of the two legs. If a and b represent the legs and c represents and hypotenuse, then $a^2 + b^2 = c^2$.

Applications

Example 3
Find the hypotenuse of a right triangle whose legs are 15 inches and 8 inches.

Solution
Let $a = 8$ and $b = 15$. Using the Pythagorean Theorem, $c^2 = a^2 + b^2$:
$$c^2 = 8^2 + 15^2$$
$$c^2 = 64 + 225$$
$$c^2 = 289$$
Using the square root property and taking the square root of both sides of this equation, we have $c = \pm\sqrt{289}$, or $c = \pm 17$. Since the length of the side of a triangle cannot be negative, we drop the solution of -17 and say $c = 17$.

Summary

To Solve a Quadratic Equation by Completing the Square

1. Use the multiplication (or division) property of equality if necessary to make the leading coefficient term equal to 1.

2. Rewrite the equation with the constant isolated on the right side of the equation.

3. Take one-half the numerical coefficient of the first-degree term, square it, and add this quantity to both sides of the equation.

4. Replace the trinomial with the square of a binomial.

5. Use the square root property to take the square root of both sides of the equation.

6. Solve for the variable.

7. Check your answer in the original equation.

Example 4
Solve $x^2 - 8x + 3 = 0$ by completing the square.

Solution
Notice that the numerical coefficient of the x^2 term is already 1 so step 1 is accomplished.

2. Subtract 3 from both sides of the equation to isolate the constant on the right side.
$$x^2 - 8x = -3$$

3. Take one-half of the numerical coefficient of x term; square it and add the result to both sides of the equation.

$$\left(\frac{1}{2}\right)(-8) = -4 \text{ and } (-4)^2 = 16$$

So we have $x^2 - 8x + 16 = -3 + 16$, or $x^2 - 8x + 16 = 13$.

4. Rewrite the trinomial as the square of a binomial: $x^2 - 8x + 16 = (x-4)^2$. Our equation now looks like $(x-4)^2 = 13$.

5. Take the square root of both sides of this new equation: $x - 4 = \pm\sqrt{13}$.

6. Solve the equation for x: $x = 4 \pm \sqrt{13}$. The solutions are $4 + \sqrt{13}$ and $4 - \sqrt{13}$. A check shows that both values work.

Example 5

Solve $2x^2 - x = -5$ by completing the square.

Solution

Notice the numerical coefficient of the x^2 term is 2 and 2 is not equal to 1. Therefore, we must divide both sides of the equation by 2 to obtain a coefficient of 1 for x^2 term:

$$\frac{2}{2}x^2 - \frac{1x}{2} = -\frac{5}{2} \text{ or } x^2 - \frac{1}{2}x = -\frac{5}{2}$$

2. The constant term is already isolated on the right side of the equation so step 2 is not necessary.

3. Take one-half of the coefficient of the x term, square this number and add the result to both sides of the equation:

$$\frac{1}{2}\left(-\frac{1}{2}\right) = -\frac{1}{4} \text{ and } \left(-\frac{1}{4}\right)^2 = \frac{1}{16}$$

Now add $\frac{1}{16}$ to both sides of the equation:

$$x^2 - \frac{1}{2}x + \frac{1}{16} = -\frac{5}{2} + \frac{1}{16}$$

4. Replace $x^2 - \frac{1}{2}x + \frac{1}{16}$ with $\left(x-\frac{1}{4}\right)^2$. Our equation becomes $\left(x-\frac{1}{4}\right)^2 = -\frac{5}{2} + \frac{1}{16} = -\frac{40}{16} + \frac{1}{16} = -\frac{39}{16}$.

5. Take the square root of both sides of the equation:

$$\left(x-\frac{1}{4}\right) = \pm\frac{\sqrt{-39}}{\sqrt{16}}$$

$$\left(x-\frac{1}{4}\right) = \pm\frac{i\sqrt{39}}{4}$$

6. Solve for x: $x = \dfrac{1}{4} \pm \dfrac{i\sqrt{39}}{4} = \dfrac{1 \pm i\sqrt{39}}{4}$.

The solutions are $\dfrac{1}{4} + \dfrac{i\sqrt{39}}{4}$ and $\dfrac{1}{4} - \dfrac{i\sqrt{39}}{4}$.

Exercise Set 8.1

Use the square root property to solve each equation.

1. $3x^2 = 48$ **2.** $y^2 + 50 = 0$ **3.** $(x+1)^2 = 25$

4. $(x+4)^2 = -27$ **5.** $(x-5)^2 - 36 = 0$ **6.** $(3x-4)^2 = -18$

Use the Pythagorean Theorem to find the unknown lengths.

7.   **8.**

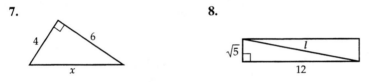

Solve each equation by completing the square.

9. $x^2 + 2x - 4 = 0$ **10.** $x^2 + 2x + 4 = 0$

11. $3x^2 + 4x - 6 = 0$ **12.** $3x^2 + 9x - 1 = 0$

Answers to Exercise Set 8.1

1. ± 4 **2.** $\pm 5i\sqrt{2}$ **3.** $-6, 4$

4. $-4 \pm 3i\sqrt{3}$ **5.** $-1, 11$ **6.** $\dfrac{4 \pm 3i\sqrt{2}}{3}$

7. $x = \sqrt{52} \approx 7.21$ **8.** $l = \sqrt{149} \approx 12.21$ **9.** $-1 \pm \sqrt{5}$

10. $-1 + i\sqrt{3}$ **11.** $\dfrac{-2 \pm \sqrt{22}}{3}$ **12.** $\dfrac{-9 \pm \sqrt{93}}{6}$

8.2 Solving Quadratic Equations by the Quadratic Formula

Summary

```
                To Solve a Quadratic Equation by
                      the Quadratic Formula

   1.  Write the quadratic equation in standard form
       ax² + bx + c = 0 and determine the numerical
       values for a, b, and c.

   2.  Substitute the values for a, b, c in the quadratic
       formula and then evaluate the formula to obtain
       the solution.
```

Quadratic Formula

$$x = \frac{-b \pm \sqrt{b^2 - 4ac}}{2a}$$

Example 1

Solve $x^2 - 6x - 16 = 0$ using the quadratic formula.

Solution

$a = 1$, $b = -6$ and $c = -16$.

$$x = \frac{-b \pm \sqrt{b^2 - 4ac}}{2a}$$

$$x = \frac{-(-6) \pm \sqrt{(-6)^2 - 4(1)(-16)}}{2(1)}$$

$$x = \frac{6 \pm \sqrt{36 + 64}}{2}$$

$$x = \frac{6 \pm \sqrt{100}}{2}$$

$$x = \frac{6 \pm 10}{2}$$

$$x = \frac{6 + 10}{2} \quad \text{or} \quad x = \frac{6 - 10}{2}$$

$$x = 8 \quad \text{or} \quad x = -2$$

The problem $x^2 - 6x - 16 = 0$ could also have been solved using factoring: $x^2 - 6x - 16 = (x - 8)(x + 2) = 0$.
So $x = 8$, or $x = -2$.

A common student error is to interpret the quadratic formula as $x = -b \pm \dfrac{\sqrt{b^2 - 4ac}}{2a}$ or as $-\dfrac{b}{2a} \pm \sqrt{b^2 - 4ac}$.

Remember to divide the **entire expression** $-b \pm \sqrt{b^2 - 4ac}$ by $2a$.

Example 2

Solve $x^2 + 4 = 3x$ using the quadratic formula.

Solution

We need to write $x^2 + 4 = 3x$ in the form $ax^2 + bx + c = 0$.

$x^2 + 4 = 3x$ becomes $x^2 - 3x + 4 = 0$.

Now $a = 1$, $b = -3$, and $c = 4$. Substitute these values into the quadratic formula and evaluate it.

$$x = \frac{-b \pm \sqrt{b^2 - 4ac}}{2a}$$

$$x = \frac{-(-3) \pm \sqrt{(-3)^2 - 4(1)(4)}}{2(1)}$$

$$= \frac{3 \pm \sqrt{9 - 16}}{2}$$

$$= \frac{3 \pm \sqrt{-7}}{2}$$

$$= \frac{3 \pm i \cdot \sqrt{7}}{2}$$

The solutions are $\dfrac{3 + i\sqrt{7}}{2}$ and $\dfrac{3 - i\sqrt{7}}{2}$.

Example 3

Solve $\dfrac{1}{2}x^2 - \dfrac{3}{8}x + \dfrac{1}{4} = 0$.

Solution

When a quadratic equation contains fractions, it is advisable to multiply both sides of the equation by the LCD of all fractions that appear in the equation. This will clear all fractions in the equation.

$$8\left(\frac{1}{2}x^2 - \frac{3}{8}x + \frac{1}{4}\right) = 8(0)$$

$$4x^2 - 3x + 2 = 0$$

Now $a = 4$, $b = -3$, and $c = 2$.

$$x = \frac{-b \pm \sqrt{b^2 - 4ac}}{2a}$$

$$x = \frac{-(-3) \pm \sqrt{(-3)^2 - 4(4)(2)}}{2(4)}$$

$$= \frac{3 \pm \sqrt{9 - 32}}{8}$$

$$= \frac{3 \pm \sqrt{-23}}{8}$$

$$= \frac{3 \pm i \cdot \sqrt{23}}{8}$$

The solutions are $\dfrac{3+i\sqrt{23}}{8}$ and $\dfrac{3-i\sqrt{23}}{8}$.

If we are given the solutions of a quadratic equation, then we can find the factors of the quadratic equation which gives us the quadratic equation, upon multiplication.

Example 4
Write an equation whose solutions are –4 and 5.

Solution
If –4 and 5 are the solutions of a quadratic equation, then $(x + 4)(x - 5)$ are the factors. Multiplying out $(x + 4)(x - 5)$ gives $x^2 - 5x + 4x - 20$ or $x^2 - x - 20$.
The equation is $x^2 - x - 20 = 0$.

Summary

Solutions of a Quadratic Equation

For a quadratic equation of the form $ax^2 + bx + c = 0$ with a not equal to zero:

If $b^2 - 4ac > 0$, then the quadratic equation has two distinct real number solutions.

If $b^2 - 4ac = 0$, then the quadratic equation has a single real number solution.

If $b^2 - 4ac < 0$, then the quadratic equation has no real number solution.

Note: $b^2 - 4ac$ is called the discriminant.

Example 5
Use the discriminant to determine the nature of the solutions of the equation $2x^2 + 5 = 4x$.

Solution
This equation is equivalent to $2x^2 - 4x + 5 = 0$, in which $a = 2$, $b = -4$, and $c = 5$. The value of the discriminant is given by $b^2 - 4ac = (-4)^2 - 4(2)(5) = -24$. Since this value is less than zero, the quadratic equation has no real number solution.

Example 6
Let $f(x) = 2x^2 + x + 6$. Find the values of x for which $f(x) = 8$.

Solution

Since $f(x) = 2x^2 + x + 6$ and $f(x) = 8$, the equation becomes $8 = 2x^2 + x + 6$, or $0 = 2x^2 + x - 2$.

Use the quadratic formula with $a = 2$, $b = 1$, and $c = -2$ to get

$$x = \frac{-b \pm \sqrt{b^2 - 4ac}}{2a}$$

$$= \frac{-1 \pm \sqrt{1^2 - 4(2)(-2)}}{2(2)}$$

$$= \frac{-1 \pm \sqrt{17}}{4}$$

The values of x are $\dfrac{-1 + 17}{4}$ and $\dfrac{-1 - \sqrt{17}}{4}$.

Example 7

An apple thrown from a height of 10 feet straight up into the air with an initial velocity of 78 feet per second reaches a distance (in feet) above the ground after t seconds given by the formula $h = 10 + 78t - 16t^2$.

    a. When does the apple reach a height of 100 feet?

    b. When does the apple hit the ground?

Solution

    a. When the apple reaches 100 feet, the h value is 100. We have

$$100 = 10 + 78t - 16t^2$$
$$0 = -90 + 78t - 16t^2$$
$$0 = -16t^2 + 78t - 90$$

Now, $a = -16$, $b = 78$, and $c = -90$.

Use the quadratic formula:

$$t = \frac{-b \pm \sqrt{b^2 - 4ac}}{2a}$$

$$= \frac{-78 \pm \sqrt{78^2 - 4(-16)(-90)}}{2(-16)}$$

$$= \frac{-78 \pm \sqrt{6084 - 5760}}{-32}$$

$$= \frac{-78 \pm \sqrt{324}}{-32}$$

$$= \frac{-78 \pm 18}{-32}$$

Then, $t = \dfrac{-78 + 18}{-32}$ or $t = \dfrac{-78 - 18}{-32}$

$t = \dfrac{-60}{-32}$ or $t = \dfrac{-96}{-32}$

$t = 1.875$ or $t = 3$

Thus, the apple reaches a height of 100 feet after 1.875 seconds and again after 3 seconds.

b. When the apple hits the ground, the h value is zero. The equation becomes $0 = 10 + 78t - 16t^2$ or
$0 = -16t^2 + 78t + 10$.
Now, $a = -16$, $b = 78$, and $c = 10$.
Use the quadratic formula.

$$t = \frac{-b \pm \sqrt{b^2 - 4ac}}{2a}$$

$$= \frac{-78 \pm \sqrt{78^2 - 4(-16)(10)}}{2(-16)}$$

$$= \frac{-78 \pm \sqrt{6084 + 640}}{-32}$$

$$= \frac{-78 \pm \sqrt{6724}}{-32}$$

$$= \frac{-78 \pm 82}{-32}$$

Then, $t = \dfrac{-78 + 82}{-32}$ or $t = \dfrac{-78 - 82}{-32}$
$t = \dfrac{4}{-32}$ or $t = \dfrac{-160}{-32}$
$t = -0.125$ or $t = 5$

Since t cannot be a negative number, the reasonable value is $t = 5$ seconds.

Exercise Set 8.2

Solve the given equations using the quadratic formula.

1. $y^2 + 3y - 4 = 0$ **2.** $x^2 + 3x - 2 = 0$ **3.** $5t^2 + 33t = 14$

4. $2x^2 - 3x + 2 = 0$ **5.** $x^2 - \dfrac{7}{6}x + \dfrac{2}{3} = 0$

Write an equation whose solutions are

6. $\dfrac{1}{2}, 3$ **7.** $\dfrac{3}{5}, \dfrac{1}{4}$

8. Set $g(x) = x^2 - 5x + 9$. Find the values of x for which $g(x) = 2$.

9. Set $p(a) = 5x^2 + 2x$. Find the values of a for which $p(a) = 1$.

10. An object is thrown upward with an initial velocity of 60 feet per second. The distance above the ground, h, after t seconds is given by $h = 60t - 16t^2$. When does the object reach a height of 56 feet.

Answers to Exercise Set 8.2

1. $-4, 1$

2. $\dfrac{-3 \pm \sqrt{17}}{2}$

3. $-7, \dfrac{2}{5}$

4. $\dfrac{3 \pm i\sqrt{7}}{4}$

5. $\dfrac{7 \pm i\sqrt{47}}{12}$

6. $2x^2 - 7x + 3$

7. $20x^2 - 17x + 3$

8. $\dfrac{5 \pm i\sqrt{3}}{2}$

9. $\dfrac{-1 \pm \sqrt{6}}{5}$

10. 1.75 seconds, 2 seconds

8.3 Quadratic Equations: Applications and Problem Solving

One goal of this section is to apply quadratic equations to real life situations.

Motion Problem

Example 1
Bob drove 20 miles at a constant speed then increased his speed by 10 miles per hour for the next 30 miles. If the time required to travel the 50 miles was 0.9 hours, find the speed he drove during the first 20 minutes.

Solution
Use $d = r \cdot t$ and orgainize the information in a chart: Let x represent the speed during the first 20 miles of the trip. Recall, $t = \dfrac{d}{r}$.

d	r	t
20 miles	x (mph)	$\dfrac{20}{x}$
30 miles	$x + 10$	$\dfrac{30}{x+10}$

Since the total time of travel is 0.9 hours, the equation is $\dfrac{20}{x} + \dfrac{30}{x+10} = 0.9$. The LCD is $x(x + 10)$ so the equation can be rewritten as

$$\frac{20(x+10)}{x(x+10)} + \frac{30x}{(x+10)x} = 0.9$$

$$\frac{20x + 200 + 30x}{x(x+10)} = \frac{9}{10}$$

$$\frac{50x + 200}{x(x+10)} = \frac{9}{10}$$

Cross multiply: $10(50x + 200) = 9x(x + 10)$

$$500x + 2000 = 9x^2 + 90x$$

$$0 = 9x^2 - 410x - 2000$$

Use quadratic formula: $x = \dfrac{-(-410) \pm \sqrt{(-410)^2 - 4(9)(-2000)}}{2(9)}$

$$x = 50 \text{ miles per hour or } x = -4.44 \text{ miles per hour}$$

Since x cannot be negative, the only answer which makes sense is $x = 50$ miles per hour.

Work Problem

Example 2
Two painters take 6 hours to paint a room when they work together. If they worked alone, the more experienced painter could complete the job 1 hour faster than the less experienced painter. How long would it take each of them to paint the room working alone?

Solution
Let $x =$ number of hours needed by the less experienced painter to paint the room. Then $x - 1$ is the number of hours needed by the more experienced painter.

In **1 hour**, the less experienced painter can paint $\dfrac{1}{x}$ of the room. Also in 1 hour, the more experienced painter can paint $\dfrac{1}{x-1}$ of the room. Finally, in 1 hour working together, **both painters** can paint $\dfrac{1}{6}$ of the room. Then the portion of the job each painter can do in an hour **combined** should equal $\dfrac{1}{6}$ or $\dfrac{1}{x} + \dfrac{1}{x-1} = \dfrac{1}{6}$. Multiply both sides by the LCD or $6x(x - 1)$:

$$6x(x-1)\left(\frac{1}{x} + \frac{1}{x-1}\right) = \frac{1}{6} \cdot 6x(x-1)$$

$$6(x-1) + 6x = x(x-1)$$

$$6x - 6 + 6x = x^2 - x$$

$$12x - 6 = x^2 - x$$

$$0 = x^2 - 13x + 6$$

Using the quadratic formula,

$$x = \frac{-(-13) \pm \sqrt{(-13)^2 - 4(1)(6)}}{2(1)} = \frac{13 \pm \sqrt{145}}{2}$$

$x = 12.52$
or $x \approx 0.48$.
The solution of 0.48 does not make sense, so the only solution is 12.52 hours.
It takes the painters 12.52 hours and 13.52 hours to paint the room working alone.

Summary

When the square of a variable appears in a formula, you may need to use the square root property to solve for the variable. However, when you use the square root property in most formulas, you will use only the positive or principle root.

Example 3

The surface area of a sphere is $A = \pi r^2$ where A is the area and r is the radius.

    a. Find the the surface area when r is 5 cm.

    b. Solve the equation for r.

Solution

    a. Substitute $r = 5$ to obtain
$$A = \pi(5)^2$$
$$= \pi(25)$$
$$= 25\pi \approx 78.54 \text{ sq. cm}$$

    b.　$A = \pi r^2$

$$\frac{A}{\pi} = r^2 \quad \text{Divide by } \pi.$$

$$\sqrt{\frac{A}{\pi}} = r \quad \text{Take square root.}$$

Example 4

Solve $p = \sqrt{a^2 - b^2}$ for a.

Solution
$$p = \sqrt{a^2 - b^2}$$
$$p^2 = a^2 - b^2 \quad \text{Square both sides.}$$
$$p^2 + b^2 = a^2 \quad\quad \text{Add } b^2 \text{ to both sides.}$$
$$\sqrt{p^2 + b^2} = a \quad\quad \text{Take square root.}$$

Exercise Set 8.3

    1. Two molding machines can complete an order in 12 hours. The larger machine can complete the order by itself in one hour less time than the smaller machine can by itself. How long will it take each machine to complete the order working by itself.

2. Carmen canoed downstream going with the current for 3 miles, then turned around and canoed upstream against the current back to the starting point. If the total time she spent canoeing was 4 hours, and the speed of the current was 0.4 miles per hour, what is the speed of the canoe in still water.

3. Solve $F = \dfrac{1}{3}mv^2$ for v.

4. Solve $a^2 + b^2 = c^2$ for a.

5. Solve $p = \sqrt{b^2 - 7c + d^2}$ for d.

Answers to Exercise Set 8.3

1. Larger machine in 23.51 hours, smaller machine in 24.51 hours

2. 1.6 miles per hour

3. $v = \sqrt{\dfrac{3F}{m}}$

4. $a = \sqrt{c^2 - b^2}$

5. $d = \sqrt{p^2 - b^2 + 7c}$

8.4 Writing Equations in Quadratic Form

Summary

To Solve Equations Quadratic in Form

1. If necessary rewrite the equation in descending order of the variable with one side of the equation equal to zero.

2. Rewrite the variable in the highest degree term as the square of the variable in the middle term.

3. Make a substitution that will result in an equation of the form $au^2 + bu + c = 0$, where u is a function of the original variable.

4. Solve the equation $au^2 + bu + c = 0$ by factoring, by the quadratic formula, or by completing the square.

5. Substitute the original variable expression for u and solve the resulting equation for the original variable.

6. Check your solutions.

Example 1
Solve $x^4 + 3x^2 = 18$.

Solution

1. $x^4 + 3x^2 - 18 = 0$ (standard form)

2. $(x^2)^2 + 3(x^2) - 18 = 0$

3. Let $u = x^2$. Then the equation becomes $u^2 + 3u - 18 = 0$.

4. Solve the equation by factoring: $(u + 6)(u - 3) = 0$
   Thus, $u + 6 = 0$ or $u - 3 = 0$
      $u = -6$ or $u = 3$

5. $u = -6$ becomes $x^2 = -6$ so that $x = \pm\sqrt{-6} = \pm i\sqrt{6}$
   $u = 3$ becomes $x^2 = 3$ so that $x = \pm\sqrt{3}$

6. A check shows all four values work. The solutions are $i\sqrt{6}$, $-i\sqrt{6}$, $\sqrt{3}$, and $-\sqrt{3}$.

Example 2

Solve $x^{1/2} - 2x^{1/4} = 8$.

Solution

1. Rewrite the equation with the right side equal to zero: $x^{1/2} - 2x^{1/4} - 8 = 0$.

2. $(x^{1/4})^2 - 2x^{1/4} - 8 = 0$

3. Let $u = x^{1/4}$ so that the equation becomes $u^2 - 2u - 8 = 0$.

4. Solve by factoring,
$$u^2 - 2u - 8 = 0$$
$$(u - 4)(u + 2) = 0$$
$$u - 4 = 0 \quad \text{or} \quad u + 2 = 0$$
$$u = 4 \quad \text{or} \quad u = -2$$

5. $u = 4$ becomes $x^{1/4} = 4$ so that $x = 4^4 = 256$ upon raising to the fourth power.
   $u = -2$ becomes $x^{1/4} = -2$ so that $x = (-2)^4 = 16$.

6. A check shows both values work.
   The solutions are 16 and 256.

Example 3

Solve $2 + \dfrac{5}{x^2} = \dfrac{6}{x}$.

Solution

Multiply both sides by x^2 to clear fractions.

$$x^2\left(2 + \frac{5}{x^2}\right) = x^2\left(\frac{6}{x}\right)$$

$$2x^2 + 5 = 6x$$

$$2x^2 - 6x + 5 = 0$$

To solve, use the quadratic formula.

$$x = \frac{-b \pm \sqrt{b^2 - 4ac}}{2a}$$

$$= \frac{-(-6) \pm \sqrt{(-6)^2 - 4(2)(5)}}{2(2)}$$

$$= \frac{6 \pm \sqrt{36 - 40}}{4}$$

$$= \frac{6 \pm \sqrt{-4}}{4}$$

$$= \frac{6 \pm 2i}{4}$$

$$= \frac{3 \pm i}{2}$$

Exercise Set 8.4

Solve the given equations.

1. $3 = \dfrac{-4}{x} + \dfrac{15}{x^2}$

2. $2x - \dfrac{20}{x} = 0$

3. $2 = \dfrac{3}{x} + \dfrac{1}{x^2}$

4. $y^4 - 4y^2 + 3 = 0$

5. $x^4 - 3x^2 - 4 = 0$

6. $x^{2/3} - 2x^{1/3} - 3 = 0$

7. $x^{1/2} - 4x^{1/4} + 3 = 0$

8. $x - 13\sqrt{x} + 40 = 0$

Answers to Exercise Set 8.4

1. $-3, \dfrac{5}{3}$

2. $\pm\sqrt{10}$

3. $\dfrac{3 \pm \sqrt{17}}{4}$

4. $\pm 1, \pm\sqrt{3}$

5. $\pm 2, \pm i$

6. $-1, 27$

7. $1, 81$

8. $25, 64$

8.5 Graphing Quadratic Functions

Summary

Graphing Quadratic Functions

The graph of $f(x) = ax^2 + bx + c$ *(or $y = ax^2 + bx + c$)*
for $a \neq 0$ is a **parabola**. The parabola opens upward if a
> 0 and opens downward if $a < 0$.

The **axis of symmetry** is $x = -\dfrac{b}{2a}$.

The **vertex** is $\left(-\dfrac{b}{2a}, f\left(-\dfrac{b}{2a}\right)\right)$ or $\left(-\dfrac{b}{2a}, \dfrac{4ac - b^2}{4a}\right)$.

To find the **y-intercept**, set $x = 0$ and solve for y.

To find the **x-intercept**, set $f(x) = 0$ (or $y = 0$) and solve
for x.

Example 1
Consider the function $f(x) = x^2 + 2x - 3$.

   a. Determine whether this parabola opens upward or downward.

   b. Find the y-intercept.

   c. Find the vertex.

   d. Find the x-intercepts (if they exist).

   e. Sketch the graph.

Solution
Since $f(x) = x^2 + 2x - 3$, then $a = 1$, $b = 2$, and $c = -3$.

   a. Since $a > 0$, the parabola opens upward.

   b. To find the y-intercept, substitue zero for x and solve the resulting equation for y: $y = 0^2 + 2(0) - 3 = -3$.
   Thus, $(0, -3)$ is the y-intercept.

   c. To find the x coordinate of the vertex, the formula $x = -\dfrac{b}{2a}$ can be used: $x = -\dfrac{2}{2(1)} = -1$. Substitute
   $x = -1$ in the equation and solve for y: $y = (-1)^2 + 2(-1) - 3 = -4$. Thus, the vertex is located at $(-1, -4)$.

d. To find the x-intercepts, substiutte $y = 0$ in the equation and solve the resulting equation for x:
$$0 = x^2 + 2x - 3$$
$$0 = (x + 3)(x - 1)$$
Thus, $x = -3$ or $x = 1$.

e. The graph can now be sketched using the information from parts a–d.

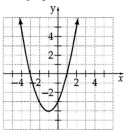

Example 2
Consider the function $g(x) = -x^2 + 2x + 2$.

   a. Determine whether this parabola opens upward or downward.

   b. Find the axis of symmetry.

   c. Find the vertex.

   d. Find the y-intercept.

   e. Sketch a graph.

Solution
Since $g(x) = -x^2 + 2x + 2$. Then $a = -1$, $b = 2$, and $c = 2$.

   a. Since $a < 0$, the parabola opens downward.

   b. Axis of symmetry: Use $x = -\dfrac{b}{2a} = -\dfrac{2}{2(-1)} = 1$. The parabola will be symmetric about the line $x = 1$.

   c. The x coordinate of the vertex is 1. Evaluate $f(1)$ to find the y coordinate of the vertex:
$$f(1) = -(1)^2 + 2(1) + 2 = 3; \text{ vertex is } (1, 3).$$

   d. To find the y-intercept, let $x = 0$ and solve.
$$y = -(0)^2 + 2(0) + 2 = 2$$

e. The graph can be sketched using the information from parts a–d.

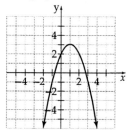

Summary

Maximum and Minimum Values

A parabola that opens upward has a **minimum value** at its vertex.

A parabola that opens downward has a **maximum value** at its vertex.

Given $f(x) = ax^2 + bx + c$, the maximum or minimum value will occur at $-\dfrac{b}{2a}$ and the value will be

$\dfrac{4ac - b^2}{4a}$. There are many real-life applications that require finding minimum and maximum values.

Example 3
Find the maximum value of $f(x) = 2x^2 - 4x + 17$.

Solution
Let $a = 2$, $b = -4$, and $c = 17$.

The maximum value occurs at $x = -\dfrac{b}{2a} = -\dfrac{-4}{2(2)} = 1$ and the value is

$\dfrac{4ac - b^2}{4a} = \dfrac{4(2)(17) - (-4)^2}{4(2)} = \dfrac{136 - 16}{8} = \dfrac{120}{8} = 15.$

Also, note that $f(1) = 2(1)^2 - 4(1) + 17 = 2 - 4 + 17 = 15$ gives the maximum value.

Example 4
An object is thrown upward with an initial velocity of 192 feet per second. The distance of the object above the ground, d, after t seconds is given by the formula $d(t) = -16t^2 + 192t$. Find the maximum height of the object.

Solution
Let $a = -16$, $b = 192$, and $c = 0$.

The maximum value occurs at $t = -\dfrac{b}{2a} = -\dfrac{192}{2(-16)} = \dfrac{192}{32} = 6$ seconds.

The maximum value is $\dfrac{4ac - b^2}{4a} = \dfrac{4(-16)(0) - (192)^2}{4(-16)} = \dfrac{-36,864}{-64} = 576$ feet.

The maximum height is 576 feet.

Summary

Translations of Parabolas

For any function $f(x) = ax^2$, the graph of $g(x) = a(x - h)^2 + k$ will have the same shape as the graph of $f(x)$. The graph of $g(x)$ will be the graph of $f(x)$ shifted as follows:

- If h is a positive real number, the graph will be shifted h units to the right.

- If h is a negative real number, the graph will be shifted $|h|$ units to the left.

- If k is a positive real number, the graph will be shifted k units up.

- If k is a negative real number, the graph will be shifted $|k|$ units down.

The graph of any function of the form $f(x) = a(x - h)^2 + k$ will be a parabola with axis of symmetry $x = h$ and vertex at (h, k).

Example 5
Graph.

   a. $f(x) = (x - 1)^2 + 5$ **b.** $g(x) = -(x + 1)^2 + 2$

Solution

a. The graph of $f(x) = (x-1)^2 + 5$ has the same shape as $y = x^2$ shifted 1 unit to the right and shifted up 5 units.

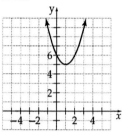

b. The graph of $g(x) = -(x+1)^2 + 2$ has the same shape as $y = -x^2$ shifted 1 unit to the left and shifted up 2 units.

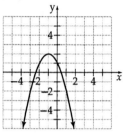

Example 6

Graph $f(x) = x^2 + 6x + 7$ by expressing $f(x)$ in the form $f(x) = a(x-h)^2 + k$.

Solution

Use the method of completing the square.

$$f(x) = x^2 + 6x + 9 - 9 + 7$$
$$= (x^2 + 6x + 9) - 2$$
$$= (x+3)^2 - 2$$

The graph has the same shape as $y = x^2$ shifted 3 units to the left and shifted down 2 units.

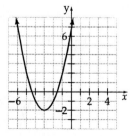

Exercise Set 8.5

For exercises 1–2,

    a. Determine whether the parabola opens upward or downward.

    b. Find the y-intercept.

    c. Find the vertex.

    d. Find the x-intercepts (if they exist).

    e. Sketch the graph.

    1. $f(x) = 2x^2 - 6x + 4$ **2.** $y = -2x^2 + 5x + 4$

Find the maximum or minimum value.

    3. $f(x) = 2x^2 - 8x + 3$ **4.** $g(x) = -4x^2 + 8x + 10$

    5. Graph $p(x) = x^2 - 4x + 5$.

Answers to Exercise Set 8.5

    1. a.   Upward   **b.** 4   **c.** $\left(\dfrac{3}{2}, -\dfrac{1}{2} \right)$

        d. $x = 1, x = 2$ **e.**

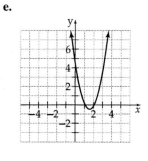

    2. a.   Downward   **b.** 4   **c.** $\left(\dfrac{5}{4}, \dfrac{57}{8} \right)$

d. $\left(\dfrac{5 \pm \sqrt{57}}{4}\right)$ **e.**

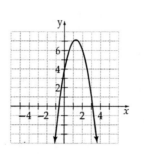

3. –5   **4.** 14   **5.**

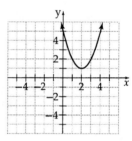

8.6 Quadratic and Other Inequalities in One Variable

Summary

Solutions of a Quadratic Inequality

1. The **solution** to a quadratic inequality is the set of all values that make the inequality a true statement.

2. One method used to solve a quadratic inequality is a **sign graph**.

Example 1
Solve $x^2 - 3x - 10 > 0$.

Solution

1. Factor $x^2 - 3x - 10$. $x^2 - 3x - 10 > 0$ is equivalent to $(x - 5)(x + 2) > 0$.

2. Find the **boundary values**. These are the values that make each factor equal to 0. If $x - 5 = 0$, then $x = 5$. If $x + 2 = 0$, then $x = -2$.

3. Draw two number lines together; one for each factor and label the boundary values. Draw vertical lines through these values.

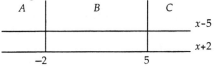

4. Notice that the two vertical lines separate the number line into three regions which are labeled A, B and C. The sign of each factor is determined for each region as well as the sign of the product of the factors. (The sign of the product is in parentheses).

```
     A          B            C
  -----      ----------   +++++   x-5

  -----      +++++++++++  +++++   x+2
 (+)  -2       (-)       5  (+)
```

5. Since we are solving $x^2 - 3x - 10 > 0$, the solutions are the numbers in the regions A and C. In interval notation, $(-\infty, -2) \cup (5, \infty)$. The boundary values are **not included** because the inequality is >.
The solution in set builder notation is $\{x | x < -2 \text{ or } x > 5\}$.

The solution can be graphed on the number line as follows:

```
  <------o          o------>
        -2          5
```

An alternate method of solving a quadratic inequality uses a single number line. For this, set up a number line with the boundary values.

```
     A          B            C
  ----+------------+----------
     -2           5
```

The boundaries form three regions (intervals). Select a test value on each interval and see if it satisfies the original inequality.

Interval A: Use $x = -4$.	Interval B: Use $x = 1$.	Interval C: Use $x = 7$.
Is $x^2 - 3x - 10 > 0$?	Is $x^2 - 3x - 10 > 0$?	Is $x^2 - 3x - 10 > 0$?
$(-4)^2 - 3(-4) - 10 > 0$	$1^2 - 3(1) - 10 > 0$	$7^2 - 3(7) - 10 > 0$
$18 > 0$	$-12 > 0$	$18 > 0$
true	false	true

The solution is $\{x | x < -2 \text{ or } x > 5\}$. In interval notation, it is $(-\infty, -2) \cup (5, \infty)$.

Summary

┌───┐

To Solve Quadratic and Other Inequalities

1. Write the inequality as an equation and solve the equation.

2. If the inequality contains a variable in any denominator, determine the value or values that make the denominator equal to 0.

3. Construct a number line. Mark each solution that is determined in step one, and values obtained in step two on the number line. Make sure you mark these values from the lowest value on the left to the greatest value on the right.

4. Select a test value in each region of the number line.

5. Test each value in step four of the inequality to determine if it satisfies the inequality.

6. Test each boundary value to determine if it is a solution to the inequality. Remember, division by 0 is not permitted.

7. Write the solution in the form requested by your instructor.

└───┘

Example 2
Solve $x^2 + 7x \geq -12$.

Solution

1. Rewrite $x^2 + 7x \geq -12$ as an equation.
    $$x^2 + 7x = -12$$
    $$x^2 + 7x + 12 = 0$$
    $$(x + 4)(x + 3) = 0$$
    Solving, we have $x = -4$ or $x = -3$.

2. Construct a number line:

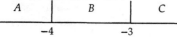

3. Select a test value in each region and determine if this value satisfies the original inequality. We shall choose -5 in region A, -3.5 in region B, and 0 in region C.

    Region A: Use $x = -5$ Region B: Use $x = -3.5$ Region C: Use $x = 0$

    Is $x^2 + 7x \geq -12$?   Is $x^2 + 7x \geq -12$?   Is $x^2 + 7x \geq -12$?

    $(-5)^2 + 7(-5) \geq -12$ $(-3.5)^2 + 7(-3.5) \geq -12$ $0^2 + 7(0) \geq -12$

    $25 + -35 \geq -12$ $-12.25 \geq -12$ False $0 \geq -12$ True

    $-10 > -12$ True

    For this problem, the boundary values are included since the sign of the original inequality is $\geq$.

4. The solution set is the values in region A along with the values in region C: $\{x|x \le -4 \text{ or } x \ge -3\}$.

Example 3

Solve $\dfrac{x-2}{x+3} \le 0$ and graph the solution set.

Solution

1. Solve $\dfrac{x-2}{x+3} = 0$. This implies that $x = 2$.

2. Determine values which make the denominator equal to zero. $x + 3 = 0$ implies that $x = -3$.

3. Construct a number line using the values found in steps 1 and 2.

$$
\begin{array}{ccc}
A & B & C \\
\hline
-3 & 2 &
\end{array}
$$

4. Use the test values of –4, 0, 3.

Region A: Use $x = -4$.

Is $\dfrac{x-2}{x+3} \le 0$?

$\dfrac{-4-2}{-4+3} \le 0$

$\dfrac{-6}{-1} \le 0$

$6 \le 0$ False

Region B: Use $x = 0$.

Is $\dfrac{x-2}{x+3} \le 0$?

$\dfrac{0-2}{0+3} \le 0$

$-\dfrac{2}{3} \le 0$ True

Region C: Use $x = 3$.

Is $\dfrac{x-2}{x+3} \le 0$?

$\dfrac{3-2}{3+3} \le 0$

$\dfrac{1}{6} \le 0$ False

5. The solutions are values of region B. Since the original inequality has a $\le$ symbol, the boundary value of 2 is included. However, the value –3 is **not included since this number makes the denominator equal to zero and we cannot divide by zero.**

In solution set form, our solution is $\{x|-3 < x \le 2\}$.

Exercise Set 8.6

Solve each inequality and graph the solution on the real number line.

1. $x^2 - 9 > 0$

2. $2x^2 + 6x + 4 \le 0$

3. $(x+4)(x+2)(x-3) \ge 0$

4. $\dfrac{x-5}{x+2} < 0$

5. $\dfrac{x+3}{x} \ge 0$

6. $\dfrac{x+6}{(x-2)(x+4)} > 0$

7. $\dfrac{x-2}{x+3} < 0$

8. $\dfrac{x+4}{x-3} > 0$

9. $\dfrac{2}{2x-1} > 2$

10. $\dfrac{y}{y+4} < 1$

Answers to Exercise Set 8.6

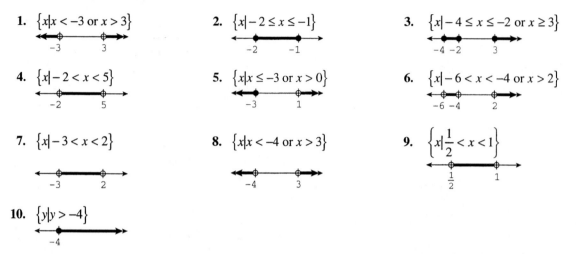

1. $\{x|x < -3 \text{ or } x > 3\}$

2. $\{x|-2 \le x \le -1\}$

3. $\{x|-4 \le x \le -2 \text{ or } x \ge 3\}$

4. $\{x|-2 < x < 5\}$

5. $\{x|x \le -3 \text{ or } x > 0\}$

6. $\{x|-6 < x < -4 \text{ or } x > 2\}$

7. $\{x|-3 < x < 2\}$

8. $\{x|x < -4 \text{ or } x > 3\}$

9. $\left\{x\left|\frac{1}{2} < x < 1\right.\right\}$

10. $\{y|y > -4\}$

Chapter 8 Practice Test

1. Use the square root property to solve $(3x - 4)^2 = 60$.

2. Solve $x^2 - 8x + 15 = 0$ by completing the square.

3. Solve $2x^2 - 8x = -64$ by completing the square.

For problems 4, 5, and 6, determine whether the equation has two distinct real solutions, a single real solution, or no real solutions.

4. $x^2 - x + 8 = 0$

5. $y^2 - 12y = -36$

6. $2x^2 + 6x + 7 = 0$

7. Solve $x^2 - 6x + 7 = 0$ using the quadratic formula.

Find the solution to the following quadratic equations by any method you choose.

8. $x^2 + 3x - 6 = 0$

9. $x^2 - x + 42 = 0$

10. $x^2 = \frac{5}{6}x + \frac{25}{6}$

Determine whether the parabola opens upward or downward, find the y-intercept, find the vertex, find the x intercepts if they exist, and sketch the graph.

11. $y = x^2 + 2x - 8$

Solve the following equations:

12. $\dfrac{5(x-1)}{x+1} = \dfrac{x-1}{x}$

13. $2y^6 - 7y^3 = -6$

Solve each inequality and express the answer in interval notation.

14. $(x - 5)(x + 2)(x + 6) \leq 0$ **15.** $\dfrac{x + 2}{x + 4} \geq 0$

Answers to Chapter 8 Practice Test

1. $\dfrac{4 \pm 2\sqrt{15}}{3}$ **2.** 3, 5   **3.** $2 \pm 2i\sqrt{7}$

4. No real   **5.** One real   **6.** No real

7. $3 \pm \sqrt{2}$ **8.** $\dfrac{-3 \pm \sqrt{33}}{2}$ **9.** $\dfrac{1 \pm i\sqrt{167}}{2}$

10. $\dfrac{5}{2}, -\dfrac{5}{3}$

11. upward; –8; (–1, –9); –4, 2

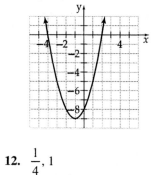

12. $\dfrac{1}{4}$, 1   **13.** $\sqrt[3]{\dfrac{3}{2}}, \sqrt[3]{2}$ **14.** $(-\infty, -6] \cup [-2, 5]$

15. $(-\infty, -4) \cup [-2, \infty)$

CHAPTER 8 SUMMARY

IMPORTANT FACTS

Square Root Property
If $x^2 = a$, then $x = \pm \sqrt{a}$

Quadratic Formula
$x = \dfrac{-b \pm \sqrt{b^2 - 4ac}}{2a}$

Discriminant $\left(b^2 - 4ac\right)$

For an equation of the form $ax^2 + bx + c = 0$

- If $b^2 - 4ac > 0$, the quadratic equation has two distinct real solutions.

- If $b^2 - 4ac = 0$, the quadratic equation has one real solution.

- If $b^2 - 4ac < 0$, the quadratic equation has no real solutions.

Parabolas

- For $f(x) = ax^2 + bx + c$, the vertex of the parabola is $\left(-\dfrac{b}{2a}, \dfrac{4ac - b^2}{4a}\right)$ or $\left(-\dfrac{b}{2a}, f\left(-\dfrac{b}{2a}\right)\right)$.

- For $f(x) = a(x - h)^2 + k$, the vertex of the parabola is (h, k).

- If $f(x) = ax^2 + bx + c$, $a > 0$, the function will have a minimum value of $\dfrac{4ac - b^2}{4a}$ at $x = -\dfrac{b}{2a}$.

- If $f(x) = ax^2 + bx + c$, $a < 0$, the function will have a maximum value of $\dfrac{4ac - b^2}{4a}$ at $x = -\dfrac{b}{2a}$.

HELPFUL HINTS

- When solving the equation $x^2 + bx + c = 0$ by completing the square, we get $x^2 + bx + \left(\dfrac{b}{2}\right)^2$ on the left side of the equal sign and a constant (c) on the right side of the equal sign. Since $x^2 + bx + \left(\dfrac{b}{2}\right)^2$ factors into $\left(x + \dfrac{b}{2}\right)\left(x + \dfrac{b}{2}\right)$, we replace $x^2 + bx + \left(\dfrac{b}{2}\right)^2$ by $\left(x + \dfrac{b}{2}\right)^2$ to get the equation $\left(x + \dfrac{b}{2}\right)^2 = c$. This equation is now ready to be solved by the Square Root Property.

- Since you are using roots and radicals again in this chapter, you may find it helpful to go back to Chapter 7 and review Evaluating and Simplifying Radicals.

- When solving an equation using substitution, make sure you remember to solve the equation for the original variable, not just the substituted variable. Otherwise, the problem will not be complete.

- If $ax^2 + bx + c = 0$, with $a > 0$, has two distinct real solutions, then:

Inequality of form	Solution is	Solution on number line
$ax^2 + bx + c \geq 0$	End intervals	⬅●———●➡
$ax^2 + bx + c \leq 0$	Center interval	⬅●━━━●➡

AVOIDING COMMON ERRORS

- When writing the quadratic formula, make sure the **entire** numerator is divided by $2a$. For example:

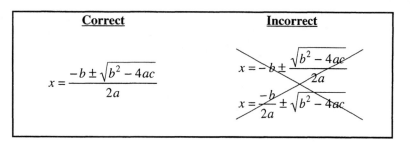

Correct	Incorrect
$x = \dfrac{-b \pm \sqrt{b^2 - 4ac}}{2a}$	$x = -b \pm \dfrac{\sqrt{b^2 - 4ac}}{2a}$ $x = \dfrac{-b}{2a} \pm \sqrt{b^2 - 4ac}$

- When using the quadratic formula, be careful when deciding whether or not to simplify in the last step. You may only divide out a common factor when **all** three terms (both terms in the numerator and the term in the denominator) have a common factor. For example:

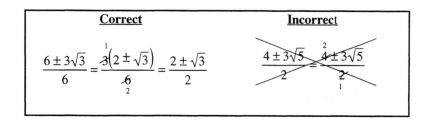

Correct	Incorrect
$\dfrac{6 \pm 3\sqrt{3}}{6} = \dfrac{\overset{1}{\cancel{3}}\left(2 \pm \sqrt{3}\right)}{\underset{2}{\cancel{6}}} = \dfrac{2 \pm \sqrt{3}}{2}$	$\dfrac{4 \pm 3\sqrt{5}}{2} = \dfrac{\overset{2}{\cancel{4}} \pm 3\sqrt{5}}{\underset{1}{\cancel{2}}}$

Chapter 9

9.1 Composite and Inverse Functions

Summary

Composition of Functions

The composition of function f with function g is denoted by $(f + g)(x)$ and is defined as $f[g(x)]$.

The composition of function g with function f is denoted by $(g + f)(x)$ and is defined as $g[f(x)]$.

Note: to find $(f + g)(x)$, we substitute $g(x)$ for x in $f(x)$ to get $f[g(x)]$.

Example 1
Let $f(x) = x^2 + 3x - 1$ and $g(x) = 3x - 2$. Find

   a. $(f + g)(x)$ **b.** $(f + g)(4)$

   c. $(g + f)(x)$ **d.** $(g + f)(4)$

Solution

   a. $f(x) = x^2 + 3x - 1$ so that
$$(f \circ g)(x) = f[g(x)] = (3x - 2)^2 + 3(3x - 2) - 1$$
$$= 9x^2 - 12x + 4 + 9x - 6 - 1$$
$$= 9x^2 - 3x - 3$$

   b. To find $(f + g)(4)$ use the above result with $x = 4$.
$$(f \circ g)(x) = 9x^2 - 3x - 3$$
$$(f \circ g)(4) = 9(4)^2 - 3(4) - 3$$
$$= 144 - 12 - 3$$
$$= 129$$

   c. $g(x) = 3x - 2$ so that
$$(g \circ f)(x) = g[f(x)] = 3(x^2 + 3x - 1) - 2$$
$$= 3x^2 + 9x - 3 - 2$$
$$= 3x^2 + 9x - 5$$

   d. To find $(g + f)(4)$ use the above result with $x = 4$.
$$(g \circ f)(x) = 3x^2 + 9x - 5$$
$$(g \circ f)(4) = 3(4)^2 + 9(4) - 5$$
$$= 48 + 36 - 5$$
$$= 79$$

Summary

One-to-One Functions

A **one-to-one function** is a function where each *y* value has a unique *x* value. For a function to be a one-to-one, it must pass not only a **vertical line test** (to determine whether or not it is a function) but also a **horizontal line test** (the criterion for a one-to-one function).

If $f(x)$ is a one-to-one function with ordered pairs of the form (a, b), then its inverse function, denoted by $f^{-1}(x)$, will be a one-to-one function with ordered pairs of the form (b, a).

To Find the Inverse Function of a One-to-One Function of the Form $y = f(x)$

1. Replace $f(x)$ with *y*.

2. Interchange the two variables *x* and *y*.

3. Solve the equation for *y*. The resulting equation will be the inverse function.

4. Replace *y* with $f^{-1}(x)$ using inverse notation.

Example 1
Determine which of the following are one-to-one functions:

a.   **b.** $\{(2, 3), (3, 9), (4, 9), (6, 10)\}$

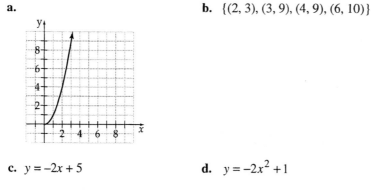

c. $y = -2x + 5$ **d.** $y = -2x^2 + 1$

Solution

a. The graph of this function passes the horizontal line test so it is one-to-one.

b. The *y* value of 9 corresponds to **both 3 and 4**. Hence, this function is **not** one-to-one since each *y* value must correspond to a **unique *x* value**.

c. The graph of $y = -2x + 5$ is a straight line with slope of -2 and y-intercept of 5. The graph of **all lines which are not vertical or horizontal** will pass the horizontal line test. Thus, these lines are one-to-one and have inverses. Thus, $y = -2x + 5$ is one-to-one and has an inverse.

d. The graph of $y = -2x^2 + 1$ is a parabola opening downward. All horizontal lines will intersect this graph **twice** (except for the horizontal line passing through the vertex of the parabola). Since the graph fails the horizontal line test, $y = -2x^2 + 1$ is **not one-to-one** and does not have an inverse.

Exmaple 2
Show that $f(x) = \{(-1, 3), (1, 4), (2, 7), (3, 9)\}$ is one-to-one and find its inverse.

Solution
Each value of the range, 3, 4, 7 and 9 corresponds to a **unique value of x**. Hence, $f(x)$ is one-to-one. To find the inverse function, denoted by $f^{-1}(x)$, simply interchange the x and y values of the original function:
$$f^{-1}(x) = \{(3, -1), (4, 1), (7, 2), (9, 3)\}.$$
Notice that the domain of $f^{-1}(x)$ is the same as the range of $f(x)$ and vice versa. **This will always be the case for functions and their inverses.**

Example 3

a. Find $f^{-1}(x)$ if $f(x) = -2x + 5$.

b. Graph $f^{-1}(x)$ and $f(x)$ on the same graph.

c. Find $(f \circ f^{-1})(x)$.

Solution

a. 1. $y = -2x + 5$ upon replacing $f(x)$ with y.

   2. Interchange x and y: $x = -2y + 5$

   3. Solve for y: $x = -2y + 5$
       $$2y = 5 - x$$
       $$y = \frac{5 - x}{2}$$

   4. or $f^{-1}(x) = \frac{5 - x}{2}$

b.

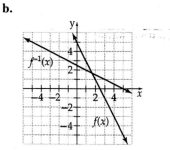

c. $f(x) = -2x + 5$ so that

$$(f \circ f^{-1})(x) = -2\left(\frac{5-x}{2}\right) + 5$$
$$= -(5-x) + 5$$
$$= -5 + x + 5$$
$$= x, \text{ as expected}$$

Exercise Set 9.1

1. Let $f(x) = x^2 + 2$ and $g(x) = x^2 - 4x + 5$. Find

    a. $(f + g)(x)$ **b.** $(f + g)(1)$

    c. $(g + f)(x)$ **d.** $(g + f)(1)$

Determine if the functions below are one-to-one.

2.   **3.**   **4.**

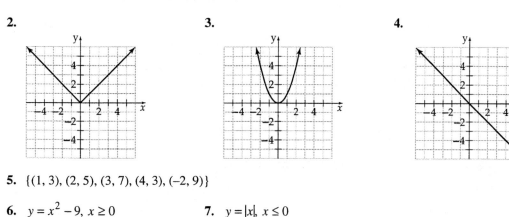

5. $\{(1, 3), (2, 5), (3, 7), (4, 3), (-2, 9)\}$

6. $y = x^2 - 9, \ x \geq 0$ **7.** $y = |x|, \ x \leq 0$

Find $f^{-1}(x)$ (problems 8, 9, and 10)

8. $f(x) = x - 3$ **9.** $f(x) = 3x + 5$ **10.** $f(x) = -3x + 7$

11. Show that $(f \circ f^{-1})(x) = x$ for $f(x) = 3x + 2$ and $f^{-1}(x) = \dfrac{x-2}{3}$.

12. Show that $(f^{-1} \circ f)(x) = x$ for $f(x) = x^3 + 1$ and $f^{-1}(x) = \sqrt[3]{x-1}$.

Answers to Exercise Set 9.1

1. a. $x^4 - 8x^3 + 26x^2 - 40x + 27$

    b. 6   **c.** $x^4 + 1$ **d.** 2

2. No   **3.** No   **4.** Yes

5. No   **6.** Yes   **7.** Yes

8. $f^{-1}(x) = x + 3$ **9.** $f^{-1}(x) = \dfrac{x-5}{3}$ **10.** $f^{-1}(x) = \dfrac{7-x}{3}$

11. $(f \circ f^{-1})(x) = f[f^{-1}(x)] = 3\left(\dfrac{x-2}{3}\right) + 2 = x - 2 + 2 = x$

12. $(f^{-1} \circ f)(x) = f^{-1}[f(x)] = \sqrt[3]{(x^3 + 1) - 1} = \sqrt[3]{x^3} = x$

9.2 Exponential Functions

Summary

> An **exponential equation** or function is one that has a variable as an exponent.

Example 1
A biologist has one cell at the start of an experiment. The number of cells doubles each day. The formula for the number of cells after x days is given by $y = 2^x$. Find the number of cells present after 20 days.

Solution
$y = 2^x$
If $x = 20$, then $y = 2^{20} = 1,048,576$ (calculator).

This example illustrates how fast the exponential function increases.

Summary

> **Exponential Function**
>
> For any real number $a > 0$ and $a \neq 1$, $f(x) = a^x$ is an exponential function.

Example 2
Graph $f(x) = 3^x$ and state the domain, range and y-intercept.

Solution
Find several ordered pairs of the function by replacing x with arbitrary values.

	Ordered pair
If $x = -3$, then $y = 3^{-3} = \dfrac{1}{3^3} = \dfrac{1}{27}$	$\left(-3, \dfrac{1}{27}\right)$
If $x = -1$, then $y = 3^{-1} = \dfrac{1}{3}$	$\left(-1, \dfrac{1}{3}\right)$
If $x = 0$, then $y = 3^0 = 1$	$(0, 1)$
If $x = 1$, then $y = 3^1 = 3$	$(1, 3)$
If $x = 2$, then $y = 3^2 = 9$	$(2, 9)$
If $x = 3$, then $y = 3^3 = 27$	$(3, 27)$

Plot the ordered pairs and connect them with a smooth curve.

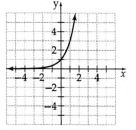

The domain is the set of real numbers: $\{x | x \text{ is a real number}\}$. The range is $\{y | y > 0\}$. The y-intercept is $(0, 1)$.

Example 3
The formula $A = p(1 + r)^n$ gives the amount, A, in an account in which p dollars is compounded annually for n years at an interest rate of r. If \$5000 is invested at 6% compounded annually for 10 years, how much will be in the account at the end of 10 years?

Solution
Use $A = p(1 + r)^n$ with $p = 5000$, $r = 0.06$, $n = 1$, and $t = 10$.
Then, $A = 5000(1 + 0.06)^{10} = 5000(1.06)^{10} \approx 5000(1.790847)$
$A \approx \$8,954.24$

Example 4
In 1998, the population in Xenobia was 103,000 people and is growing according to the function
$P(t) = 103,000(1.08)^t$ where t is the number of years after 1998. Estimate the population in 2008.

Solution
Let $t = 10$, the number of years after 1998.
Then $P(10) = 103,000(1.08)^{10}$
$$\approx 103,000(2.158925)$$
$$\approx 222,369$$

Example 5
Bob invests $100 into a savings account earning interest at 6% compounded semiannually. Find the amount in the account after 20 years.

Solution

Use $A = p\left(1 + \dfrac{r}{n}\right)^{nt}$ with $p = 100$, $n = 2$, $r = 0.06$, and $t = 20$.

Then, $A = 100\left(1 + \dfrac{0.06}{2}\right)^{2 \cdot 20}$
$$= 100(1.03)^{40}$$
$$\approx 100(3.262038)$$
$$\approx 326.20$$
At the end of 20 years, Bob will have $326.20 in the account.

Exercise Set 9.2

Graph the exponential functions.

1. $y = 4^x$

2. $y = \left(\dfrac{1}{4}\right)^x$

3. $y = 2^{-x}$

4. If $5,000 is invested at 6% compounded annually, find the amount in the account at the end of

  a. 4 years

  b. 10 years

  c. 20 years

5. In the formula $N(x) = 2^x$, N is the number of one-celled organisms after x hours.

  a. How many one-celled organisms are there after 13 hours?

  b. In how many hours will 1024 organisms be present?

Answers for Exercise Set 9.2

1.   **2.**   **3.**

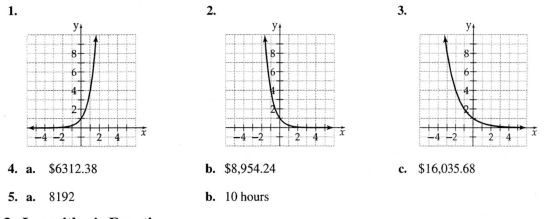

4. a. $6312.38   **b.** $8,954.24   **c.** $16,035.68

5. a. 8192   **b.** 10 hours

9.3 Logarithmic Functions

Summary

Logarithms
For all positive numbers a, where $a \neq 1$, $y = \log_a x$ means $a^y = x$.

Example 1
Write in logarithmic form.

   a. $10^2 = 100$ **b.** $\left(\dfrac{1}{3}\right)^4 = \dfrac{1}{81}$ **c.** $5^{-3} = \dfrac{1}{125}$

Solution

   a. $10^2 = 100$ is equivalent to $\log_{10} 100 = 2$.

   b. $\left(\dfrac{1}{3}\right)^4 = \dfrac{1}{81}$ is equivalent to $\log_{1/3}\left(\dfrac{1}{81}\right) = 4$

   c. $5^{-3} = \dfrac{1}{125}$ is equivalent to $\log_5\left(\dfrac{1}{125}\right) = -3$

Example 2
Write in exponential form and then find the missing value.

   a. $y = \log_6 36$ **b.** $\log_{10} x = -1$ **c.** $\log_b 4 = -2$

Solution

a. $y = \log_6 36$ is equivalent to $6^y = 36$. Thus, $y = 2$.

b. $\log_{10} x = -1$ is equivalent to $10^{-1} = x$. Thus, $x = \dfrac{1}{10}$ or 0.1.

c. $\log_b 4 = -2$ is equivalent to $b^{-2} = 4$ or $\dfrac{1}{b^2} = 4$.

Solve this equation to obtain $b^2 = \dfrac{1}{4}$ or $b = \pm\sqrt{\dfrac{1}{4}} = \pm\dfrac{1}{2}$.

Since b, the base, must be a positive number, use $b = \dfrac{1}{2}$.

Example 3
Graph $y = \log_3 x$ and state the domain and range.

Solution

$y = \log_3 x$ means $3^y = x$. It is preferable to choose the y values first and then find the corresponding x values.

x	$\frac{1}{27}$	$\frac{1}{9}$	$\frac{1}{3}$	1	3	9	27
y	-3	-2	-1	0	1	2	3

Connect the points with a smooth curve.

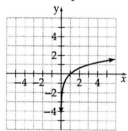

The domain is $(0, \infty)$ and the range is $(-\infty, \infty)$.
Since $y = \log_3 x$ means $3^y = x$, this function is the inverse of the function $y = 3^x$. The graphs of $y = \log_3 x$ and $y = 3^x$ are symmetric with respect to the line $y = x$.

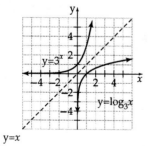

y=x

Exercise Set 9.3

Write in logarithmic form.

1. $5^4 = 625$

2. $2^{-5} = \dfrac{1}{32}$

3. $a^y = b$

Write in exponential form.

4. $\log_5 25 = 2$

5. $\log_6\left(\dfrac{1}{36}\right) = -2$

6. $\log_{1/2} y = x$

Find the value of each unknown.

7. $\log_7 1 = y$

8. $\log_b\left(\dfrac{1}{4}\right) = 2$

9. $\log_2 x = 3$

Answers for Exercise Set 9.3

1. $\log_5 625 = 4$

2. $\log_2\left(\dfrac{1}{32}\right) = -5$

3. $\log_a b = y$

4. $5^2 = 25$

5. $6^{-2} = \dfrac{1}{36}$

6. $\left(\dfrac{1}{2}\right)^x = y$

7. $y = 0$

8. $b = \dfrac{1}{2}$

9. $x = 8$

9.4 Properties of Logarithms

Summary

Product Rule for Logarithms

For positive real numbers x, y, and a, $a \neq 1$,

$$\log_a xy = \log_a x + \log_a y$$

Quotient Rule for Logarithms

$$\log_a \frac{x}{y} = \log_a x - \log_a y$$

Power Rule for Logarithms

If x and a are positive real numbers, $a \neq 1$, and n is any real number, then

$$\log_a x^n = n \log_a x$$

Additional Properties

If $a > 0$, $a \neq 1$, then $\log_a a^x = x$ and $a^{\log_a(x)} = x$

Example 1
Expand the following.

   a. $\log_6(7 \cdot 9)$ **b.** $\log_{10} y(y-3)$

Solution

   a. $\log_6(7 \cdot 9) = \log_6 7 + \log_6 9$ **b.** $\log_{10} y(y-3) = \log_{10} y + \log_{10} y - 3$

Example 2
Expand the following.

   a. $\log_5 \left(\dfrac{17}{8} \right)$ **b.** $\log_3 \sqrt{\dfrac{x}{x-2}}$

Solution

   a. $\log_5 \left(\dfrac{17}{8} \right) = \log_5 17 - \log_5 8$

b. $\log_3 \sqrt{\dfrac{x}{x-2}} = \log_3\left(\dfrac{x}{x-2}\right)^{1/2}$

$\qquad\qquad = \dfrac{1}{2}\log_3\left(\dfrac{x}{x-2}\right)$

$\qquad\qquad = \dfrac{1}{2}[\log_3 x - \log_3(x-2)]$

Example 3
Write as a logarithm of a single expression.

    a. $3\log_a x + 2\log_a y$ **b.** $\dfrac{1}{2}[\log_5(2-y) - \log_5 7]$

Solution

    a. $3\log_a x + 2\log_a y = \log_a x^3 + \log_a y^2 = \log_a(x^3 y^2)$

    b. $\dfrac{1}{2}[\log_5(2-y) - \log_5 7] = \dfrac{1}{2}\log_5\left(\dfrac{2-y}{7}\right) = \log_5\left(\dfrac{2-y}{7}\right)^{1/2}$ or $\log_5\sqrt{\dfrac{2-y}{7}}$

Example 4
Evaluate

    a. $7^{\log_7(13)}$ **b.** $(3^2)^{\log_9 5}$ **c.** $2\log_9\left(\sqrt{9}\right)$

Solution

    a. $7^{\log_7(13)}$ is of the form $a^{\log_a(x)}$. Since $a^{\log_a(x)} = x$, $7^{\log_7(13)} = 13$.

    b. $(3^2)^{\log_9 5}$ is equivalent to $9^{\log_9(5)} = 5$.

    c. $2\log_9\sqrt{9} = \log_9\left(\sqrt{9}\right)^2 = \log_9 9 = 1$

Exercise Set 9.4

Expand the following.

    1. $\log_9(8 \cdot 5)$ **2.** $\log_7 x(x-5)$ **3.** $\log_{10}\dfrac{\sqrt{y}}{y-3}$

Write as a logarithm of a single expression.

    4. $3\log_5 x + 2\log_5(x-1)$ **5.** $\log_7 6 + 4\log_7 x$ **6.** $\dfrac{1}{2}[\log_6(x-1) - \log_6 3]$

Evaluate.

7. $\log_3 3^5$ **8.** $\log_{12} 1$ **9.** $(5^3)^{\log_{125} 1}$

Answers to Exercise Set 9.4

1. $\log_9 8 + \log_9 5$ **2.** $\log_7(x) + \log_7(x-5)$ **3.** $\dfrac{1}{2}\log_{10} y - \log_{10}(y-3)$

4. $\log_5[x^3 \cdot (x-1)^2]$ **5.** $\log_7(6x^4)$ **6.** $\log_6 \sqrt{\dfrac{x-1}{3}}$

7. 5   **8.** 0   **9.** 1

9.5   Common Logarithms

Summary

Common Logarithms

The **common logarithm** of a positive real number is the **exponent** to which the base **10** is raised to obtain the number.

If $\log N = L$, then $10^L = N$

Antilogarithms

If $\log N = L$ then $N = $ antilog L.

Example 1
Find the following using a scientific or graphing calculator.

a. $\log 769$ **b.** $\log 1$

c. $\log 0.000123$ **d.** $\log (-5.9)$

Solution

a. $\log 769 = 2.8859$

b. $\log 1 = 0$ (This problem can be done without using a calculator. Log $1 = 0$ since $10^0 = 1$.)

c. $\log 0.000123 = -3.9101$

d. $\log (-5.9)$ does not exist since the domain of the logarithm function is $\{x | x > 0\}$.

Example 2
From example 1, it was found that log 769 = 2.8859. This means that $10^{2.8859} \approx 769$. We say the
antilogarithm of 2.8859 is 769 since $10^{2.8859} = 769$.

Example 3
Find N if log $N = 1.234$.

Solution
If log $N = 1.234$ then $10^{1.234} = N$ or 17.14.

Exercise Set 9.5

Find the common logarithm of the number and round answers to 4 decimal places.

  1. 983   **2.** 7   **3.** 29,541

  4. 0.00543

Find the antilog of the logarithm. Round answers to 3 decimal places.

  5. 2.123   **6.** 6.49   **7.** −2.965

Find N. Round N to 3 decimal places.

  8. log $N = 2.497$ **9.** log $N = -2.143$ **10.** log $N = 3$

Find the common logarithms without using a calculator.

  11. log 1000   **12.** log 0.001   **13.** $\log 10^7$

  14. $10^{\log 50}$ **15.** $6 \cdot \log 10^{5.2}$

Answers to Exercise Set 9.5

  1. 2.9926   **2.** .8451   **3.** 4.4704

  4. −2.2652   **5.** 132.739   **6.** 3,090,295.433

  7. 0.001   **8.** 314.051   **9.** 0.007

  10. 1000   **11.** 3   **12.** −3

  13. 7   **14.** 50   **15.** 31.2

9.6 Exponential and Logarithmic Equations

Summary

Properties for Solving Exponential and Logarithmic Equations

a. If $x = y$, then $a^x = a^y$.

b. If $a^x = a^y$, then $x = y$.

c. If $x = y$, then $\log x = \log y$. $(x > 0, y > 0)$

d. If $\log x = \log y$, then $x = y$ $(x > 0, y > 0)$

Example 1
Solve $3^{-x} = 27$.

Solution
$3^{-x} = 27$
$3^{-x} = 3^3$
$-x = 3$ (If $a^x = a^y$, then $x = y$)
$x = -3$

Example 2
Solve $3^x = 6$.

Solution
$$3^x = 6$$
$\log 3^x = \log 6$ (if $x = y$, then $\log x = \log y$)
$x \log 3 = \log 6$ (property of logarithms)
$$x = \frac{\log 6}{\log 3} = 1.631$$

Note: The numerical value was not calculated until the very last step. The reason is to minimize accumulated round off errors. For example, if log 6 was evaluated in the first step, some students would round off the answer differently. Again, in step 2, log 3 might be rounded differently by different students. The quotient of these two rounded numbers would vary depending upon the rules used for rounding log 3 and log 6. The answer might also vary depending upon the number of decimal places your calculator rounds to.

Example 3

Solve $5^x = 3^{x+1}$.

Solution

$$5^x = 3^{x+1}$$
$$\log 5^x = \log 3^{x+1} \quad \text{(if } x = y, \text{ the } \log x = \log y)$$
$$x \log 5 = (x+1) \log 3$$
$$x \log 5 = x \log 3 + \log 3$$
$$x \log 5 - x \log 3 = \log 3$$
$$x(\log 5 - \log 3) = \log 3$$
$$x = \frac{\log 3}{\log 5 - \log 3} = 2.151$$

Example 4

Solve $\log_2(x-2) = 3 - \log_2 x$.

Solution

$$\log_2(x-2) = 3 - \log_2 x$$
$$\log_2(x-2) + \log_2 x = 3$$
$$\log_2[(x-2)x] = 3$$
$$2^3 = (x-2)x$$
$$8 = x^2 - 2x$$
$$0 = x^2 - 2x - 8$$
$$0 = (x-4)(x+2)$$
$$x = 4, \ x = -2$$

Discard the solution of $x = -2$ since the domain of $\log_2 x$ must consist of numbers greater than zero. The solution is $x = 4$.

Example 5

The formula $A = p(1+r)^n$ gives the amount, A, to which a principal, p, will grow if compounded annually at an interest rate of r for n compounding periods. How long would it take \$1000 to grow to \$2000 if compounded annually at 6% interest?

Solution

Use $A = p(1+r)^n$, where $A = 2000, p = 1000, r = 0.06$ and n is unknown.

$$2000 = 1000(1 + 0.06)^n$$
$$2 = (1.06)^n$$
$$\log 2 = \log(1.06)^n$$
$$\log 2 = n \log(1.06)$$
$$\frac{\log 2}{\log 1.06} = n$$
$$11.89 = n$$

To the nearest year, $n = 12$ years.

Exercise Set 9.6

Solve the equation without using a calculator.

1. $2^{-x} = 16$

2. $5^{-x} = \dfrac{1}{125}$

3. $\left(\dfrac{1}{2}\right)^x = 16$

4. $64^x = 4^{2x-1}$

Use a calculator to solve the following equations.

5. $5^x = 75$

6. $6^x = 23$

7. $\left(\dfrac{1}{4}\right)^x = 9$

8. $5^x = 3^{x+2}$

Solve.

9. $\log_3(x+6) = \log_3(3x-2)$ **10.** $\log_3(x-2) = 1 - \log_3(x)$ **11.** $\log_7(5x+4) = 2$

12. If the initial amount of bacteria in a culture is 4500, when will the number of bacteria in this culture reach 50,000? Use the formula $N = 4500 \cdot 2^t$, where t is in hours and N represents the number of bacteria.

Answers to Exercise Set 9.6

1. –4

2. 3

3. –4

4. –1

5. 2.683

6. 1.750

7. –1.585

8. 4.301

9. 4

10. 3

11. 9

12. 3.47 hours

9.7 Natural Exponential and Natural Logarithmic Functions

Summary

Natural Exponential Function

The Natural Exponential function is

$$f(x) = e^x, \text{ where } e \approx 2.7183.$$

Natural Logarithms

Natural logarithms are logarithms to the base e. Natural logarithms are indicated by the letters ln.

$$\log_e(x) = \ln x$$

If $y = \ln x$ then $e^y = x$.

The functions $y = e^x$ and $y = \ln(x)$ are inverse functions.

Example 1
Use a calculator to evaluate each of the following.

   a. ln 3.1   **b.** ln 0.00013

   c. $e^{7.314}$ **d.** e^{-2}

Solution

   a. ln 3.1 = 1.131 to three decimal places.   **b.** ln 0.00013 = −8.948

   c. $e^{7.314} = 1501.17$ **d.** $e^{-2} = 0.135$

Example 2
Find N if

   a. ln $N = 3.48$

   b. ln $N = -0.037$

Solution

   a. If ln $N = 3.48$, then $e^{3.48} = N = 32.46$

   b. If ln $N = -0.037$, then $e^{-0.037} = N = 0.964$

Summary

Change of Base Formula

If $a > 0$, $b > 0$, $x > 0$ and neither a nor b equals 1, then

$$\log_a x = \frac{\log_b x}{\log_b a}.$$

Summary

Properties for Natural Logarithms

$$\ln xy = \ln x + \ln y, \; (x > 0 \text{ and } y > 0)$$

$$\ln \frac{x}{y} = \ln x - \ln y, \; (x > 0 \text{ and } y > 0)$$

$$\ln x^n = n \ln x, \; (x > 0)$$

Additional Properties

$$\ln e^x = x$$
$$e^{\ln x} = x, \; (x > 0)$$

Example 3
Find $\log_8 5$.

Solution
Use $\log_a x = \dfrac{\log_b x}{\log_b a}$.

$$\log_8 5 = \frac{\log 5}{\log 8} \approx 0.77398$$

Check: If $\log_8 5 = .77398$, then $8^{0.77398} = 5$ (which is true).

An alternate method of finding $\log_8 5$ would be to use the change of base formula with natural logarithms, rather than common logarithms: $\log_8 5 = \dfrac{\ln 5}{\ln 8}$.

Example 4
Solve the equation $\ln x - \dfrac{3}{2} \ln 4 = 0$.

Solution
$$\ln x - \frac{3}{2}\ln 4 = 0$$
$$\ln x = \frac{3}{2}\ln 4$$
$$\ln x = \ln 4^{3/2}$$
This implies that $x = 4^{3/2} = \left(\sqrt{4}\right)^3 = 2^3 = 8.$

Example 5
Solve $e^{-0.12t} = 0.8.$

Solution
$$e^{-0.12t} = 0.8$$
$$\ln e^{-0.12t} = \ln 0.8$$
$$-0.12t \ln e = \ln 0.8$$
$$-0.12t(1) = \ln 0.8$$
$$t = \frac{\ln 0.8}{-0.12} = 1.86$$

Example 6
How much money must be deposited today to become $15,000 in 12 years if invested at 7% compounded continuously?

Solution
Use the formula $A = pe^{rt}$ with $A = 15{,}000$, $r = 0.07$ and $t = 12$.
$$15000 = pe^{(0.07)(12)}$$
$$\frac{15{,}000}{e^{(0.07)(12)}} = p$$
$$6475.66 = p$$

Exercise Set 9.7

Find the following values correct to 3 decimal places.

  1. $\ln 397$ **2.** $\ln 0.00395$

Find the value of N rounded to 3 significant digits.

  3. $\ln N = 2.9$ **4.** $\ln N = -4.75$

Use the change of base formula to evaluate the following.

  5. $\log_7 9$ **6.** $\log_5 0.796$

Solve for the variable.

  7. $\ln x - \ln 2 + \ln(x - 1) = 0$ **8.** $\ln 8 - \ln x = 5 \cdot \ln 2$

9. $20 = 40 \cdot e^{-0.5t}$ **10.** $180 = 90 \cdot e^{3t}$

11. How much money must be deposited today to become \$40,000 in 16 years if invested at 5% compounded continuously?

12. The atmospheric pressure, P, in pounds per square inch, at an elevation of x feet above sea level can be found by the formula $P = 14.7 \cdot e^{-0.0004x}$. Find the atmospheric pressure at an elevation of 1 mile (5,280 feet).

Answers to Exercise Set 9.7

1. 5.984	**2.** −5.534	**3.** 18.174
4. 0.009	**5.** 1.129	**6.** −0.142
7. $x = 2$	**8.** $\dfrac{1}{4} = x$	**9.** $t = 1.386$
10. $t = 0.231$	**11.** $p = \$17{,}973.16$	**12.** Pressure is 1.78 pounds

Chapter 9 Practice Test

Graph the following functions.

1. $y = 2^{-x}$ **2.** $y = \log_{1/2}(x)$

Write in logarithmic form.

3. $6^3 = 216$ **4.** $16^{1/4} = 2$

Write in exponential form.

5. $\log_7 2401 = 4$ **6.** $\log_8 2 = \dfrac{1}{3}$

Use the properties of logarithms to expand each expression below.

7. $\log_4(5 \cdot 6)$ **8.** $\log_3\left(\dfrac{5}{8}\right)$

9. $\log_7 5^4$ **10.** $\log_6\left(\dfrac{x}{xy}\right)$

Solve for the variable.

11. $3 = \log_4 x\ 1$ **12.** $\log x = 2.3304$

13. $10^{\log_{10} 3} = x$ **14.** $27^x = 3^{2x+5}$

Evaluate.

15. a. log 7.96   **b.** antilog of 2.347

Solve for the variable.

16. $\log_3 x + \log_3(2x+1) = 1$ **17.** $4^x = 37$

18. If $10,000 is placed in an account paying 7% interest compounded continuously, find the time needed for the account to double in value.

19. Find the inverse of $f(x) = 2x - 7$.

20. Let $f(x) = x^2 + 10x - 5$ and $g(x) = 2x - 1$. Find $(f + g)(x)$ and $(g + f)(x)$.

Answers to Chapter 9 Practice Test

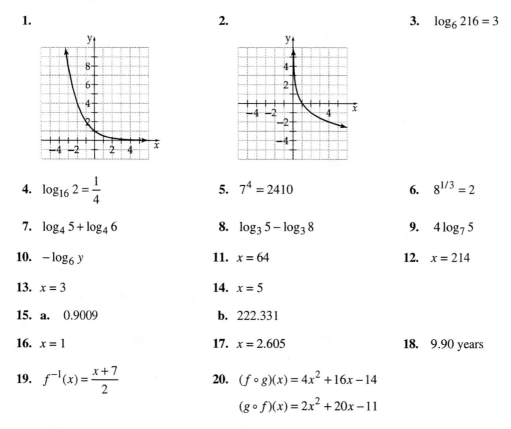

1.   **2.**   **3.** $\log_6 216 = 3$

4. $\log_{16} 2 = \dfrac{1}{4}$ **5.** $7^4 = 2410$ **6.** $8^{1/3} = 2$

7. $\log_4 5 + \log_4 6$ **8.** $\log_3 5 - \log_3 8$ **9.** $4 \log_7 5$

10. $-\log_6 y$ **11.** $x = 64$ **12.** $x = 214$

13. $x = 3$ **14.** $x = 5$

15. a. 0.9009   **b.** 222.331

16. $x = 1$ **17.** $x = 2.605$ **18.** 9.90 years

19. $f^{-1}(x) = \dfrac{x+7}{2}$ **20.** $(f \circ g)(x) = 4x^2 + 16x - 14$

$(g \circ f)(x) = 2x^2 + 20x - 11$

CHAPTER 9 SUMMARY

IMPORTANT FACTS

<table>
<tr><td>

Definition of a Logarithm

$y = \log_a x$ *means* $x = a^y$

</td><td>

Change of Base Formula

$\log_a x = \dfrac{\log_b x}{\log_b a}$

</td></tr>
</table>

Composite and Inverse Functions

- Composite function of f with g: $(f \circ g)(x) = f[g(x)]$

- Composite function of g with f: $(g \circ f)(x) = g[f(x)]$

- If $f(x)$ and $g(x)$ are inverse functions, then $(f \circ g)(x) = (g \circ f)(x) = x$

- $y = a^x$ and $y = \log_a x$ are inverse functions. Therefore, if $f(x) = a^x$, then $f^{-1}(x) = \log_a x$.

- $y = e^x$ and $y = \ln x$ are inverse functions. Therefore, if $f(x) = e^x$, then $f^{-1}(x) = \ln x$.

Exponential Functions Compared with Logarithmic Functions

	__Exponential Function__	__Logarithmic Function__
	$y = a^x,\ a > 0$ and $a \neq 1$	$y = \log_a x,\ a > 0$ and $x \neq 0$
Domain:	$(-\infty, \infty)$	$(0, \infty)$
Range:	$(0, \infty)$	$(-\infty, \infty)$
Points:	$\left(-1, \dfrac{1}{a}\right)$	$\left(\dfrac{1}{a}, -1\right)$
	$(0, 1)$	$(1, 0)$
	$(1, a)$	$(a, 1)$

x becomes *y*
y becomes *x*

Properties of Logarithms and Natural Logarithms

- $\log_a xy = \log_a x + \log_a y$

- $\log_a \dfrac{x}{y} = \log_a x - \log_a y$

- $\log_a x^n = n \log_a x$

- $\log_a a^x = x$

- $a^{\log_a x} = x \ \ (x > 0)$

- $\ln e^x = x$

- $e^{\ln x} = x \ \ (x > 0)$

Properties of Logarithms Used to Solve Exponential and Logarithmic Equations

- If $x = y$, then $a^x = a^y$.

- If $a^x = a^y$, then $x = y$.

- If $x = y$, then $\log_b x = \log_b y \ \ (x > 0, y > 0)$.

- If $\log_b x = \log_b y$, then $x = y \ \ (x > 0, y > 0)$.

HELPFUL HINTS

- Be careful not to confuse the product of two functions with a composite function.

    □ Product of functions f and g: When multiplying functions f and g, a dot is used between the f and g, such as $(f \cdot g)(x)$ or $(fg)(x)$.

    □ Composite function of f with g: When finding the composite function of f with g, a small open circle is used between the f and g, such as $(f \circ g)(x)$.

- When expanding logarithms, be careful which rule you apply first.

    □ When expanding $\log_3 \dfrac{(x-6)^2}{3}$, you would use the quotient rule first since **just the numerator** of the argument is squared.

    □ When expanding $\log_3 \left(\dfrac{x-6}{3} \right)^2$, you would use the power rule first because the **entire argument** is squared.

- Using either exponential form or the antilog to solve a logarithmic equation:

    □ If a logarithmic equation is written in base 10, it is more easily solved using the antilog. For example: $\log \dfrac{2x+6}{x} = 2.1$. Taking the antilog of both sides would give you $\dfrac{2x+6}{x} = \text{antilog } 2.1$. You would then solve for x.

    □ If a logarithmic equation is not written in base 10, you cannot use the antilog. You would solve the equation by first writing it in exponential form. For example: $\log_5(x+2)^3 = 4$ would be rewritten as $(x+2)^3 = 5^4$ and then solved for x.

AVOIDING COMMON ERRORS

- Be careful when expanding logarithms or writing a logarithm as a single expression:

<u>Correct Rules</u>	<u>Please Note</u>
$\log_a xy = \log_a x + \log_a y$ $\log_a \dfrac{x}{y} = \log_a x - \log_a y$	$\log_a(x+y) \neq \log_a x + \log_a y$ $\log_a(x-y) \neq \log_a x - \log_a y$ $\log_a(xy) \neq (\log_a x)(\log_a y)$ $\log_a(x/y) \neq \dfrac{\log_a x}{\log_a y}$

Chapter 10

10.1 The Parabola and the Circle

Summary

Parabola with Vertex at (h, k)

1. $y = a(x - h)^2 + k, \; a > 0$
   (opens upward)

2. $y = a(x - h)^2 + k, \; a < 0$
   (opens downward)

3. $x = a(y - k)^2 + h, \; a > 0$
   (opens to the right)

4. $x = a(y - k)^2 + h, \; a < 0$
   (opens to the left)

Example 1
Sketch the graph of $y = 2(x + 1)^2 - 3$.

Solution
This is of the form of equation 1 $(a = 2 > 0)$.
Therefore, vertex is at $(-1, -3)$ and it opens upward.

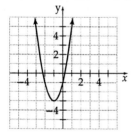

Example 2
Sketch the graph of $y = -2x^2 + 4x - 3$.

Solution
First, factor -2 from the from the two terms containing the variable to make the coefficient of the squared term equal to 1.
$y = -2(x^2 - 2x) - 3$

Now add $\left(\dfrac{2}{2}\right)^2 = (1)^2 = 1$ to complete the square. Since the added 1 must be multiplied by –2, we are really adding $(-2)(1) = -2$.

Therefore, add +2 to the –3 to keep the equation the same.

$y = \underline{-2}(x^2 - 2x + \underline{1}) - 3 + \underline{2}$

$y = -2(x - 1)^2 - 1$

The parabola opens downward since $a = -2 < 0$ and the vertex is at $(1, -1)$.

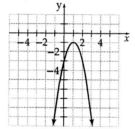

Example 3

Sketch the graph of $x = y^2 - 4y + 1$.

Solution

First we complete the square for $y^2 - 4y$ by adding $\left(\dfrac{4}{2}\right)^2 = 4$. We must add –4 to 1 to keep the equation the same.

$x = (y^2 - 4y + 4) + 1 - 4$

$x = (y - 2)^2 - 3$

This is of the form of equation 3, $a = 1 > 0$. Therefore, it opens to the right and the vertex is at $(-3, 2)$.

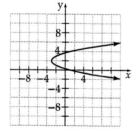

Summary

Circle with its Center at the Origin and Radius r

$$x^2 + y^2 = r^2$$

Example 4
Write the equation of a circle with center at (0, 0) and radius 4.

Solution
The radius 4 should be substituted into the equaton for r.
$$x^2 + y^2 = r^2$$
$$x^2 + y^2 = 4^2$$
$$x^2 + y^2 = 16$$

Example 5
Sketch a graph of the equation $x^2 + y^2 = 25$.

Solution
Write $x^2 + y^2 = 25$
$$x^2 + y^2 = 5^2$$
It is a circle with center at the origin and radius 5.

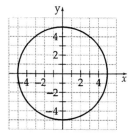

Summary

Circle with its Center at (h, k) with Radius r
$$(x - h)^2 + (y - k)^2 = r^2$$

Example 6
Write the equation of the circle with center at (2, −1) and radius 3.

Solution
Substitute $h = 2$, $k = -1$, and $r = 3$ into the equation.
$$(x - 2)^2 + (y - (-1))^2 = 3^2$$
$$(x - 2)^2 + (y + 1)^2 = 9$$

Example 7

Sketch a graph of the equation of $x^2 - 4x + y^2 + 2y - 11 = 0$.

Solution

Since the coefficients of x^2 and y^2 are equal (in this case, 1), we know we have the equation of a circle. Rewrite the equation by keeping the variables on the left side of the equation and moving the constant to the right side.

$$x^2 - 4x + y^2 + 2y = 11$$

Complete the square for each variable.

$$x^2 - 4x + \underline{4} + y^2 + 2y + \underline{1} = 11 + \underline{4} + \underline{1}$$
$$(x - 2)^2 + (y + 1)^2 = 16$$
$$(x - 2)^2 + (y - (-1))^2 = 4^2$$

So the center is at $(2, -1)$ and the radius is 4.

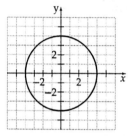

Exercise Set 10.1

Sketch the graph of each equation.

1. $y = -(x - 2)^2 + 4$ **2.** $y = 3(x + 1)^2 + 2$

3. $x = (y + 3)^2 - 1$ **4.** $x = -2(y - 2)^2 + 5$

Write each equation in the form $y = a(x - h)^2 + k$ or $x = a(y - k)^2 + h$ and then sketch the graph of the equation.

5. $y = -2x^2 + 4x$ **6.** $y = x^2 - 4x + 2$

7. $x = -2y^2 + 12y - 13$ **8.** $x = y^2 + 2y$

Write the equation of the circle with the given center and radius.

9. Center $(0, 0)$; radius 6   **10.** Center $(0, 0)$; radius $\sqrt{3}$

11. Center $(3, 5)$; radius 5   **12.** Center $(-2, 5)$; radius $\sqrt{10}$

Write the equation of the circle in standard form. Determine its center and radius. Then sketch a graph.

13. $x^2 + y^2 - 4 = 0$

14. $2x^2 + 2y^2 - 2 = 0$

15. $x^2 + y^2 + 2x + 4y - 4 = 0$

16. $x^2 + y^2 - 8x - 6y = 0$

17. $x^2 + y^2 + 12x - 2y + 1 = 0$

18. $x^2 + y^2 - 10x + 2y + 10 = 0$

Answers to Exercise Set 10.1

1.

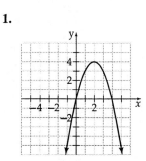

2.

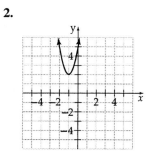

3.

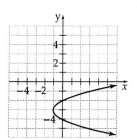

4.

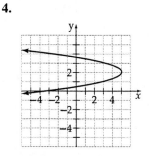

5. $y = -2(x-1)^2 + 2$

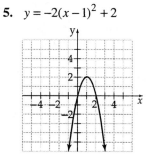

6. $y = (x-2)^2 - 2$

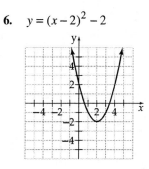

7. $x = -2(y-3)^2 + 5$

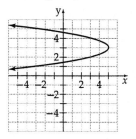

8. $x = (y+1)^2 - 1$

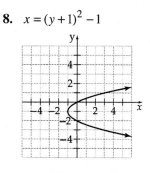

9. $x^2 + y^2 = 36$

10. $x^2 + y^2 = 3$

11. $(x-3)^2 + (y-5)^2 = 25$

12. $(x+2)^2 + (y-5)^2 = 10$

13. $x^2 + y^2 = 4$; center (0, 0); radius 2

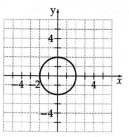

14. $x^2 + y^2 = 1$; center (0, 0); radius 1

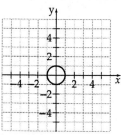

15. $(x+1)^2 + (y+2)^2 = 9$; center (−1, −2); radius 3

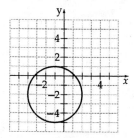

16. $(x-4)^2 + (y-3)^2 = 25$; center (4, 3); radius 5

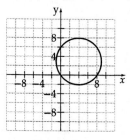

17. $(x+6)^2 + (y-1)^2 = 36$; center $(-6, 1)$; radius 6

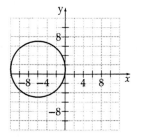

18. $(x-5)^2 + (y+1)^2 = 16$; center $(5, -1)$; radius 4

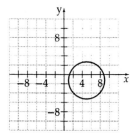

10.2 The Ellipse

Summary

Ellipse with Its Center at the Origin

$\dfrac{x^2}{a^2} + \dfrac{y^2}{b^2} = 1$, where $(a, 0)$ and $(-a, 0)$ are the

x-intercepts and $(0, b)$ and $(0, -b)$ are the y-intercepts.

Example 1

Sketch the graph of $\dfrac{x^2}{16} + \dfrac{y^2}{9} = 1$.

Solution

Rewrite $\dfrac{x^2}{16}+\dfrac{y^2}{19}=1$ as $\dfrac{x^2}{4^2}+\dfrac{y^2}{3^2}=1$.

The *x*-intercepts are –4 and 4. The *y*-intercepts are –3 and 3.

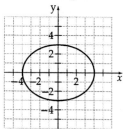

Example 2

Sketch the graph of $9x^2+4y^2=36$.

Solution

Divide each side of the equation by 36.

$$\dfrac{9x^2}{36}+\dfrac{4y^2}{36}=\dfrac{36}{36}=\dfrac{x^2}{4}+\dfrac{y^2}{9}=1=\dfrac{x^2}{2^2}+\dfrac{y^2}{3^2}=1$$

The *x*-intercepts are –2 and 2. The *y*-intercepts are –3 and 3.

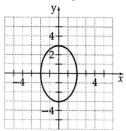

Exercise Set 10.2

Sketch the graph of each equation.

1. $\dfrac{x^2}{4}+\dfrac{y^2}{25}=1$ 2. $\dfrac{x^2}{9}+\dfrac{y^2}{50}=1$ 3. $2x^2+8y^2=32$

4. $4x^2+25y^2=100$ 5. $4x^2+y^2=1$

Answers to Exercise Set 10.2

1.
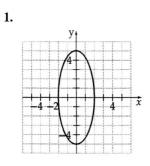

2.
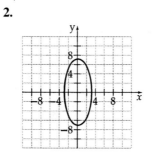

3.
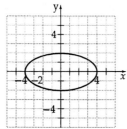

4.
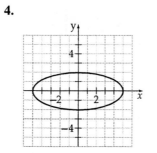

5.
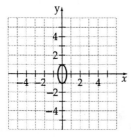

10.3 The Hyperbola

Summary

Hyperbola with its Center at the Origin

Transverse axis along x-axis (opens to right and left)

$$\frac{x^2}{a^2} - \frac{y^2}{b^2} = 1$$

Transverse axis along y-axis (opens upward and downward)

$$\frac{y^2}{b^2} - \frac{x^2}{a^2} = 1$$

Asymptotes

$$y = \frac{b}{a}x \text{ and } y = -\frac{b}{a}x$$

This may be given as $y = \pm\frac{b}{a}x$.

Example 1

Consider the equation $\dfrac{x^2}{4} - \dfrac{y^2}{9} = 1$.

  a. Determine the equation of the asymptotes of the hyperbola.

  b. Sketch the hyperbola using the asymptotes.

Solution

  a. Here, $a^2 = 4$ and $b^2 = 9$, so $a = 2$ and $b = 3$.

    Using $y = \dfrac{b}{a}x$ and $y = -\dfrac{b}{a}x$, we have $y = \dfrac{3}{2}x$ and $y = -\dfrac{3}{2}x$.

b. First graph the asymptotes. Since the x term is positive, the transverse axis is along the x-axis. The denominator of the x term is positive, thus the x-intercepts are $\pm\sqrt{4}$ or ± 2.

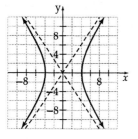

Example 2

Consider $4y^2 - 16x^2 = 64$.

　　a. Show that the equation is a hyperbola by expressing the equation in standard form.

　　b. Determine the asymptotes and sketch a graph.

Solution

　　a. Divide both sides by 64 to obtain 1 on the right side:

$$\frac{4y^2}{64} - \frac{16x^2}{64} = \frac{64}{64}$$

$$\frac{y^2}{16} - \frac{x^2}{4} = 1$$

　　b. Here $b^2 = 16$ so $b = 4$ and $a^2 = 4$ so $a = 2$. The asymptotes are $y = \pm\dfrac{4}{2}x = \pm 2x.$

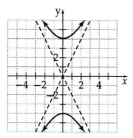

Summary

Another form of the hyperbola is $xy = c$, where c is a nonzero constant.

Example 3
Sketch the graph of $xy = 1$.

Solution

$xy = 1$ or $y = \dfrac{1}{x}$. We will make a table with x values less than zero and a similar table with x values greater than zero.

x	y	x	y
-4	$-\frac{1}{4}$	4	$\frac{1}{4}$
-2	$-\frac{1}{2}$	2	$\frac{1}{2}$
-1	-1	1	1
$-\frac{1}{2}$	-2	$\frac{1}{2}$	2
$-\frac{1}{4}$	-4	$\frac{1}{4}$	4
$-\frac{1}{8}$	-8	$\frac{1}{8}$	8

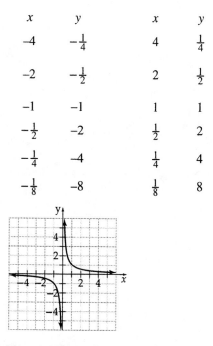

Exercise Set 10.3

Determine the equations of the asymptotes and sketch a graph of the equation.

1. $\dfrac{x^2}{4} - \dfrac{y^2}{36} = 1$

2. $\dfrac{x^2}{25} - \dfrac{y^2}{25} = 1$

3. $\dfrac{y^2}{36} - \dfrac{x^2}{49} = 1$

4. $\dfrac{y^2}{16} - \dfrac{x^2}{1} = 1$

Write each equation in standard form, determine the equation of the asymptotes, and then sketch the graph.

5. $25x^2 - 4y^2 = 100$

6. $9x^2 - 4y^2 = 36$

7. $4x^2 - y^2 = 4$

8. $10y^2 - 90x^2 = 90$

Sketch a graph of the equation.

9. $xy = 8$

10. $y = -\dfrac{2}{x}$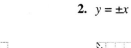

Answers to Exercise Set 10.3

1. $y = \pm 3x$

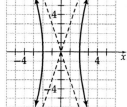

2. $y = \pm x$

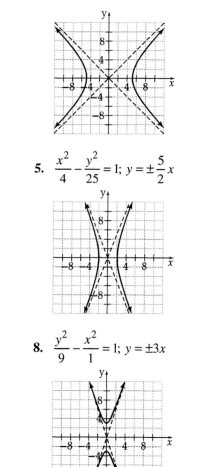

3. $y = \pm \dfrac{6}{7}x$

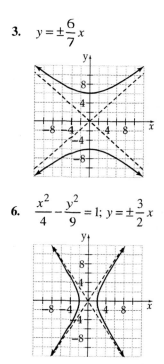

4. $y = \pm 4x$

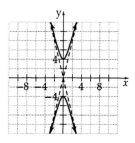

5. $\dfrac{x^2}{4} - \dfrac{y^2}{25} = 1$; $y = \pm \dfrac{5}{2}x$

6. $\dfrac{x^2}{4} - \dfrac{y^2}{9} = 1$; $y = \pm \dfrac{3}{2}x$

7. $\dfrac{x^2}{1} - \dfrac{y^2}{4} = 1$; $y = \pm 2x$

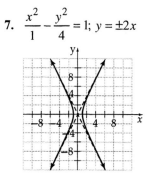

8. $\dfrac{y^2}{9} - \dfrac{x^2}{1} = 1$; $y = \pm 3x$

9.

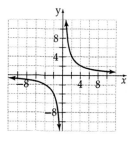

10.

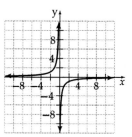

10.4 Nonlinear Systems of Equations and Their Applications

Summary

A **system of nonlinear equations** is a system of equations in which at least one equation is not a linear equation (that is, one whose graph is not a straight line).

One approach to solving a system of nonlinear equations is to graph its equation and determine the intersection of the graphs.

Example 1
Solve the system of equations graphically.
$$x^2 + y^2 = 4$$
$$x - y = 2$$

Solution
Graph each equation on the same axes and determine the intersection.

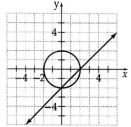

From the graph, the intersection is $(2, 0)$ and $(0, -2)$.

Check: $(2, 0)$: $x^2 + y^2 = 4$ $x - y = 2$
                $2^2 + 0^2 = 4$ $2 - 0 = 2$
                $4 + 0 = 4$ $2 = 2$ is true.
                    $4 = 4$ is true.

Check: $(0, -2)$: $x^2 + y^2 = 4$ $x - y = 2$
                 $0 + (-2)^2 = 4$ $0 - (-2) = 2$
                 $0 + 4 = 4$ $2 = 2$ is true.
                     $4 = 4$ is true.

Summary

> To solve a system of equations algebraically, we often solve one or more of the equations for one of the variables and then use substitute.

Example 2
Solve the system of equations algebraically using substitution.
$$2x^2 + y^2 = 9$$
$$2x - y = 3$$

Solution
Solve the linear equation for x or y. We select to solve for y (since its coefficient is -1).
$$2x - y = 3$$
$$-y = -2x + 3$$
$$y = 2x - 3$$

Substitute $y = 2x - 3$ for y in the equation $x^2 + y^2 = 9$ and solve for the remaining variable.
$$x^2 + y^2 = 9$$
$$x^2 + (2x - 3)^2 = 9$$
$$x^2 + 4x^2 - 12x + 9 = 9$$
$$5x^2 - 12x = 0$$
$$x(5x - 12) = 0$$
$$x = 0 \quad \text{or} \quad 5x - 12 = 0$$
$$5x = 12$$
$$x = \frac{12}{5}$$

Next, find the corresponding value of y by substituting each value of x in the equation solved for y.
If $x = 0$, and $y = 2x - 3$, then $y = 2(0) - 3 = -3$ so $(0, -3)$ is a solution.
If $x = \dfrac{12}{5}$, and $y = 2x - 3$, then $y = \dfrac{24}{5} - 3 = \dfrac{9}{5}$ so $\left(\dfrac{12}{5}, \dfrac{9}{5} \right)$ is a solution.

Summary

> We can often solve systems of equations more easily using the addition method that was discussed in section 4.1. As with the substitution method, our objective is to obtain a single equation containing only one variable.

Example 3
Solve the system of equations using the addition method.
$$x^2 + y^2 = 26$$
$$x^2 - y^2 = 24$$

Solution
We can eliminate a variable by adding the two equations together.

$x^2 + y^2 = 26$
$x^2 - y^2 = 24$

$\quad 2x^2 = 50$

$\quad\quad x^2 = 25$

$\quad\quad x = \pm\sqrt{25} = \pm 5$

Finally, find the corresponding y values by substituting into the equation $x^2 + y^2 = 26$ and solving for y.
If $x = 5$, then $(5)^2 + y^2 = 26$

$\quad\quad\quad 25 + y^2 = 26$

$\quad\quad\quad\quad\quad y^2 = 1$

$\quad\quad\quad\quad\quad y = \pm 1$

Thus $(5, 1)$ and $(5, -1)$ are two ordered pair solutions.
If $x = -5$, then $(-5)^2 + y^2 = 26$

$\quad\quad\quad 25 + y^2 = 26$

$\quad\quad\quad\quad\quad y^2 = 1$

$\quad\quad\quad\quad\quad y = \pm 1$

So $(-5, 1)$ and $(-5, -1)$ are also solutions.
There are four solutions: $(5, 1)$, $(5, -1)$, $(-5, 1)$, $(-5, -1)$.

Example 4
The area of a rectangle is 30 square feet. The perimeter is 26 feet. Find the length and width of the rectangle.

Solution
Let l = length of the rectangle and w = width of the rectangle.
Since the area of a rectangle is length times width, one equation is $lw = 30$.
The perimeter of a rectangle is the sum of twice the length and twice the width, thus a second equation is $2l + 2w = 26$.
Now, solve the system: $lw = 30$
$\quad\quad\quad\quad\quad\quad\quad 2l + 2w = 26$
Solving the second equation for l we obtain
$2l + 2w = 26$

$\quad 2l = 26 - 2w$

$\quad\quad l = 13 - w$

Substituting that expression for l in the first equation, we obtain
$\quad\quad\quad lw = 30$

$(13 - w)(w) = 30$

$\quad 13w - w^2 = 30$

$\quad\quad\quad\quad 0 = w^2 - 13w + 30$

$\quad\quad\quad\quad 0 = (w - 10)(w - 3)$

$w - 10 = 0 \quad$ or $\quad w - 3 = 0$

$\quad\quad w = 10 \quad$ or $\quad\quad\quad w = 3$

If $w = 10$,   If $w = 3$
$l = 13 - w$ $l = 13 - w$
$l = 13 - 10 = 3$ $l = 13 - 3$
                                      $l = 10$
So the dimensions of the rectangle are 3 feet by 10 feet.

Exercise Set 10.4

Solve the system of equations by the substitution method.

1. $y = x^2 + 2x$ **2.** $y = x^2 - 4x + 4$
   $y = x$ $x + y = 2$

3. $x^2 + y^2 = 1$ **4.** $x - y = 2$
   $x + 2y = 1$ $x^2 - y^2 = 16$

Solve the system of equations using the addition method.

5. $x^2 + y^2 = 4$ **6.** $2x^2 + 3y^2 = 6$
   $x^2 - y^2 = 4$ $x^2 + 3y^2 = 3$

7. $5x^2 - 2y^2 = -13$ **8.** $4x^2 + 4y^2 = 16$
   $3x^2 + 4y^2 = 39$ $2x^2 + 3y^2 = 5$

9. The area of a rectangle is 84 square feet. The perimeter is 38 feet. Find the dimensions of the rectangle.

Answers to Exercise Set 10.4

1. (0, 0), (–1, –1)   **2.** (2, 0), (1, 1)   **3.** $(1, 0), \left(-\dfrac{3}{5}, \dfrac{4}{5}\right)$

4. (5, 3)   **5.** (2, 0), (–2, 0)   **6.** $\left(\sqrt{3}, 0\right), \left(-\sqrt{3}, 0\right)$

7. (1, 3), (1, –3), (–1, 3), (–1, –3)

8. No real solution   **9.** 7 feet by 12 feet

Chapter 10 Practice Test

1. Write the equation of the circle with the center at (–2, 4) and radius 5.

2. Write the equation in standard form. The, sketch the graph.
   $x^2 + y^2 - 4x + 8y - 5 = 0$

3. Sketch the graph of $9x^2 + 25y^2 = 225$.

4. Sketch the graph of $y = -3(x + 2)^2 - 4$.

5. Sketch the graph of $x = y^2 + 4y + 3$.

6. Sketch the graph of $\dfrac{y^2}{9} - \dfrac{x^2}{81} = 1$.

7. Sketch the graph of $y = -\dfrac{6}{x}$.

8. Solve the system of equations.
$$4x^2 - y^2 = 7$$
$$y = 2x^2 - 3$$

9. Solve the system of equations.
$$6x^2 + y^2 = 9$$
$$3x^2 + 4y^2 = 36$$

10. The product of two numbers is 65. Their sum is 18. Find the numbers.

Answers to Chapter 10 Practice Test

1. $(x+2)^2 + (y-4)^2 = 25$ **2.** $(x-2)^2 + (y+4)^2 = 25$ **3.**

4.   **5.**   **6.**

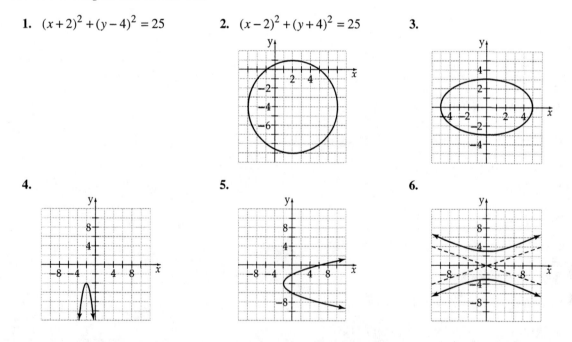

7.

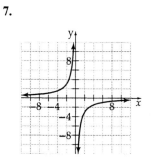

8. $\left(\sqrt{2}, 1\right), \left(-\sqrt{2}, 1\right)$

9. $(0, 3), (0, -3)$

10. 5 and 13

CHAPTER 10 SUMMARY

IMPORTANT FACTS

Distance Formula
$d = \sqrt{\left(x_2 - x_1\right)^2 + \left(y_2 - y_1\right)^2}$

Midpoint Formula
$\left(\dfrac{x_1 + x_2}{2}, \dfrac{y_1 + y_2}{2}\right)$

Circle
$\left(x - h\right)^2 + \left(y - k\right)^2 = r^2$
center at (h, k)
radius r

Ellipse
$\dfrac{\left(x - h\right)^2}{a^2} + \dfrac{\left(y - k\right)^2}{b^2} = 1$
center at (h, k)

- **Parabola Information**

$$y = a(x - h)^2 + k \qquad\qquad\qquad x = a(y - k)^2 + h$$

<table>
<tr><td align="center">vertex at (h, k)
opens upward when a > 0
opens downward when a < 0</td><td align="center">vertex at (h, k)
opens to the right when a > 0
opens to the left when a < 0</td></tr>
</table>

- **Hyperbola Information**

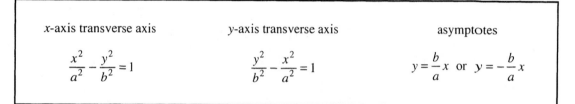

x-axis transverse axis y-axis transverse axis   asymptotes

$$\frac{x^2}{a^2} - \frac{y^2}{b^2} = 1 \qquad\qquad \frac{y^2}{b^2} - \frac{x^2}{a^2} = 1 \qquad\qquad y = \frac{b}{a}x \ \text{ or } \ y = -\frac{b}{a}x$$

HELPFUL HINTS

- When solving nonlinear systems of equations, you use the same methods (substitution method and addition method) as used to solve linear systems of equations. You may find it helpful to go back and review these methods which were introduced in Chapter 4.

- When solving a nonlinear system of equations, make sure that you solve for both variables in order to get an ordered pair solution. In addition, remember that the solution to a system in two variables (if one exists) may consist of *more than one* ordered pair.

AVOIDING COMMON ERRORS

- When using the distance formula, $d = \sqrt{(x_2 - x_1)^2 + (y_2 - y_1)^2}$, make sure that you complete every step. Don't forget the step of taking the square root. Also remember, $\sqrt{a^2 + b^2} \neq a + b$.

Chapter 11

11.1 Sequences and Series

Summary

Sequences

A **sequence (or progression)** of numbers is a list of numbers arranged in a specific order.

An **infinite sequence** is a function whose domain is the set of natural numbers.

A **finite sequence** is a function whose domain includes only the first n natural numbers.

Example 1

Write the first five terms of the sequence $a_n = n^2 - 2$.

Solution

$$a_1 = 1^2 - 2 = -1$$
$$a_2 = 2^2 - 2 = 2$$
$$a_3 = 3^2 - 2 = 7$$
$$a_4 = 4^2 - 2 = 14$$
$$a_5 = 5^2 - 2 = 23$$

Example 2

For the sequence $a_n = \dfrac{2n}{n+1}$, find

   a. the tenth term in the sequence.

   b. the fifteenth term in the sequence.

Solution

   a. For the tenth term, $n = 10$. So $a_{10} = \dfrac{2(10)}{10+1} = \dfrac{20}{11}$.

   b. For the fifteenth term, $n = 15$. Thus, $a_{15} = \dfrac{2(15)}{15+1} = \dfrac{30}{16} = \dfrac{15}{8}$.

Summary

Series

A **series** is the sum of the terms of a sequence. A **series** may be finite or infinite depending upon whether the sequence it is based on is finite or infinite.

A **partial sum of a series** is the sum of a finite number of consecutive terms of the series, beginning with the first term.

Example 3
Given the sequence $a_n = 2n - 1$, find the first, third, and fifth partial sum.

Solution
For the first partial sum, we need $a_1 = 2(1) - 1 = 1$, $s_1 = 1$.
For the third partial sum, we need $a_1 = 2(1) - 1 = 1$, $a_2 = 2(2) - 1 = 3$ and $a_3 = 2(3) - 1 = 5$.
Now, $s_3 = 1 + 3 + 5 = 9$.
For the fifth partial sum, we need $a_1 = 1$, $a_2 = 3$, $a_3 = 5$, $a_4 = 7$, and $a_5 = 9$. $s_5 = 1 + 3 + 5 + 7 + 9 = 25$.

Summary

A $\sum$ symbol is used to indicate which terms of a finite series are to be added.

Example 4
Write out the series and then find the sum of the series.

$$\sum_{k=1}^{4} (k^2 + 2)$$

Solution
Make a table:

k	$k^2 + 2$
1	$1^2 + 2 = 3$
2	$2^2 + 2 = 6$
3	$3^2 + 2 = 11$
4	$4^2 + 2 = 18$

$$\sum_{k=1}^{4}(k^2 + 2) = 3 + 6 + 11 + 18 = 38$$

Exercise Set 11.1

Write the first five terms of the sequence whose nth term is shown.

1. $a_n = 3n$

2. $a_n = n^2 + 5$

3. $a_n = \dfrac{2n}{n+1}$

Find the indicated term of the sequence whose nth term is shown.

4. $a_n = 4n - 3$; sixth term

5. $a_n = \dfrac{n^2}{n^2 + 1}$; fifth term

6. $a_n = (-1)n^3$; fourth term

Find the first, second, and fourth partial sums for the given sequence.

7. $a_n = 3n - 4$

8. $a_n = 2n^2 - 10$

9. $a_n = \left(\dfrac{1}{2}\right)^n$

Write out the series, and then find the sum of the series.

10. $\displaystyle\sum_{k=1}^{3}(2k + 3)$

11. $\displaystyle\sum_{k=1}^{5}\dfrac{k-1}{k}$

12. $\displaystyle\sum_{n=1}^{4}\dfrac{n(n+1)}{2}$

Answers to Exercise Set 11.1

1. 3, 6, 9, 12, 15

2. 6, 9, 14, 21, 30

3. $1, \dfrac{4}{3}, \dfrac{3}{2}, \dfrac{8}{5}, \dfrac{5}{3}$

4. $a_6 = 21$

5. $a_5 = \dfrac{25}{26}$

6. $a_4 = -64$

7. $s_1 = -1$; $s_2 = 1$; $s_4 = 14$

8. $s_1 = -8$; $s_2 = -10$; $s_4 = 20$

9. $s_1 = \dfrac{1}{2}$; $s_2 = \dfrac{3}{4}$; $s_4 = \dfrac{15}{16}$

10. $5 + 7 + 9 = 21$ **11.** $0 + \dfrac{1}{2} + \dfrac{2}{3} + \dfrac{3}{4} + \dfrac{4}{5} = \dfrac{163}{60}$ **12.** $1 + 3 + 6 + 10 = 20$

11.2 Arithmetic Sequences and Series

Summary

Arithmetic Sequence

A sequence in which each term after the first differs from the preceding term by a constant number is called an **arithmetic sequence** or **arithmetic progression.**

The constant amount by which each pair of successive terms differs is called the **common difference.**

nth term of an arithmetic sequence is
$a_n = a_1 + (n-1)d.$

Example 1

    a. Write an expression for the general or nth term a_n, of the arithmetic sequence whose first term is 5 and whose common difference is –2.

    b. Find the tenth term of that sequence.

Solution

    a. Use $a_n = a_1 + (n-1)d$, with $a_1 = 5$ and $d = -2$.
$$a_n = 5 + (n-1)(-2)$$
$$a_n = 5 - 2n + 2$$
$$a_n = 7 - 2n$$

    b. Use $a_n = 7 - 2n$ with $n = 10$: $a_{10} = 7 - 2(10) = -13$.

Example 2
Find the number of terms in the arithmetic sequence 11, 16, 21, …, 121.

Solution
The first term, a_1, is 11. The common difference, d, is 5. The nth term, a_n, is 121.
$$a_n = a_1 + (n-1)d$$
$$121 = 11 + (n-1)5$$
$$121 = 11 + 5n - 5$$
$$121 = 6 + 5n$$
$$115 = 5n$$
$$23 = n$$
The sequence has 23 terms.

Summary

---

nth Partial Sum of an Arithmetic Sequence

$$s_n = \frac{n(a_1 + a_n)}{2}$$

Example 3

Find the sum of the first 10 terms of the arithmetic sequence 4, 7, 10, …

Solution

Use $s_n = \dfrac{n(a_1 + a_n)}{2}$. First, find a_n using $a_1 = 4$, $d = 3$ and $n = 10$.

$a_{10} = 4 + (10 - 1)(3) = 4 + 9(3) = 31$

Now, $s_{10} = \dfrac{10(4 + 31)}{2} = \dfrac{(10)(35)}{2} = 175$

Example 4

The first term of an arithmetic series is 1. The last term is 21. If $s_n = 121$, find the number of terms in the sequence and the common difference.

Solution

$a_1 = 1$, $a_n = 21$, $s_n = 121$

$s = \dfrac{n(a_1 + a_n)}{2}$

$121 = \dfrac{n(1 + 21)}{2} = \dfrac{n(22)}{2}$

$121 = 11n$

$n = 11$

There are 11 terms in the sequence.

Now,

$a_n = a_1 + (n - 1)d$

$21 = 1 + (11 - 1)d$

$21 = 1 + 10d$

$20 = 10d$

$2 = d$

The common difference is 2.

Example 5

If a person has a starting salary of $1,000 per month and receives a $20 raise each month, how much will have been earned in total at the end of 12 months?

Solution

Here, $a_1 = 1000$, $n = 12$, $d = 20$.

First, determine a_{12}.

$a_{12} = a_1 + (n-1)d$

$a_{12} = 1000 + (12-1)20$

$a_{12} = 1000 + 11(20)$

$a_{12} = 1220$

Now, use $s_n = \dfrac{n(a_1 + a_n)}{2} = \dfrac{12(1000 + 1220)}{2} = \dfrac{12(2220)}{2} = 13,320.$

A total of $13,320 will have been earned.

Exercise Set 11.2

Write the first five terms and an expression for the nth term of the arithmetic sequence with the given first term and common difference.

1. $a_1 = 1$, $d = -2$ **2.** $a_1 = -9$, $d = 3$ **3.** $a_1 = 3$, $d = \dfrac{3}{4}$

Find the desired quantity of the arithmetic sequence.

4. $a_1 = 4$, $d = 3$, find a_{25}.   **5.** $a_1 = 5$, $d = 4$, $a_n = 77$, find n.   **6.** $a_1 = 2$, $a_{24} = 48$, find d.

Find the sum, s_n, and the common difference, d.

7. $a_1 = 4$, $a_n = 28$, $n = 7$ **8.** $a_1 = 3$, $a_n = -84$, $n = 30$

9. A seating section in a theater-in-the-round has 20 seats in the front row, 22 in the second row, 24 in the third row and so on for 25 rows. How many seats are there in the last row? How many seats are there in the section?

Answers to Exercise Set 11.2

1. $1, -1, -3, -5, -7$; $a_n = 3 - 2n$

2. $-9, -6, -3, 0, 3$; $a_n = 3n - 12$

3. $3, \dfrac{15}{4}, \dfrac{9}{2}, \dfrac{21}{4}, 6$; $a_n = \dfrac{9}{4} + \dfrac{3}{4}n$

4. 76   **5.** 19   **6.** 2

7. $d = 4$; $s_7 = 112$ **8.** $d = -3$; $s_{30} = -1215$

9. 68 seats in the last row; 1100 seats in the section.

11.3 Geometric Sequences and Series

Summary

Geometric Sequence

A **geometric sequence** (or **geometric progression**) is a sequence in which each term after the first is a multiple of the preceding term.

The common multiple is called the **common ratio, r.**

Example 1
Determine the first four terms of the geometric sequence if $a_1 = 1$ and $r = 2$.

Solution
$a_1 = 1,\ a_2 = 1 \cdot 2 = 2,\ a_3 = 2 \cdot 2 = 4,\ a_4 = 4 \cdot 2 = 8,\ a_5 = 8 \cdot 2 = 16$
The first five terms are 1, 2, 4, 8, and 16.

Summary

---

nth Term of a Geometric Sequence

$$a_n = a_1 \cdot r^{n-1}$$

Example 2

    a. Write an expression for the general (or nth) term, a_n, of the geometric sequence with $a_1 = 2$ and $r = -3$.

    b. Find the eight term of the sequence.

Solution

    a. $a_1 = 2,\ r = -3$ so
      $a_n = a_1 \cdot r^{n-1}$
      $a_n = 2 \cdot (-3)^{n-1}$

    b. $a_n = 2 \cdot (-3)^{n-1},\ a_8 = 2(-3)^{(8-1)} = 2(-3)^7 = -4374$

Example 3
Find r and a_1 for the geometric sequence with $a_2 = 6$ and $a_6 = 486$.

Solution

Consider the sequence ____, 6, ____, ____, ____, 486.

Let $a_1 = 6$. Therefore, $a_5 = 486$. So, $a_n = a_1 \cdot r^{n-1}$

$$486 = 6 \cdot r^{5-1}$$
$$486 = 6 \cdot r^4$$
$$81 = r^4$$
$$3 = r$$

To find a_1, use $a_n = a_1 \cdot r^{n-1}$

$$a_2 = a_1 3^{2-1}$$
$$6 = a_1 3^1$$
$$2 = a_1$$

Summary

---

nth Partial Sum of a Geometric Series

$$s_n = \frac{a_1(1-r^n)}{1-r}, \ r \neq 1$$

Example 4

Find the sixth partial sum of a geometric sequence whose first term is 27 and whose common ratio is $\dfrac{1}{3}$.

Solution

$$s_n = \frac{a_1(1-r^n)}{1-r}$$

$$s_6 = \frac{27\left(1-\left(\frac{1}{3}\right)^6\right)}{1-\frac{1}{3}} = \frac{27\left(1-\frac{1}{729}\right)}{1-\frac{1}{3}}$$

$$s_6 = \frac{27\left(\frac{728}{729}\right)}{\frac{2}{3}} = \frac{364}{9}$$

Example 5
Given $s_n = 363$, $a_1 = 3$, $r = 3$, find n.

Solution

$$s_n = \frac{a_1(1-r^n)}{1-r}$$

$$363 = \frac{3(1-3^n)}{1-3}$$

$$363 = \frac{3(1-3^n)}{-2}$$

$$-242 = 1-3^n$$

$$-243 = -3^n$$

$$243 = 3^n$$

$$5 = n$$

Example 6
A city has a population of 100,000. If the population grows at a rate of 5% per year, find

    a. the population in 10 years.

    b. the number of years for the population to double.

Solution

    a. Here, $a_1 = 100,000$, $r = 1.05$, $n = 10$.

$$a_n = a_1 \cdot r^{n-1}$$

$$a_{10} = 100,000 \cdot (1.05)^{10-1} \approx 155,133$$

    b. Here, $a_1 = 100,000$, $a_n = 200,000$, $r = 1.05$ and n is unknown.

Use the formula $a_n = a_1 \cdot r^{n-1}$.

$$200,000 = 100,000 \cdot (1.05)^{n-1}$$

$$2 = (1.05)^{n-1}$$

$$\ln 2 = (n-1) \cdot \ln(1.05)$$

$$\frac{\ln 2}{\ln 1.05} = n-1$$

$$\frac{\ln 2}{\ln 1.05} + 1 = n$$

$$15.2 = n$$

The population will double in a little more than 15 years.

Summary

Sum of an Infinite Geometric Series
$$S_\infty = \frac{a_1}{1-r}, \; |r| < 1$$

Example 7

Find the sum of the terms of the sequence $4, \dfrac{2}{3}, \dfrac{1}{9}, \ldots$

Solution

$a_1 = 4$, $r = \dfrac{1}{6}$, since $4 \cdot \dfrac{1}{6} = \dfrac{2}{3}$.

Since $|r| < 1$, the formula for the sum of an infinite geometric series can be used:

$$S_\infty = \frac{a_1}{1-r} = \frac{4}{1-\frac{1}{6}} = \frac{4}{\frac{5}{6}} = 4 \cdot \frac{6}{5} = \frac{24}{5} = 4.8$$

Example 8

Find the sum of the infinite series below.

$$3 + \frac{3}{5} + \frac{3}{25} + \cdots$$

Solution

$a_1 = 1$, $r = \dfrac{1}{5}$, since $3 \cdot \dfrac{1}{5} = \dfrac{3}{5}$. Since $|r| < 1$, the formula for the sum of an infinite geometric series can be used

once again:

$$S_\infty = \frac{a_1}{1-r} = \frac{3}{1-\frac{1}{5}} = \frac{3}{\frac{4}{5}} = 3 \cdot \frac{5}{4} = \frac{15}{4} = 3\frac{3}{4} = 3.75$$

Example 9

Write the rational number $0.121212\ldots$ as a ratio of two integers using an infinite geometric series.

Solution

The decimal number $0.121212\ldots$ can be written as a series: $0.12 + 0.0012 + 0.000012 + \cdots$

Here, $a_1 = 0.12$ and $r = 0.01$ and the formula for the sum of an infinite geometric series can again be used:

$$S_\infty = \frac{a_1}{1-r} = \frac{0.12}{1-0.01} = \frac{0.12}{0.99} = \frac{12}{99} = \frac{4}{33}$$

Exercise Set 11.3

Determine the first five terms of the geometric sequence.

    1. $a_1 = 4$, $r = 2$ **2.** $a_1 = 81$, $r = -\dfrac{1}{3}$

Find the indicated term of the geometric sequence.

3. $a_1 = 5$, $r = \dfrac{1}{2}$, find a_5. **4.** $a_1 = 1$, $r = 5$, find a_8.

Find the sum.

5. $a_1 = -2$, $r = 3$, find s_6. **6.** $a_1 = 12$, $r = -\dfrac{1}{2}$, find s_5.

7. In a geometric sequence $a_3 = -12$ and $a_6 = 96$. Find r and a_1.

8. In a geometric sequence, $a_2 = 64$, $a_8 = 1$, find r and a_1.

9. The population of a city is 500,000 and grows at the rate of 4% per year.

   a. What will the population be in 10 years?

   b. In how many years will the population double?

Find the sums.

10. $7 + \dfrac{7}{3} + \dfrac{7}{9} + \cdots$ **11.** $\dfrac{5}{3} + \dfrac{5}{12} + \dfrac{5}{48} + \cdots$ **12.** $243 + 162 + 108 + \cdots$

13. $16 + 12 + 9 + \cdots$ **14.** $10 - 5 + \dfrac{5}{2} - \dfrac{5}{4} + \cdots$

Write the decimal number as a ratio of two integers.

15. $0.232323\ldots$ **16.** $0.123123123\ldots$

Answers to Exercise Set 11.3

1. 4, 8, 16, 32, 64 **2.** 81, –27, 9, –3, 1 **3.** $\dfrac{5}{16}$

4. 78,125 **5.** –728 **6.** $\dfrac{33}{4}$

7. $a_1 = -3$, $r = -2$ **8.** $a_1 = 128$, $r = \dfrac{1}{2}$

9. a. 711,656 **b.** 18.7 years

10. $\dfrac{21}{2}$ **11.** $\dfrac{20}{9}$ **12.** 729

13. 64

14. $\dfrac{20}{3}$

15. $\dfrac{23}{99}$

16. $\dfrac{123}{999}$

11.4 The Binomial Theorem

Summary

---

n Factorial

$n! = n(n-1)(n-2)(n-3) \dots (1)$
for any positive integer n

$0! = 1$

Example 1
Find

   a. 4!   **b.** 7!

Solution

   a. $4! = 4 \cdot 3 \cdot 2 \cdot 1 = 24$ **b.** $7! = 7 \cdot 6 \cdot 5 \cdot 4 \cdot 3 \cdot 2 \cdot 1 = 5040$

Summary

Binomial Coefficients

For n and r nonnegative integers, $n > r$

$$\binom{n}{r} = \frac{n!}{r! \cdot (n-r)!}$$

Example 2
Evaluate

   a. $\dbinom{7}{3}$ **b.** $\dbinom{8}{4}$

   c. $\dbinom{6}{0}$ **d.** $\dbinom{6}{6}$

Solution

a. $\begin{pmatrix} 7 \\ 3 \end{pmatrix} = \dfrac{7!}{3!(7-3)!} = \dfrac{7 \cdot 6 \cdot 5 \cdot 4 \cdot 3 \cdot 2 \cdot 1}{3 \cdot 2 \cdot 1 \cdot 4 \cdot 3 \cdot 2 \cdot 1} = 35$

b. $\begin{pmatrix} 8 \\ 4 \end{pmatrix} = \dfrac{8!}{4!(8-4)!} = \dfrac{8 \cdot 7 \cdot 6 \cdot 5 \cdot 4 \cdot 3 \cdot 2 \cdot 1}{4 \cdot 3 \cdot 2 \cdot 1 \cdot 4 \cdot 3 \cdot 2 \cdot 1} = 70$

c. $\begin{pmatrix} 6 \\ 0 \end{pmatrix} = \dfrac{6!}{0!(6-0)!} = \dfrac{6!}{6!} = 1$

d. $\begin{pmatrix} 6 \\ 6 \end{pmatrix} = \dfrac{6!}{6!(6-6)!} = \dfrac{6!}{6! \cdot 0!} = 1$

Summary

Binomial Theorem
For any positive integer n, $(a+b)^n = \begin{pmatrix} n \\ 0 \end{pmatrix} a^n \cdot b^0 + \begin{pmatrix} n \\ 1 \end{pmatrix} a^{n-1} \cdot b^1 + \begin{pmatrix} n \\ 2 \end{pmatrix} a^{n-2} \cdot b^2 + \begin{pmatrix} n \\ 3 \end{pmatrix} a^{n-3} \cdot b^3 + \cdots + \begin{pmatrix} n \\ n \end{pmatrix} a^0 \cdot b^n$

Example 3

Expand $(3x+y)^5$ using the binomial formula.

Solution

Use $(a+b)^n = \begin{pmatrix} n \\ 0 \end{pmatrix} a^n \cdot b^0 + \begin{pmatrix} n \\ 1 \end{pmatrix} a^{n-1} \cdot b^1 + \begin{pmatrix} n \\ 2 \end{pmatrix} a^{n-2} \cdot b^2 + \begin{pmatrix} n \\ 3 \end{pmatrix} a^{n-3} \cdot b^3 + \cdots + \begin{pmatrix} n \\ n \end{pmatrix} a^0 \cdot b^n$

$a = 3x$, $b = y$ and $n = 5$:

$\begin{pmatrix} 5 \\ 0 \end{pmatrix}(3x)^5 y^0 + \begin{pmatrix} 5 \\ 1 \end{pmatrix}(3x)^4 y^1 + \begin{pmatrix} 5 \\ 2 \end{pmatrix}(3x)^3 y^2 + \begin{pmatrix} 5 \\ 3 \end{pmatrix}(3x)^2 y^3 + \begin{pmatrix} 5 \\ 4 \end{pmatrix}(3x)^1 y^4 + \begin{pmatrix} 5 \\ 5 \end{pmatrix}(3x)^0 y^5$

$= 3^5 x^5 + 5(3^4)x^4 y + 10(3^3)x^3 y^2 + 10(3^2)x^2 y^3 + 5(3x)y^4 + 1 \cdot y^5$

$= 243x^5 + 405x^4 y + 270x^3 y^2 + 90x^2 y^3 + 15xy^4 + y^5$

Exercise Set 11.4

Evaluate the following.

1. $3!$

2. $5!$

3. $\begin{pmatrix} 4 \\ 0 \end{pmatrix}$

4. $\begin{pmatrix} 4 \\ 1 \end{pmatrix}$

5. $\begin{pmatrix} 7 \\ 2 \end{pmatrix}$

6. $\begin{pmatrix} 8 \\ 3 \end{pmatrix}$

Use the binomial formula to expand each of the following.

7. $(r+s)^3$ **8.** $(a-b)^4$ **9.** $(3x-y)^5$

10. $(2x+3y)^4$

Answers to Exercise Set 11.4

1. 6   **2.** 120   **3.** 1

4. 4   **5.** 21   **6.** 56

7. $r^3 + 3r^2s + 3rs^2 + s^2$ **8.** $a^4 - 4a^3b + 6a^2b^2 - 4ab^3 + b^4$

9. $243x^5 - 405x^4y + 270x^3y^2 - 90x^2y^3 + 15xy^4 - y^5$

10. $16x^4 + 96x^3y + 216x^2y^2 + 216xy^3 + 81y^4$

Chapter 11 Practice Test

1. Write the first five terms of the sequence with $a_n = \dfrac{2n}{n+1}$.

2. Find the first and third partial sum of $a_n = \dfrac{n^2}{n+4}$.

3. Write out the series and find the sum of the series $\displaystyle\sum_{n=1}^{5}(3n-2)$.

4. Write the general term for the arithmetic sequence.
   4, 11, 18, …

5. Write the general term for the geometric sequence.
   12, 6, 3, …

6. Write the first four terms of the sequence where $a_1 = 10$, $d = -4$.

7. Write the first four terms of the sequence where $a_1 = 8$ and $r = \dfrac{3}{4}$.

8. Find a_8 when $a_1 = -3$ and $d = -4$.

9. Find s_{10} if $a_1 = 8$ and $d = 3$.

10. Find the number of terms in the arithmetic sequence.
   $-3, 1, 5, 9, …, 45$

11. Find a_6 if $a_1 = 8$ and $r = -\dfrac{1}{2}$.

12. Find s_4 if $a_1 = 10$ and $r = \dfrac{1}{5}$.

13. Find the common ratio and write a general term for the sequence.
$8, -4, 2, -1$

14. Find the sum of the infinite geometric series.
$10 + 2 + \dfrac{2}{5} \cdots$

15. Use the binomial theorem to expand $(2x - y)^5$.

Answers to Chapter 11 Practice Test

1. $1, \dfrac{4}{3}, \dfrac{3}{2}, \dfrac{8}{5}, \dfrac{5}{3}$ **2.** $s_1 = \dfrac{1}{5}, s_3 = \dfrac{226}{105}$ **3.** $1 + 4 + 7 + 10 + 13 = 35$

4. $a_n = 7n - 3$ **5.** $a_n = 12\left(\dfrac{1}{2}\right)^{n-1}$ **6.** $10, 6, 2, -2$

7. $8, 6, \dfrac{9}{2}, \dfrac{27}{8}$ **8.** -31 **9.** 215

10. 13 **11.** $-\dfrac{1}{4}$ **12.** $\dfrac{312}{25}$

13. $r = -\dfrac{1}{2}; a_n = 8\left(-\dfrac{1}{2}\right)^{n-1}$ **14.** $\dfrac{25}{2}$

15. $32x^5 - 80x^4y + 80x^3y^2 - 40x^2y^3 + 10xy^4 - y^5$

CHAPTER 11 SUMMARY

IMPORTANT FACTS

Summation Notation

$$\sum_{i=1}^{n} x_i = x_1 + x_2 + x_3 + \cdots + x_n$$

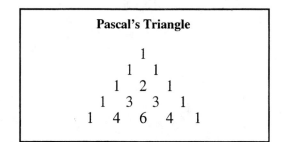

Pascal's Triangle

```
        1
      1   1
    1   2   1
  1   3   3   1
1   4   6   4   1
```

nth Terms and Partial Sums of Sequences and Series

nth Term of an Arithmetic Sequence	nth Term of a Geometric Sequence
$a_n = a_1 + (n-1)d$	$a_n = a_1 r^{n-1}$
nth Partial Sum of an Arithmetic Series	**nth Partial Sum of a Geometric Series**
$s_n = \dfrac{n(a_1 + a_n)}{2}$	$s_n = \dfrac{a_1(1 - r^n)}{1 - r}, r \neq 1$

n Factorial	Sum of an Infinite Geometric Series
$n! = n(n-1)(n-2)\cdots(2)(1)$	$s_\infty = \dfrac{a_1}{1-r}, |r| < 1$

Binomial Information

- Binomial Coefficients: $\dbinom{n}{r} = \dfrac{n!}{r! \cdot (n-r)!}$

- Binomial Theorem: $(a+b)^n = \dbinom{n}{0}a^n b^0 + \dbinom{n}{1}a^{n-1}b^1 + \dbinom{n}{2}a^{n-2}b^2 + \dbinom{n}{3}a^{n-3}b^3 + \cdots + \dbinom{n}{n}a^0 b^n$

HELPFUL HINTS

- You are working again with exponents in this chapter. If you have any difficulties, it would be a good idea to go back to Section 1.5 to review and practice the rules for exponents.